ARCHES &
CANYONLANDS
NATIONAL PARKS

JUDY JEWELL & W. C. McRAE

Contents

Although every effort was made to make sure the information in this book was accurate when going to press, research was impacted by the COVID-19 pandemic and things may have changed since the time of writing. Be sure to confirm specific details, like opening hours, closures, and travel guidelines and restrictions, when making your travel plans. For more detailed information, see p. 181.

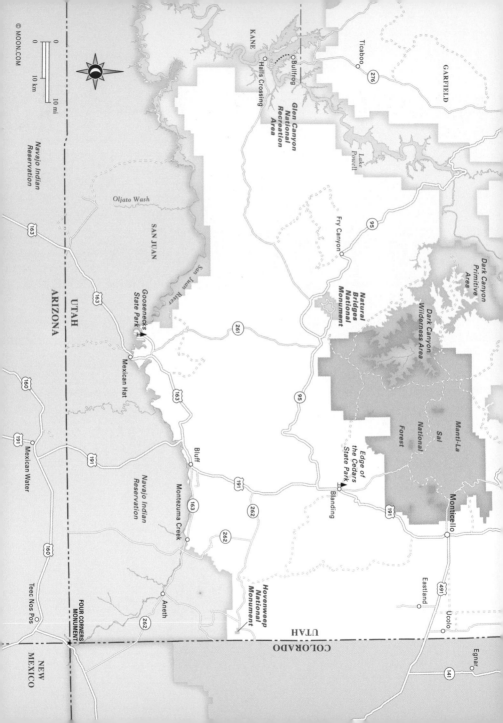

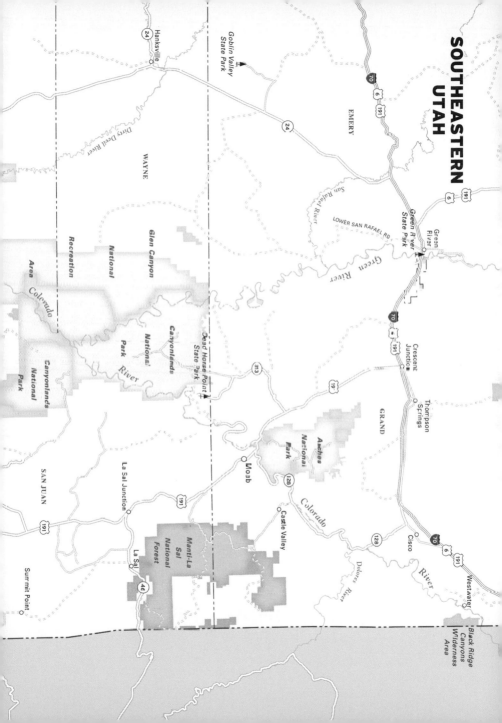

SOUTHEASTERN UTAH

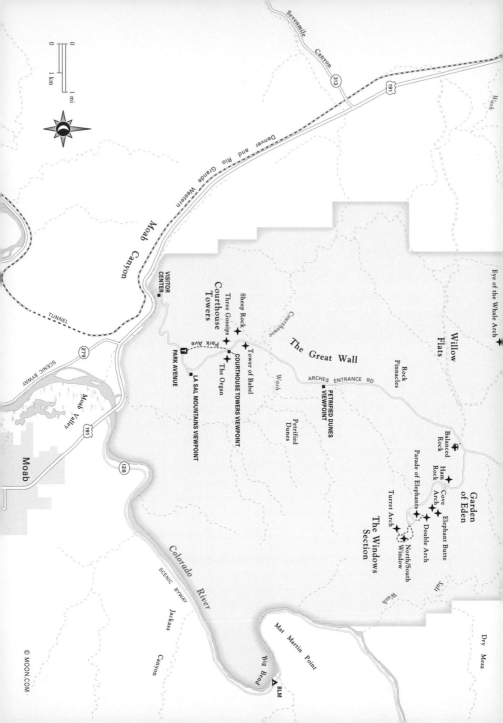

0
0
1 km
1 mi

© MOON.COM

Sevenmile Canyon

313

191

Wash

Denver and Rio Grande Western

Moab Canyon

TUNNEL

SCENIC BYWAY

279

191

128

Moab Valley

Moab

Colorado River

SCENIC BYWAY

Jackass Canyon

VISITOR CENTER

PARK AVENUE

Park Ave

Sheep Rock
Three Gossips
Courthouse Towers
Tower of Babel
COURTHOUSE TOWERS VIEWPOINT
The Organ
LA SAL MOUNTAINS VIEWPOINT

The Great Wall

Courthouse

ARCHES ENTRANCE RD

Wash

Petrified Dunes

PETRIFIED DUNES VIEWPOINT

Rock Pinnacles

Willow Flats

Eye of the Whale Arch

Balanced Rock

Parade of Elephants
Ham Rock
Cove Arch
Elephant Butte
Turret Arch
North/South Window
Double Arch

Garden of Eden

The Windows Section

Salt Wash

Mat Martin Point

Big Bend

BLM

Dry Mesa

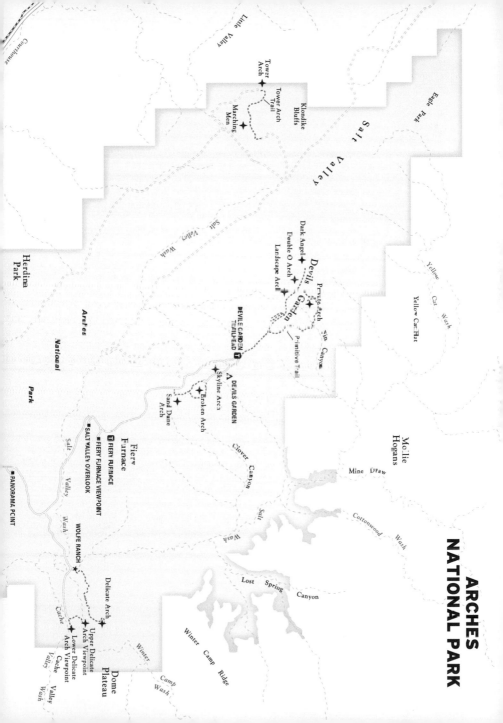

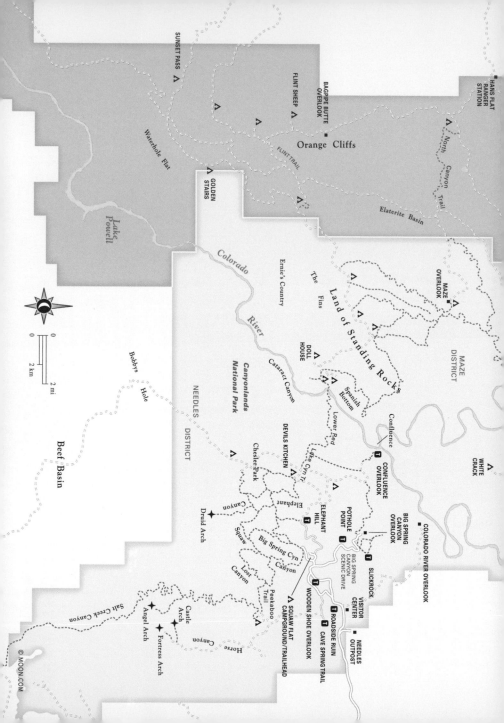

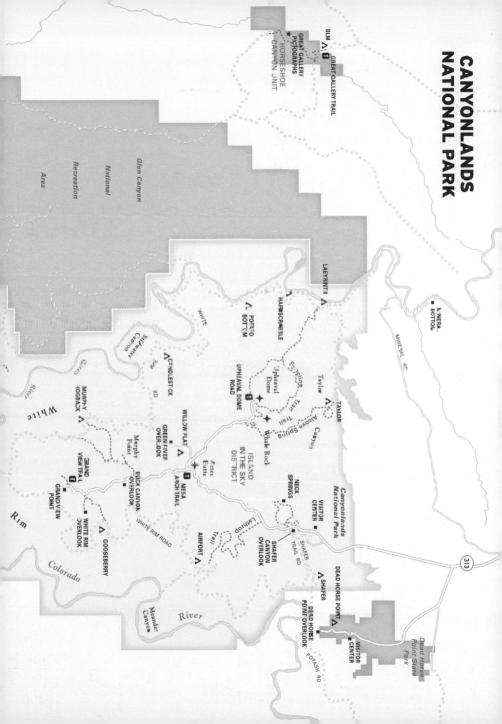

Arches & Canyonlands

Southeastern Utah is so filled with staggering beauty, drama, and power that it seems like a place of myth. Two national parks, several national monuments and recreation areas, and multiple state parks are all within a day's drive of each other. The colorful canyons, arches, and mesas found within this high, dry area are surprisingly diverse, and each park has its own characteristic landscape.

Nor are the riches here restricted to natural beauty: These rugged landscapes hold the remains of ancient indigenous cultures, while the haunting beauty of their rock art is on display at hundreds of locations. The area's modern hub, and one of Utah's most vibrant communities, is Moab, a recreational mecca known for its mountain biking and comfortable, even sophisticated, dining and lodging.

The beauty of Arches National Park, where delicate rock arches provide vast windows into the solid rock, is awe-inspiring and nearly mystical. Short trails draw hikers into a dramatic landscape of slickrock promontories and stone bridges.

In Canyonlands National Park, the Colorado River carves through deep red

Clockwise from top left: a kiva at Edge of the Cedars State Park; rafting down the Green River; Island in the Sky vista; Rough Mules Ear grow in Arches National Park; biking the Slickrock Trail; South Window at Arches National Park.

sandstone. From the Island in the Sky unit, expansive vistas take in hundreds of miles of canyon country, while rafting the Colorado's Cataract Canyon is the wet and thrilling climax of many a vacation.

Beyond the national park boundaries, much of the land is publicly owned. In many cases it vies with the national parks in terms of beauty and grandeur. No trip to Island in the Sky should neglect a side trip to Dead Horse Point State Park, with its astonishing views into the Colorado River Canyon. Hikers looking for their own patch of wildlands should check out Fisher Towers, a Bureau of Land Management recreation area upriver from Moab. A bit off the beaten path, Hovenweep National Monument preserves a wondrous series of Ancestral Puebloan villages perched on the edge of a cliff.

Although many people first visit southeastern Utah as part of a grand tour of the Southwest, they often return here to further explore a smaller and distinctive corner of this vast landscape. Best of all, you can still find special places that you will have all to yourself.

Clockwise from top left: Mesa Arch; Hovenweep National Monument; hiking through slot canyons in Arches National Park; Colorado River flowing through Glen Canyon National Recreation Area.

6 TOP EXPERIENCES

1 **Take in the Views:** This is a landscape that invites you to stare. Above it are some of the most gorgeous skies you'll ever see, whether painted with fiery sunsets or glowing with countless stars (page 24).

2 **Stare at Picture Perfect Arches:** Delicate Arch (page 42), Mesa Arch (page 63), and the Windows Section (page 36) are just some of the stunning rock formations that are endlessly photographed by visitors.

3 **Admire Ancient Rock Art:** The Colorado Plateau contains a rich tapestry of pictographs and petroglyphs (page 29).

4 **Go Off-Road Biking:** When it comes to mountain biking, **Moab's Slickrock Trail** may get all the love but Southern Utah offers an abundance of off-road adventures (page 28).

∧
∧
∧

5 **Take a Hike:** Wander through epic canyons, arches, and needles of sandstone (page 27).

6 **Explore Ancestral Puebloan Villages:** Wander amid the stone structures built around 900 years ago at Edge of the Cedars State Park Museum (page 129) and Hovenweep National Monument (page 133).

Planning Your Trip

Where to Go

Arches National Park

Just up the road from Moab is Arches National Park, with its **famous natural bridges.** Arches is a **great family park:** It's not too large and there are lots of accessible hikes to explore. Unlike other Utah national parks, there's plenty to see even if you can't get out of the car and hike. Be sure to hike the **Windows Section,** a series of arches and rock fins at the center of the park, and to **Delicate Arch,** overlooking the Colorado River.

Canyonlands National Park

Canyonlands National Park is made up of four sections: the **River District,** containing the canyons of the Colorado and Green Rivers; the **Needles District,** with **hiking trails** and backcountry roads through a standing-rock desert; the **Maze District,** a remote area filled with **geologic curiosities** and labyrinthine canyons; and the **Island in the Sky District,** a flat-topped mesa that overlooks the rest. A separate area, the **Horseshoe Canyon Unit,** lies to the west and contains a significant cache of **prehistoric rock art.**

Moab

At the heart of Utah's slickrock country, Moab is the recreation capital of southeastern Utah. Although **mountain biking** put Moab on the map, old mining roads make **four-wheel-driving** an increasingly popular alternative. Arches National Park is just minutes from downtown, and Canyonlands' districts are an easy drive from Moab. But Moab is a destination in itself: a youthful, high-energy town that offers good **restaurants and brewpubs.**

The Southeastern Corner

Although Arches and Canyonlands National Parks get most of the attention from first-time visitors, veterans of the area know that southeastern Utah has abundant other wonders in **national recreation areas, national monuments,** and **state parks.** After you have explored the national parks, take time to visit such fascinating destinations as **Natural Bridges** and **Hovenweep National Monuments,** and the lovely alpine glades of **Manti-La Sal National Forest.**

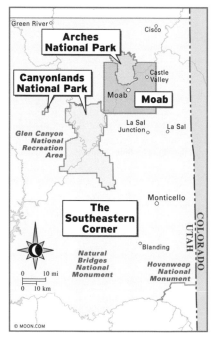

rock-climbing at Indian Creek National Monument

- **Hiking:** In Arches, check out the Delicate Arch Trail or Devils Garden Loop. Over in Canyonlands, take the Cave Spring Trail for an introduction to slickrock hiking or head out on Grand View or Great Gallery Trails.

- **Mountain Biking:** Moab gets all the press, and serious mountain bikers must visit, but Red Canyon (just outside Bryce) has good biking without the hype.

- **Rock Climbing:** The hot spot is just east of Canyonlands' Needles District, in the new Indian Creek National Monument.

- **Scenic Driving:** Following the White Rim Road below the sheer cliffs of Island in the Sky makes driving an adventure

- **Rafting:** The Colorado River picks up speed through Cataract Canyon, ensuring a wild ride.

- **Kid-Friendly Activities:** There's something magical about the sandstone spans and hoodoos in Arches, and exploring these awe-inspiring landmarks doesn't require a lot of stamina from little legs.

- **Solitude:** Plan a backcountry trek in Natural Bridges National Monument to have the wilderness to yourself.

- **Views:** It's hard to beat the views of Delicate Arch, Mesa Arch, and the Windows Section. Make time to see them all.

biking the White Rim Trail

Know Before You Go

High Season
(APRIL-SEPTEMBER)

The parks are all open year-round, although **spring** (Apr.-early June) and **early fall** (Sept.-Oct.) are the most pleasant times to visit. They are also the busiest seasons, and travelers may find that popular campgrounds and hotels are booked well in advance.

Spring rain can dampen trails, and late winter-early spring storms can play havoc with backcountry roads. Thunderstorms are also fairly common in **summer** (late July-early Sept.) and bring the threat of flash flooding, especially in slot canyons. In **Canyonlands, Arches,** and **Moab,** summer temperatures can exceed 100°F.

Low Season
(OCTOBER-MARCH)

Winter days tend to be bright and sunny, but nighttime temperatures can dip into the teens or lower. However, The **lack of crowds** and **brilliant sunshine** can make this a wonderful time to visit, if you don't mind layering your outer wear.

Park Fees and Passes

Entrance fees to both Arches National Park and Canyonlands National Park are $30 per vehicle. If you're planning on visiting more than two parks over the course of the year, buy an **America the Beautiful—National Parks and Federal Recreational Lands Pass** (valid for one year, $80) at your first stop to cover entrance to all national parks. Senior passes (lifetime pass $80) and free passes for residents with permanent disabilities are also available. Paid fees are good for seven days.

Camping Reservations

Many national parks now offer **reserved**

Delicate Arch

Avoid the Crowds

Goblin Valley State Park

Many areas outside the national parks are often less crowded but equally compelling.

- **Hovenweep National Monument** (page 133) contains the ruins of Ancestral Puebloan stone villages.

- **Natural Bridges National Monument** (page 142) contains rock formations that rival Arches National Park.

- **Dead Horse Point State Park** (page 94), on the road into Canyonlands, provides an eagle's-eye view over the Colorado River canyon.

- **Goblin Valley State Park** (page 151) has trails among goblin-shaped hoodoos.

campsites. If you want to camp in a park, reserve ahead, especially at **Arches**—or plan to arrive early in the day to get an unreserved site. Reservations at **Devils Garden Campground** (www.recreation.gov) must be made no less than 4 days and no more than 240 days in advance.

In **Canyonlands**, all campgrounds are open year-round. Reservations can be made at the **Needles Campground** (Mar. 15-June 30 and Sept. 1-Oct. 31) in the Needles District. If Needles Campground is full, head east to the first-come, first-served campgrounds, either at the private **Needles Outpost** or at **Bureau of Land Management** sites along Lockhart Basin Road, east of the park entrance.

Wherever you plan to camp, it's a good idea to arrive early in the day to get an unreserved site. If you don't have a reservation, **Moab** offers lodgings and campsites, from primitive sites along the Colorado River to shady comfort in town at the private tents-only **Up the Creek** campground.

What to Pack

Unless you want to return from Utah looking like a leather handbag, remember to use lots of **sunscreen.** Prepare for wide variations in temperature; nights in the desert can be very chilly even when summer highs soar above 100°F. There's no need to pack dressy clothes. **Casual**

Monument Valley

Characterized by mountain peaks, deep canyons, and fanciful arches, this is a landscape filled with big views.

- **Delicate Arch:** Looking across the Colorado River Canyon to the distant La Sal Mountains through Delicate Arch is a memory-of-a-lifetime experience (page 38).

- **Natural Bridges National Monument:** Often overlooked, the incredible rock spans here are some of the largest and most dramatic in Utah (page 142).

- **Monument Valley:** These towering pinnacles of stone have served as backdrop to innumerable Western movies (page 140).

- **Dead Horse Point State Park and Grand View Point:** From the main access road into the Island in the Sky section of Canyonlands, two road-end vista points provide swallow-your-gum views over the incredible Colorado River canyon. From Dead Horse Point State Park (page 94), a 30-foot-wide neck of land extends into the void over the twisting channels of the river 2,000 feet (610 m) below. Continue to Grand View Point, above the confluence of the Colorado and the Green Rivers, for vistas of canyons, sheer rock walls, pinnacles, and distant mountains (page 60).

clothes are acceptable nearly everywhere, even in what passes for a classy restaurant. Bring your **cell phone,** but don't count on reception in the canyons of southern Utah.

Visitors Centers

The **Arches Visitor Center** (8am-5pm daily Mar.-Oct., 9am-4pm daily Nov.-mid-Mar.) is just past the park entrance booth.

In Canyonlands, there are visitors centers at the entrances to the **Island in the Sky District** 435/259-4712, 8am-6pm daily late Apr.-late-Sept., 8am-5pm early spring and fall, closed late Dec.-early Mar.) and the **Needles District** (435/259-4711, 8am-6pm daily spring and fall, 8am-5pm daily July-Aug.).

The **Hans Flat Ranger Station** (435/259-2652, 8am-4:30pm daily year-round) is on a remote

Exploring slickrock country on all-terrain vehicles is a popular activity near Moab.

plateau above the even more isolated canyons of the Maze District and the Horseshoe Canyon Unit.

The **National Park Service Office** (2282 SW Resource Blvd., Moab, 435/719-2313, 8am-4pm Mon.-Fri.) covers the River District, but can generally handle inquiries for all districts of the park.

For **backcountry information,** or to make backcountry reservations, call 435/259-4351.

The **Moab Information Center** (8am-4pm daily) can handle inquiries about the town and the nearby parks, Arches and Canyonlands.

Getting Around

The rugged topography can make **driving challenging.** Unpaved back roads can serve as shortcuts if you have a high-clearance vehicle, but check locally before setting out to determine current conditions. Rainstorms and snowmelt can render these roads impassable.

The Best of Arches and Canyonlands

If you're a hiker or biker, it's easy to spend a week exploring Southeast Utah—and if you're a fan of the backcountry, you could easily spend another week investigating such remote and otherworldly destinations as the Maze District and the Green River canyon.

Moab is an excellent hub for visiting Arches and Canyonlands, as it affords comfortable lodgings and very good dining in addition to a lively nightlife scene. But each of the parks also offers campgrounds, and the region also has a selection of guest ranches and B&Bs. In the southern part of the region, the tiny town of Bluff is a handsome destination with good hotels and restaurants and is a good center for visits to Hovenweep and Cedar Mesa.

Seven Days in the Parks

Day 1

Drive into **Moab** and claim your hotel room (or head to your campsite at Arches National Park). Take the rest of the day to explore this hip and youthful town with its obsessive regard for mountain biking and microbrews. It's not hard to find good food and convivial company, all with the splendid backdrop of red rock canyons.

Day 2

Explore **Arches National Park,** with a drive around the ring parkway and frequent stops for short hikes. Be sure to hike to the dramatic **Windows** section and stand below these massive stone bridges. Save some time and energy to climb up the slickrock bluff to **Delicate Arch,** perhaps the park's most famed beauty spot.

Day 3

Get an early start on the day by joining a ranger-led hike of Arches' **Fiery Furnace** area (you'll need advance reservations for these popular and moderately strenuous tours), and then return to Moab to join a half-day **raft trip** that explores the canyons of the **Colorado River.**

Day 4

Check out the mesa-top vistas from Canyonlands' **Island in the Sky District.** On the way to the mother of all belvederes at **Grand View Point,** be sure to stop by **Dead Horse Point State Park** and take the short hike to cliff's edge or **bike** the park's **Intrepid Trail System.**

Day 5

Drive south from Moab to the **Needles District** of Canyonlands. On the way into the park, be sure to stop at **Newspaper Rock,** one of Utah's top caches of ancient Native American rock art. Plan to explore some of the Needles backcountry on hiking trails before driving south to **Bluff** to spend the night.

Day 6

From Bluff, drive east to **Hovenweep National Monument,** a well-preserved series of Ancestral Puebloan stone-built villages at the edge of high-desert canyons. In the afternoon, return to Bluff and explore some of the many **rock art** panels in the area.

Day 7

From Bluff, drive back north to Highway 95, stopping to view the Ancestral Puebloan ruins at **Butler Wash,** and detour into the wonder of

Best Day Hikes

Devils Garden Loop trail

It's difficult to imagine more dramatic landscapes than those found in Southeastern Utah's national parks. These day hikes through epic canyons, arches, and needles of sandstone invite you to get out of your vehicle and explore.

CANYONLANDS

- **Great Gallery Trail:** This hike to the phenomenal rock art in verdant Horseshoe Canyon is a near-mystical experience for many. The 7-mi (11.2-km) roundtrip trail requires negotiating a steep canyon wall, but experiencing the stunning petroglyphs is well worth the effort. The trailhead is roughly 30 mi (48 km) east of Highway 24 on gravel roads.

- **Neck Springs Trail:** In the **Island in the Sky District,** the landscape is nearly all vertical, and hiking trails explore the rock faces and canyon walls. This 5.8-mi (9.3-km) trail drops from the Island in the Sky road down to a series of springs in Taylor Canyon, a tiny oasis with songbirds and luxuriant plant life, then loops back up the canyon wall to complete the delightful, not-too-arduous hike.

- **Confluence Overlook Trail:** Even though the Colorado River is responsible for trenching the incredible landscapes of Canyonlands, it's often difficult to see the river in its canyon. In the **Needles District,** this trail allows hikers to look down on the confluence of the Green and Colorado Rivers from thousand-foot cliffs. This fairly easy 11-mi (17.8 km) round-trip trail starts from the end of Big Spring Canyon Overlook Scenic Drive.

ARCHES

- **Delicate Arch Trail:** This 3-mi (4.8-km) round-trip hike is a fantastic experience, a moderately demanding trail up a slickrock formation to the aptly named arch and transcendent views over the Colorado River Canyon.

- **Devils Garden Loop:** If you'd prefer a trail without crowds, go to the end of the paved parkway and hike the 6-mi (9.6-km) loop trail past eight arches and the weird formations in Fin Canyon. Crowds drop off after the first mile or so.

- **Fiery Furnace Trail:** Though this challenging backcountry trail is only 2 mi (4.8 km) round-trip, you can easily spend half a day or longer in this maze of narrow canyons. Access is restricted: You'll need a permit to hike on your own, or sign up in advance to join a ranger-led hike.

Natural Bridges National Monument. Then, if you're visiting during summer, take Highway 276 south and cross the Colorado River's **Lake Powell** on the **Halls Crossing and Bullfrog ferry.** Outside the ferry's season, you can continue on Highway 95 to cross the Colorado on the **Hite Bridge,** with no loss of scenic value. Once on the west side of the river, follow paved roads north to **Hanksville** for the night and dream of more Utah adventures.

Best Bike Rides

Moab is the center for some of the most noteworthy mountain bike trails in the West. However, most of the trails here aren't for novices—you need to be proficient on your bike and ready for extreme weather before heading out on your two-wheeled steed. If you'd rather explore these backcountry routes with a guide, simply contact one of the many bike shops in Moab, and they can set you up with a tour.

Slickrock Bike Trail

This is the trail that started the mountain-bike craze in Moab, and it's a challenge even to strong riders. The aptly named trail traverses steep, **exposed slickrock faces** over 10.5 mi (16.9 km), passing a succession of canyon and mountain viewpoints.

Gemini Bridges Trail

You'll find dramatic scenery along this trail (14 mi, 22.5 km one-way) that drops though the rock fins and arches of the **Wingate Formation.** The trick is getting to the trailhead, which is 12.5 mi uphill from Moab. The best answer is to hire a shuttle bus as transportation—from that point onward, this is one of the more moderate biking trails in the Moab area.

biking on slickrock in Moab

The Legacy of Ancient Rock Art

Southeastern Utah contains a rich tapestry of pictographs (drawings painted on rock using natural dyes) and petroglyphs (images carved into stone). Searching out rock-art panels can easily become an obsession, and it's a good one, since it will lead you far off the beaten path and deep into canyons that were once central for the area's ancient inhabitants.

Great Gallery

- **Delicate Arch:** On this popular hiking trail in Arches is an often-overlooked panel of Ute-style rock-art images.

- **Great Gallery:** One of the most important rock-art sites in the United States is in Canyonlands' Horseshoe Canyon Unit.

- **Holly Ruins:** You'll find many petroglyphs at Hovenweep National Monument, one of Utah's best-preserved Ancestral Puebloan villages.

- **Newspaper Rock:** Near Canyonlands' Needles District, this is another easily reached showcase of rock art.

- **Sego Canyon:** An hour north of Moab, you'll find hundreds of etched images, starting with ghostly, shamanic-looking creatures right out of sci-fi movies.

- **Utah Scenic Byway 279:** Follow this highly scenic route roughly 6 mi (9.7 km) west of Moab, where a series of petroglyphs appear at the base of 800-ft (244 m) cliffs. Just look for the sign pointing to "Indian Writing."

Lower Monitor and Merrimac Trail

A good introduction to the varied terrains of the Moab area, the 7.5 mi (12 km) Lower Monitor and Merrimac Trail includes lots of slickrock riding and a bit of sand. This is a **good training ride** for the more challenging rides in the area. Reach the trailhead by traveling 15 mi (24 km) north of Moab on U.S. 191 and turning west (left) onto Mill Canyon Road, just past milepost 141. Make sure to go on the lower trail, not the Monitor and Merrimac Jeep Trail. After your ride, explore the nearby Mill Canyon Dinosaur Trail (foot traffic only).

MOAB Brand Trails

This trail system joins four interconnecting routes. The **Bar-M trail** is easy enough for families, while other trails include thrills and spills aplenty for more seasoned riders. Catch the trailhead 7 mi (11.3 km) north of Moab near the sign for the Bar M Chuckwagon.

River Trips

The Colorado River is the big name in river trips here, but there are certainly other options for those looking for more remote and challenging adventures. And even on the Colorado, you have a choice of white water, easy-going family tours, jet boats, and tours with light shows and meals—you'll find a plethora of outfitters in Moab ready to get you out on a river.

Cataract Canyon

This is the **most adventurous** white-water trip in the Moab area, with lots of **Class III and IV rapids** through the Canyonlands and Glen Canyon area of the Colorado River. Most Cataract Canyon trips take four days to complete, although some outfitters offer motorized trips that conclude the trip in just two days.

Westwater Canyon

Upstream along the Colorado River from Moab, near the Colorado border, Westwater Canyon offers lots of white-water adventure in a **day-long trip.** If you're looking for an intense day of rafting but can't devote four days to Cataract Canyon, this is the trip for you.

Fisher Towers Section

If you're an **all-ages family group** or not comfortable with white water, trips through the Fisher Towers section of the Colorado River just upstream from Moab might be the answer. The rapids are fun without being frightening, and the scenery is top-notch. Full-day and half-day

trips are available. This is also a trip that experienced rafters could easily negotiate on their own—just arrange to rent gear in Moab.

The Green River

For an **easygoing backcountry experience,** the Green River, which flows into the Colorado at Canyonlands National Park, offers stellar scenery and mild enough river conditions for canoeists. To make the full journey from the town of Green River to Mineral Bottom takes five days.

The San Juan River

Board a raft in Bluff and paddle through some of the **most remote canyons** in the West. A three-day trip will get you to the town of Mexican Hat; add a few more days to navigate the meanders of the Goosenecks and pull out at Lake Powell.

Jet Boats and Tour Boats

If you're just looking for an easy way to get out on the Colorado River and experience its canyon landscapes, consider half-day or full-day jet-boat tours that explore the river on high-speed boats. Popular trips leave from Moab and race downriver to the boundary of Canyonlands National Park (jet boats aren't allowed in the park). Another option is the colorful sound-and-light tours provided by **Canyonlands by Night & Day** (435/259-5261 or 800/394-9978, www.canyonlandsbynight.com), which also offer the option of dinner cruises.

Arches National Park

A concentration of rock arches of marvelous variety has formed within the maze of sandstone fins at Arches National Park, one of the most popular national parks in the United States. Balanced rocks and tall spires add to the splendor.

Paved roads and short hiking trails provide easy access to some of the more than 1,500 arches in the park. If you're short on time, a drive to the Windows Section (23.5 mi/38 km round-trip) affords a look at some of the largest and most spectacular arches. To visit all the stops and hike a few short trails takes a full day.

Although Native Americans were in the area for thousands of years and left rock art, most of the early settlers and cowboys who passed through the Arches area paid little attention to the scenery.

Highlights

Look for ★ to find recommended sights, activities, dining, and lodging.

★ **See Balanced Rock:** Rising 128 feet (39 m) from the desert, this unbelievable spire-upon-spire balancing act will give your camera a warm-up (page 36).

★ **Explore the Windows Section:** The park's largest must-see arches are here, drawing large crowds. Escape them by hiking the more primitive trail behind the North Window (page 36).

★ **Trek the Delicate Arch Trail:** Beautiful from afar, Delicate Arch is mystical up close. It's worth the tough 1.5-mile (2.4-km) hike that leads to its base (page 42).

★ **Tour the Fiery Furnace Trail:** Take a ranger-led expedition of this wonderland of rock mazes, fins, and turrets (page 43).

★ **Hike the Devils Garden Loop:** The park's best day hike is on this 7.2-mile (11.6-km) trail through a landscape of bizarre rock fins (page 47).

★ **Discover Tower Arch Trail:** This trail leads to a spire in the backcountry, one of the park's most beautiful but neglected sights (page 47).

Arches National Park

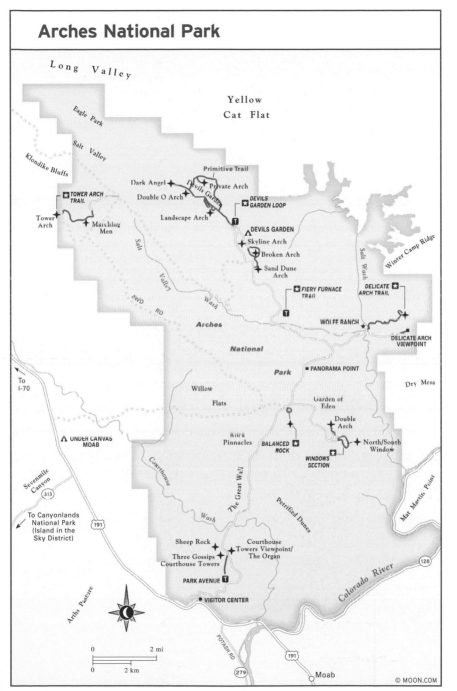

Long Valley

Yellow
Cat Flat

Eagle Park

Salt Valley

Klondike Bluffs

Primitive Trail

Dark Angel   Private Arch
Double O Arch   Devils Garden
TOWER ARCH TRAIL
DEVILS GARDEN LOOP

Tower Arch   Marching Men   Landscape Arch

Salt   DEVILS GARDEN
Skyline Arch

Valley   Broken Arch

Wash   Sand Dune Arch
4WD RD

Salt Wash   Winter Camp Ridge

FIERY FURNACE TRAIL   DELICATE ARCH TRAIL

Arches   WOLFE RANCH

National   DELICATE ARCH VIEWPOINT

Park   PANORAMA POINT   Dry Mesa

To I-70

Willow Flats   Garden of Eden
Double Arch

UNDER CANVAS MOAB   Rock Pinnacles   North/South Window
BALANCED ROCK   WINDOWS SECTION

Courthouse

Sevenmile Canyon   313

To Canyonlands National Park (Island in the Sky District)   191

The Great Wall   Petrified Dunes

Wash

Sheep Rock   Courthouse Towers Viewpoint/ The Organ
Three Gossips   128
Courthouse Towers

PARK AVENUE

Arches Pasture   VISITOR CENTER

Colorado River

Mat Martin Point

N

0   2 mi
0   2 km

POTASH RD

191

279   Moab

© MOON.COM

Arches in One Day

- Get to the park early to avoid lines at the entrance station. Stop at the **visitors center** to learn about the natural and human history of the park.

- Drive 11 miles (17.7 km) to the **Windows** trailhead, where a number of easy trails lead to arches carved into fins of rock.

- Continue to the **Delicate Arch** trailhead to hike up to the iconic arch before the day gets too hot.

- Enjoy a **picnic lunch** and views from the picnic area at **Devils Garden** trailhead, 7 miles (11.3 km) north of the Windows (18 mi /29 km from the park entrance). Then explore a bit of the trail: **Tunnel** and **Pine Tree Arches** are less than a mile in from the trailhead.

- If you still have some time, stop on the way back out of the park and take a stroll on the **Park Avenue Trail.**

- There are no dining facilities in the park, so enjoy a refined meal at the **Desert Bistro** in Moab, 6 miles (9.7 km) south of the park entrance.

In 1923, however, a prospector by the name of Alexander Ringhoffer interested officials of the Rio Grande Railroad in the scenic attractions at what he called Devils Garden, now known as Klondike Bluffs. The railroad people liked the area and contacted Stephen Mather, the first director of the National Park Service. Mather started the political process that led to designating two small areas as a national monument in 1929, but Ringhoffer's Devils Garden wasn't included until later. The monument grew in size over the years and became Arches National Park in 1971. The park now comprises 76,519 acres—small enough to be appreciated in one day, yet large enough to warrant extensive exploration.

Thanks to unrelenting erosion, the arches themselves are constantly changing. Every so often there's a dramatic change, as there was during the summer of 2008 when Wall Arch, a 71-foot (22-m) span on the Devils Garden Trail, collapsed.

PLANNING YOUR TIME

If you only have part of the day to explore, drive the 18-mile (29-km) length of the main park road with a brief stop at Balanced Rock and the Windows Section, where short trails lead to enormous arches in the skyline. At the road's end, set out on the Devils Garden Trail, but take only the trip to Tunnel and Pine Tree Arches.

A full day in the park allows plenty of time to stop at the visitors center and then hike the full Delicate Arch Trail and explore Devils Garden. Energetic hikers may want to do the entire 7.2-mile (11.6-km) loop in Devils Garden; those who want less of a workout can walk the 1-mile (1.6-km) trail to Landscape Arch. Often overlooked, the Park Avenue Trail leads to views of massive towers and hoodoos, and it's an easy 1-mile (1.6-km) hike that's fine even if you're not totally in shape.

If you have more than one day to spend, plan ahead and register online for a ranger-led hike into the Fiery Furnace area of the park. This takes about half a day; for the other half, head out via car or mountain bike to Tower Arch Trail.

Although Arches is known more for day hiking than backpacking, park rangers can help you put together a backpacking trip and issue the required backcountry permit.

Previous: the Delicate Arch Trail; Windows Section; sandstone towers in the Fiery Furnace.

Exploring the Park

The entrance to **Arches National Park** (435/719-2299, www.nps.gov/arch, $30 per vehicle for seven days, $25 motorcyclists, $15 bicyclists and pedestrians, $50 annual Southeast Utah Parks Pass) is 5 miles (8 km) north of downtown Moab on U.S. 191. With less than 30 miles (48 km) of paved road in the entire park, the traffic can be heavy in the spring and summer high seasons.

Come prepared with a picnic lunch; there are no accommodations and no restaurants inside the park.

VISITORS CENTER

Located just past the park entrance booth, the expansive **visitors center** (8am-5pm daily Mar.-Oct., 9am-4pm daily Nov.-mid-Mar.) provides a good introduction to what you can expect ahead. A short film on the geology of the park runs regularly, and exhibits identify the rock layers, describe the geologic and human history, and illustrate some of the wildlife and plants of the park. A large outdoor plaza is a good place to trawl for information when the visitors center is closed.

Staff members are available to answer your questionsand check you in for a ranger-led tour in the Fiery Furnace area of the park.

Look for the posted list of special activities; rangers host campfire programs and lead a wide variety of **guided walks** (Apr.-Sept.). You'll find checklists, pamphlets, books, maps, posters, postcards, and T-shirts available for purchase. An audio tour of the park's scenic main road is also available for rent or purchase. An audio version of the park brochure is available on CD (or can be downloaded from www.nps.gov/arch), and you may also request large-print or braille publications at the visitors center. See the rangers for advice and the **free backcountry permit** required for overnight trips.

Desert bighorn sheep frequent the area around the visitors center and can sometimes be seen from U.S. 191 just south of the park entrance. A sheep crossing about 3 miles (4.8 km) north of the visitors center is also a good place to scan the steep talus slopes for these nimble animals.

If your plans include visiting Canyonlands National Park plus Hovenweep and Natural Bridges National Monuments, consider the **Southeast Utah Parks Pass** ($50), which buys annual entry to all of these federal preserves. Purchase the pass at any of the park or national monument entrances.

Sights

MOAB FAULT

The park road begins a long but well-graded climb from the visitors center up the cliffs to the northeast. A pullout on the right after 1.1 miles (1.8 km) offers a good view of Moab Canyon and its geology. The rock layers on this side of the canyon have slipped down more than 2,600 feet (792 m) in relation to the other side. This movement took place about six million years ago along the Moab Fault, which follows the canyon floor. Rock layers at the top of the far cliffs are nearly the same age as those at the bottom on this side. If you could stack the rocks of this side on top of rocks on the other side, you'd have a complete stratigraphic column of the Moab area—more than 150 million years' worth.

PARK AVENUE

The South Park Avenue overlook and trailhead are on the left 2.1 miles (3.4 km) from the visitors center. Great sandstone slabs form a skyline on each side of this dry wash. A trail goes north 1 mile (1.6 km) down the wash to the North Park Avenue trailhead (1.3 mi /2.1 km ahead by road). Arrange to be picked up there, or backtrack to your starting point. The large rock monoliths of Courthouse Towers rise north of Park Avenue. Only a few small arches exist now, although major arches may have formed there in the past. One striking feature, visible from the road and the trail, is the group of sandstone towers forming the Three Gossips.

★ BALANCED ROCK

This gravity-defying formation is on the right, 8.5 miles (13.7 km) from the visitors center. A boulder more than 55 feet (17 m) high rests precariously atop a 73-foot (22-m) pedestal. Chip Off the Old Block, a much smaller version of Balanced Rock, stood nearby until it collapsed in the winter of 1975-1976. For a closer look at Balanced Rock, take the 0.3-mile (0.5-km) trail encircling it. There's a picnic area across the road. Author Edward Abbey lived in a trailer near Balanced Rock for a season as a park ranger in the 1950s; his journal became the basis for the classic *Desert Solitaire.*

TOP EXPERIENCE

★ WINDOWS SECTION

The Windows Section of Arches is located 2.5 miles (4 km) past Balanced Rock, on a paved road to the right. Short trails (0.25-1 mi /0.4-1.6 km one-way) lead from the road's end to some massive arches. The Windows trailhead is the start for North Window (an opening 51 ft/16 m high and 93 ft/28 m wide), South Window (66 ft/20 m high and 105 ft/32 m wide), and Turret Arch (64 ft/20 m high and 39 ft/12 m wide). Cut across the parking area for the trail to Double Arch, an unusual pair of arches. The larger opening—105 feet (32 m) high and 163 feet (50 m) wide—is best appreciated by walking inside. The smaller opening is 61 feet (19 m) high and 60 feet (18 m) wide. Together, the two arches frame a large opening overhead.

Garden of Eden Viewpoint, on the way back to the main road, promises a good panorama of Salt Valley to the north. Under the valley floor, the massive body of salt and gypsum that's responsible for the arches comes close to the surface. Far-off Delicate Arch can be seen across the valley on a sandstone ridge. Early visitors to the Garden of Eden saw rock formations resembling Adam (with an apple) and Eve. Two other viewpoints of the Salt Valley area lie farther north on the main road.

1: the aptly named Balanced Rock 2: a ranger-led hike in the Windows Section 3: Delicate Arch

DELICATE ARCH AND WOLFE RANCH

A bit of pioneer history survives at Wolfe Ranch, 2.5 miles (4 km) north on the main road from the Windows junction (turn right and drive 1.8 mi/2.9 km to the parking area). John Wesley Wolfe came to this spot in 1888, hoping the desert climate would provide relief for health problems related to a Civil War injury. He found a good spring high in the rocks, grass for cattle, and water in Salt Wash to irrigate a garden. The ranch that he built provided a home for him and some of his family for more than 20 years, and cattlemen later used it as a line ranch. Then sheepherders brought in their animals, which so overgrazed the range that the grass has yet to recover. A trail guide available at the entrance tells about the Wolfe family and the features of their ranch. The weather-beaten cabin built in 1906 still survives. A short trail leads to petroglyphs above Wolfe Ranch; figures of horses indicate that Ute people, rather than earlier inhabitants, did the artwork. Park staff can give directions to other rock-art sites; great care should be taken not to touch the fragile artwork.

Delicate Arch stands in a magnificent setting atop gracefully curving slickrock. Distant canyons and the La Sal Mountains lie beyond. The span is 45 feet (14 m) high and 33 feet (10 m) wide. A moderately strenuous 3-mile (4.8 km) round-trip hike leads to the arch. Another perspective on Delicate Arch can be obtained by driving 1.2 miles (1.9 km) beyond Wolfe Ranch. Look for the small arch high above. A short wheelchair-accessible trail and a slightly longer, steeper trail (0.5 mi/0.8 km round-trip) provide views onto the arch.

FIERY FURNACE

The Fiery Furnace Viewpoint and trailhead are 3 miles (4.8 km) from the Wolfe Ranch junction, on the right side of the main road. The Fiery Furnace gets its name from sandstone fins that turn flaming red on occasions when thin cloud cover at the horizon reflects the warm light of sunrise or sunset. The shady recesses beneath the fins provide a cool respite from the hot summer sun.

Closely packed sandstone fins form a maze of deep slots, with many arches and at least one natural bridge inside. Both for safety reasons (it's easy to get a bit lost in here) and to reduce human impact on this sensitive area, which harbors several species of rare plants, hikers are encouraged to join a ranger-led hike. The hike is moderately strenuous and involves steep ledges, squeezing through narrow cracks, a couple of jumps, and hoisting yourself up off the ground. There is no turning back once the hike starts, so make sure you're physically prepared and properly equipped.

Rangers offer two different guided hikes into the Fiery Furnace (May–Sept.). Ranger-led loop hikes are roughly three hours long and cover 2 miles/3.2 kilometers ($16 adults, $8 ages 5-12), while ranger-led out-and-back hikes ($10 adults, $5 ages 5-12) are about 2.5 hours long and cover about 1.25 miles (2 km). Tours are offered both in the morning and in the afternoon; only the morning tours are reservable in advance. The afternoon tickets are only sold in person at the visitors center up to a week in advance.

Group size is limited to about 20 people, and children under age five are not allowed. An adult must accompany children 12 and under. Morning walks often fill weeks in advance. Make reservations for the morning hikes online at www.recreation.gov. To visit the Fiery Furnace without a ranger, visitors must obtain a **permit** at the visitors center ($10 adults, $5 ages 5-12). Several Moab outfitters also lead hikes into the Fiery Furnace; these cost considerably more, but there's usually space available.

SKYLINE ARCH

This arch is on the right, 1 mile (1.6 km) past the Sand Dune/Broken Arch trailhead. In desert climates, erosion can proceed imperceptibly for centuries until a cataclysmic event happens. In 1940 a giant boulder fell from the

Why Are There Arches?

The park's distinctive arches are formed by an unusual combination of geologic forces. About 300 million years ago, evaporation of inland seas left behind a salt layer more than 3,000 feet (915 m) thick in the Paradox Basin of this region. Sediments, including those that later became the arches, then covered the salt. Unequal pressures caused the salt to gradually flow upward in places, bending the overlying sediments as well. These upfolds, or anticlines, later collapsed when groundwater dissolved the underlying salt.

The faults and joints caused by the uplift and collapse opened the way for erosion to carve hundreds of thin freestanding formations that look like shark fins. Alternate freezing and thawing action and exfoliation (flaking caused by expansion when water or frost penetrates the rock) continued to peel away more rock until holes formed in some of the fins. Rockfalls within the holes helped enlarge the arches. Nearly all arches in the park eroded out of Entrada sandstone. The towering stone walls of **Courthouse Towers** and the **Fin Canyon** section of Devils Garden are good examples of complete rock fins, while **Turret Arch,** in the Windows Section, is an example of a smaller arch being formed within a rock fin.

Eventually all the present arches will collapse, as Wall Arch did in 2008, but there should be plenty of new ones by the time that happens. The fins' uniform strength and hard upper surfaces have proved ideal for arch formation. Not every hole in the rock is considered an arch. To qualify, the opening must be at least 3 feet (0.9 m) in one direction, and light must be able to pass through. Although the term *windows* often refers to openings in large walls of rock, windows and arches are really the same.

Water seeping through the sandstone from above has created a second type of arch—the pothole arch. **Pothole Arch,** near Balanced Rock off Windows Road, and **Ring Arch** are good examples. (You can see them from the Courthouse Wash trail, accessible from a parking lot off U.S. 191 just north of the Colorado River Bridge near Moab.) You may also come across a few natural bridges cut from the rock by perennial water runoff. Rock bridges are different from arches as they have water flowing through them at least part of the year.

A succession of rock layers is on display at Arches. The rocks on top of the salt beds—the rocks you actually see at Arches—are mostly Entrada sandstone, which is a pretty general category of rock. Within this Entrada Formation are three distinct types of sandstone. The formation's dark red base layer is known as the Dewey Bridge Member. It's softer than the formation's other sandstones and erodes easily. Dewey Bridge rocks are topped by the pinkish-orange Slick Rock Member, the park's most visible rocks. The Slick Rock layer is much harder than the Dewey Bridge, and the combination of the two layers—softer rocks overlaid by harder—is responsible for the differential erosion that forms hoodoos and precariously balanced rocks. The thin top layer of Entrada sandstone, a white rock similar to Navajo sandstone, is called the Moab Tongue.

opening of Skyline Arch, doubling the size of the arch in seconds. The hole is now 45 feet (14 m) high and 69 feet (21 m) wide. A short trail leads to the base of the arch.

DEVILS GARDEN

The Devils Garden trailhead, picnic area, and campground are all near the end of the main park road. Devils Garden offers fine scenery and more arches than any other section of the park. The hiking trail leads past large sandstone fins to Landscape and six other named arches. Carry water, even if

you think you're just going for a short stroll, this is an area where it's tempting to keep on hiking! Adventurous hikers could spend days exploring the maze of canyons among the fins.

KLONDIKE BLUFFS AND TOWER ARCH

Relatively few visitors come to the spires, high bluffs, and fine arch in this northwestern section of the park. A fair-weather dirt road turns off the main drive 1.3 miles (2.1 km) before Devils Garden trailhead, winds down into Salt Valley, and heads northwest. After 7.5 miles (12 km), turn left on the road to Klondike Bluffs and proceed 1 mile (1.6 km) to the Tower Arch trailhead. These roads may have washboards, but they are usually passable by cars in dry weather; don't drive on them if storms threaten. The trail to Tower Arch winds past the Marching Men and other rock formations (3 mi/4.8 km round-trip). Alexander Ringhoffer, who discovered the arch in 1922, carved an inscription on the south column. The area can also be fun to explore off-trail with a map and compass or a GPS receiver. Those with 4WD vehicles can drive close to the arch on a separate jeep road. Tower Arch has an opening 34 feet (10 m) high by 92 feet (28 m) wide. A tall monolith nearby gave the arch its name.

4WD ROAD

A rough road near Tower Arch in the Klondike Bluffs turns southeast past **Eye of the Whale Arch** in Herdina Park to Balanced Rock on the main park road, 10.8 miles (17.4 km) away. The road isn't particularly difficult for 4WD enthusiasts, although normal backcountry precautions should be taken. A steep sand hill north of Eye of the Whale Arch is difficult to climb for vehicles coming from Balanced Rock; it's better to drive from the Tower Arch area instead. (Trust us and don't try this road in a big pickup truck, even one with 4WD!)

Recreation

Because of its great popularity and proximity to Moab, Arches sees a lot of visitors (about 1.8 million people visit the park yearly). Most are content, however, to drive the parkways and perhaps saunter to undemanding viewpoints. You can quickly leave the crowds behind by planning a hike to more outlying destinations. Arches' outback offers magnificent rewards for hikers willing to leave the pavement behind and get dusty on a backcountry trail.

HIKING

Established hiking trails lead to many fine arches and overlooks that can't be seen from the road. You're free to wander cross-country too, but stay on rock or in washes to avoid damaging the fragile cryptobiotic soils. Wear good walking shoes with rubber soles for travel across slickrock. The summer sun can be especially harsh on the unprepared hiker—don't forget water, a hat, and sunscreen. The desert rule is to carry at least one gallon of water per person for an all-day hike. Take a map and compass or a map and GPS unit for off-trail hiking. Be cautious on the slickrock, as the soft sandstone can crumble easily. Also,

remember that it's easier to go up a steep slickrock slope than it is to come back down.

You can reach almost any spot in the park on a day hike, although you'll also find some good overnight camping possibilities. Areas for longer trips include Courthouse Wash in the southern part of the park and Salt Wash in the eastern part. All backpacking is done off-trail. A **backcountry permit** must be obtained from a ranger before camping in the backcountry.

Backcountry regulations prohibit fires and pets, and they allow camping only out of sight of any road (at least 1 mi/1.6 km away), or trail (at least 0.5 mi/0.8 km away), and at least 300 feet (91 m) from a recognizable archaeological site or nonflowing water source.

Park Avenue

Distance: 1 mile (1.6 km) one-way
Duration: 30 minutes one-way; 1 hour round-trip
Elevation change: 320 feet (98 m)
Effort: easy-moderate
Trailheads: Park Avenue or North Park Avenue trailhead

Get an eyeful of massive stone formations and a feel for the natural history of the park

Arches Hikes

Trail	Effort	Distance	Duration
Broken and Sand Dune Arches	easy	1 mi/1.6 km round-trip	45 minutes
The Windows	easy	1 mi/1.6 km round-trip	1 hour
Landscape Arch	easy	2 mi/3.2 km round-trip	1 hour
Delicate Arch Viewpoint	easy-moderate	0.5 mi/0.8 km round-trip	15-30 minutes
Park Avenue	easy-moderate	1 mi/1.6 km one-way	30 minutes
★ **Fiery Furnace Trail**	moderate-strenuous	2 mi/3.2 km round-trip	3 hours
★ **Delicate Arch Trail**	moderate-strenuous	3 mi/4.8 km round-trip	2 hours
★ **Tower Arch Trail**	moderate-strenuous	3.4 mi/5.5 km round-trip	2.5 hours
★ **Devils Garden Loop**	strenuous	7.2 mi/11.6 km round-trip	4 hours

on the easy-moderate Park Avenue Trail. The Park Avenue trailhead, just past the crest of the switchbacks that climb up into the park, is the best place to start. The vistas from here are especially dramatic: Courthouse Towers, the Three Gossips, and other fanciful rock formations loom above a natural amphitheater. The trail drops into a narrow wash before traversing the park highway at the North Park Avenue trailhead. Hikers can be dropped off at one trailhead and picked up 30 minutes later at the other.

The Windows

Distance: 1 mile (1.6 km) round-trip
Duration: 1 hour
Elevation change: 140 feet (43 m)
Effort: easy
Trailhead: end of Windows Road

Ten miles (16 km) into the park, just past the impossible-to-miss Balanced Rock, follow signs and a paved road to the Windows Section. A 1-mile (1.6-km) loop along a sandy trail leads to the Windows—a cluster of enormous arches that are impossible to see from the road. Highlights include the **North** and **South Windows** and **Turret Arch.** Unmarked trails lead to vistas and scrambles along the stone faces that make up the ridge. If this easy loop leaves you eager for more exploration in the area, a second trail starts from just across from the Windows parking area and goes to **Double Arch.** This 0.5-mile (0.8-km) trail leads to two giant spans that are joined at one end. These easy trails are good for family groups because younger or more ambitious hikers can scramble to their hearts' content along rocky outcrops.

Delicate Arch Viewpoint

Distance: 0.5 mile (0.8 km) round-trip
Duration: 15-30 minutes
Elevation change: 100 feet (30 m)
Effort: easy-moderate
Trailhead: 1.2 miles (1.9 km) past Wolfe Ranch, at the end of Wolfe Ranch Road

Park Avenue

If you don't have the time or the endurance for the relatively strenuous hike to Delicate Arch, you can view the astonishing arch from a distance at the Delicate Arch Viewpoint. From the viewing area, hikers can scramble up a steep trail to a rim with views across Cache Valley. Even though this is a short hike, it's a good place to wander around the slick-rock for a while. It's especially nice to linger around sunset, when the arch captures the light and begins to glow. If you'd rather not scramble around on the slickrock, a short wheelchair-accessible path leads about 100 yards from the parking area to a decent view of the arch.

TOP EXPERIENCE

★ Delicate Arch Trail
Distance: 3 miles (4.8 km) round-trip
Duration: 2 hours
Elevation change: 500 feet (152 m)
Effort: moderate-strenuous
Trailhead: Wolfe Ranch

For those who are able, the hike to the base of Delicate Arch is one of the park's highlights. Shortly after the trail's start at Wolfe Ranch, a spur trail leads to some petroglyphs depicting horses and their riders and a few bighorn sheep. Horses didn't arrive in the area until the mid-1600s, so these petroglyphs are believed to be the work of the Ute people.

The first stretch of the main trail is broad, flat, and not especially scenic, except for a good display of spring wildflowers. After about half an hour of hiking, the trail climbs steeply up onto the slickrock and the views open up across the park to the La Sal Mountains in the distance.

Just before the end of the trail, walk up to the small, decidedly indelicate Frame Arch for a picture-perfect view of the final destination. The classic photo of Delicate Arch is taken late in the afternoon or in the evening when the sandstone glows with golden hues. Standing at the base of Delicate Arch is a magical moment: The arch rises out of the barren, almost lunar, rock face, yet it seems ephemeral. Views

© MOON.COM

The Windows

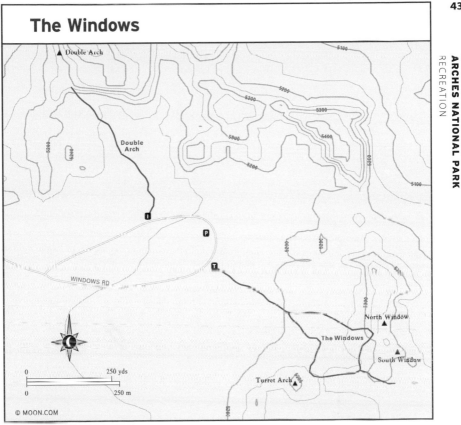

from the arch over the Colorado River valley are amazing.

★ Fiery Furnace Trail

Distance: 2-mile (3.2-km) loop
Duration: 3 hours
Elevation change: 250 feet (76 m)
Effort: moderate-strenuous
Trailhead: Fiery Furnace Viewpoint

The Fiery Furnace area is open only to hikers with **permits** ($6 adults, $3 ages 5-12) or to those joining a ranger-led hike. From May through September there are two daily hike options: Ranger-led **loop hikes** are roughly three hours long and cover 1.5 miles/2.4 kilometers ($16 adults, $8 ages 5-12), while ranger-led **out-and-back hikes** ($10 adults, $5 ages 5-12) are about 2.5 hours long and cover 1.25

miles (2 km). Tours are offered both in the morning and in the afternoon; only the morning tours are reservable in advance online at www.recreation.gov. The afternoon tickets are only sold in person at the visitors center up to a week in advance. These hikes are popular and are often booked weeks in advance, so plan accordingly.

Hiking in the Fiery Furnace is not along a trail; hikers navigate a maze of narrow sandstone canyons. The route through the area is sometimes challenging, requiring hands-and-knees scrambling up cracks and ledges. Navigation is difficult: Route-finding can be tricky because what look like obvious paths often lead to dead ends. Drop-offs and ridges make straight-line travel impossible. It's easy to become disoriented. Even if you're

Delicate Arch

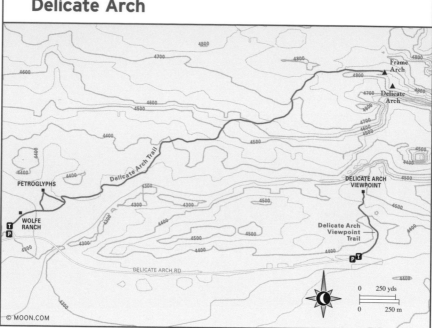

© MOON.COM

an experienced hiker, the ranger-led hikes provide the best introduction to the Fiery Furnace.

If you're not able to get in on a ranger-led hike and aren't strapped for cash, several Moab outfitters, including **Canyonlands By Night** (1861 N. U.S. 191, Moab, 435/259-2628 or 800/394-9978, www.canyonlandsbynight. com, $89 adults, $67 ages 5-15) offer guided tours in the Fiery Furnace.

Broken and Sand Dune Arches

Distance: 1 mile (1.6-km) round-trip
Duration: 45 minutes
Elevation change: 140 feet (43 m)
Effort: easy
Trailhead: on the right side of the road, 2.4 miles (3.9 km) past the Fiery Furnace turnoff

A short, sandy trail leads to small Sand Dune Arch (its opening is 8 ft/2.4 m high and 30

ft/9.1 m wide), tucked within fins. A longer trail (1 mi/1.6 km round-trip) crosses a field to Broken Arch, which you can also see from the road. The opening in this arch is 43 feet (13 m) high and 59 feet (18 m) wide. Up close, you'll see that the arch isn't really broken. These arches can also be reached by a trail across from campsite 40 at Devils Garden Campground. Another beautiful arch, **Tapestry Arch,** requires a short detour off the trail between the campground and Broken Arch.

Look for low-growing Canyonlands biscuit root, found only in areas of Entrada sandstone, colonizing the sand dunes. Hikers can protect the habitat of the biscuit root and other fragile plants by keeping to washes or rock surfaces.

1: Delicate Arch **2:** sandstone towers in the Fiery Furnace **3:** Broken Arch isn't really broken, it's just wearing a little thin on top.

Devils Garden Loop

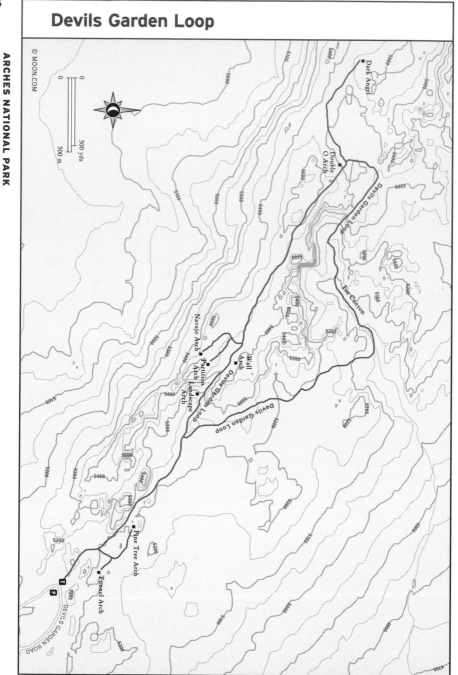

© MOON.COM

0
0
500 yds
500 m

Dark Angel

Double O Arch

Devils Garden Loop

Fin Canyon

5055

Navajo Arch

Partition Arch

Wall Arch

Landscape Arch

Devils Garden Loop

Devils Garden Loop

Pine Tree Arch

Tunnel Arch

DEVILS GARDEN ROAD

★ Devils Garden Loop

Distance: 7.2 miles (11.6 km) round-trip
Duration: 4 hours
Elevation change: 350 feet (107 m)
Effort: strenuous
Trailhead: Devils Garden trailhead

From the end of the paved park road, a full tour of Devils Garden leads to eight named arches and a vacation's worth of scenic wonders. This is one of the park's most popular areas, with several shorter versions of the full loop hike that make the area accessible to nearly every hiker. Don't be shocked to find quite a crowd at the trailhead—it will most likely dissipate after the first two or three arches.

The first two arches are an easy walk from the trailhead and are accessed via a short side trail to the right. **Tunnel Arch** has a relatively symmetrical opening 22 feet (6.7 m) high and 27 feet (8.3 m) wide. The nearby **Pine Tree Arch** is named for a pinon pine that once grew inside; the arch has an opening 48 feet (15 m) high and 46 feet (14 m) wide.

Continue on the main trail to **Landscape Arch.** The trail narrows past Landscape Arch and continues to the remains of **Wall Arch,** which collapsed in August 2008. A short side trail branches off to the left beyond the stubs of Wall Arch to **Partition Arch** and **Navajo Arch.** Partition was so named because a piece of rock divides the main opening from a smaller hole. Navajo Arch is a rock-shelter type; prehistoric Native Americans may have camped here.

The main trail climbs up slickrock, offering great views of the La Sal Mountains and Fin Canyon. At the Fin Canyon viewpoint, the trail curves left (watch for rock cairns) and continues northwest, ending at **Double O Arch** (4 mi/6.4 km round-trip from the trailhead). Double O has a large oval-shaped opening (45 ft/14 m high and 71 ft/22 m wide) and a smaller hole underneath. **Dark Angel** is a distinctive rock pinnacle 0.25 mile (0.4 km) northwest; cairns mark the way. Another primitive trail loops back to Landscape Arch via **Fin Canyon.** This route goes through a

different part of Devils Garden but adds about 1 mile (1.6 km) to your trip (3 mi/4.8 km back to the trailhead instead of 2 mi/3.2 km). Pay careful attention to the trail markers to avoid getting lost.

Landscape Arch

Distance: 2 miles (3.2 km) round-trip
Duration: 1 hour
Elevation change: 60 feet (18 m)
Effort: easy
Trailhead: Devils Garden trailhead

Landscape Arch, with an incredible 306-foot (93 m) span—6 feet (1.8 m) longer than a football field—is one of the longest unsupported rock spans in the world. It's also one of the park's more precarious arches to observe up close. The thin arch looks ready to collapse at any moment. Indeed, a spectacular rockfall from the arch on September 1, 1991, accelerated its disintegration, which is the eventual fate of every arch. Now the area directly underneath the arch is fenced off; when you look at the photos of the 1991 rockfall, you'll be happy to stand back a ways.

On the way to Landscape Arch, be sure to take the short side trails to Tunnel and Pine Tree Arches.

★ Tower Arch Trail

Distance: 3.4 miles (5.5 km) round-trip
Duration: 2.5 hours
Elevation change: 450 feet (137 m)
Effort: moderate-strenuous
Trailhead: Klondike Bluffs parking area
Directions: From the main park road, take Salt Valley Road (a dirt road; usually fine for passenger cars but not for RVs) west 7.5 miles (12 km) to the Klondike Bluffs turnoff.

Most park visitors don't venture into this area of sandstone fins and big dunes. It's a bit like Devils Garden, but without the crowds.

After a short but steep climb, the trail levels out and opens up to views of Arches' distinctive sandstone fins and, in the distance, the La Sal and Abajo Mountains. The trail drops down to cross a couple of washes, then climbs onto the fin-studded slickrock

Klondike Bluffs. Tower Arch is actually both an arch and a tower, and there's no mistaking the tower for just another big sandstone rock.

Because of the dirt-road access to this hike, it's best to skip it if there has been recent rain or if rain is threatening.

BIKING

Cyclists are required to keep to established roads in the park; there is no single-track or trail riding allowed. You'll also have to contend with heavy traffic on the narrow paved roads and dusty washboard surfaces on the dirt roads. Beware of deep sand on the 4WD roads, traffic on the main park road, and summertime heat wherever you ride.

One good, not-too-hard ride is along the Willow Springs Road. Allow two to three hours for an out-and-back, starting from the Balanced Rock parking area and heading west.

Perhaps the best bet for relatively fit mountain bikers is the 24-mile (39-km) ride to Tower Arch and back. From the Devils Garden parking area, ride out the **Salt Valley Road,** which can be rough. After about 7.5 miles (12 km), turn left onto a jeep road that leads to the "back door" to Tower Arch.

Nearby, Bureau of Land Management and Canyonlands National Park areas offer world-class mountain biking.

CLIMBING

Rock climbers should stop by a kiosk outside the visitors center for a **free permit** (also available online at https://archespermits.nps. gov). Groups are limited to five climbers, and Balanced Rock, the "Arches Boulders," and all arches with openings greater than 3 feet (0.9 m) are closed to climbing. Check at the visitors center or online for temporary closures, often due to nesting raptors. Slacklining and BASE jumping are prohibited in the park. There are still plenty of long-standing routes for advanced climbers to enjoy, although the rock in Arches is sandier and softer than in other areas around Moab.

Several additional climbing restrictions are in place. No new permanent climbing hardware may be installed in any fixed location. If an existing bolt or other hardware item is unsafe, it may be replaced. This effectively limits all technical climbing to existing routes or new routes not requiring placement of fixed anchors. Other restrictions are detailed on the park's website.

The most commonly climbed areas are along the sheer stone faces of **Park Avenue.**

Devils Garden Campground

Another popular destination is **Owl Rock,** the small, owl-shaped tower located in the Windows Section of the park. For more information on climbing in Arches, consult *Desert Rock* by Eric Bjørnstad or *High on Moab* by Karl Kelley, or ask for advice at **Pagan Mountaineering** (59 S. Main St., Moab, 435/259-1117, www.paganclimber.com), a climbing and outdoor-gear store.

CAMPGROUNDS

Devils Garden Campground (elev. 5,355 ft/1,632 m, year-round, $25) is near the end of the 18-mile (29-km) main park road. It's an excellent place to camp, with some sites tucked under rock formations and others offering great views, but it's extremely popular. The well-organized traveler must plan accordingly and reserve a site in advance for March to October. Reservations (www.recreation. gov) must be made no less than 4 days and no more than 240 days in advance. All campsites can be reserved, so during the busy spring, summer, and fall seasons, campers without reservations are pretty much out of luck. In winter, sites 1-24 are available first come, first served. There are two accessible sites, close to an accessible bathroom, for people with limited physical mobility. A camp host is on-site, firewood is for sale ($5), and water is available, but there are no other services or amenities.

If you aren't able to score a coveted Arches campsite, all is not lost. There are many Bureau of Land Management (BLM) campsites within an easy drive of the park. Try the primitive BLM campgrounds on Highway 313, just west of U.S. 191 and on the way to Canyonlands National Park's Island in the Sky District. Another cluster of BLM camp grounds is along the Colorado River on Highway 128, which runs northeast from U.S. 191 at the north end of Moab.

Getting There

Arches National Park is 26 miles (42 km) south of I-70 and 5 miles (8 km) north of Moab, both off U.S. 191. If you're driving from Moab, allow 15 minutes to reach the park, as there is often slow moving RV traffic along the route. If you're on a bike, a paved bike path parallels the highway between Moab and the park.

Canyonlands National Park

The canyon country stages its supreme performance in this vast park, which spreads across 527 square miles (1,365 sq. km). The deeply entrenched Colorado and Green Rivers meet in its heart, after which the Colorado continues south through the tumultuous Cataract Canyon Rapids.

The park is divided into four districts and a separate noncontiguous unit. The Colorado and Green Rivers form the River District and divide Canyonlands National Park into three other regions. Island in the Sky is north, between the rivers; the Maze is to the west; and Needles is to the east. The small Horseshoe Canyon Unit, farther west, preserves a canyon on Barrier Creek, a tributary of the Green River, in which astounding petroglyphs and ancient rock paintings are protected.

Highlights

Look for ★ to find recommended sights, activities, dining, and lodging.

★ **Take a Ride on White Rim Road:** Only high-clearance 4WD rigs or sturdy mountain bikes can make this scenic drive along the Colorado and Green Rivers (page 60).

★ **Hit the Mesa Arch Trail:** This easy trail leads to a dramatic cliff-side arch. If you have time for just one hike, make it this one—the sun rising through the arch is a sight to behold (page 63).

★ **Hike Grand View Trail:** This short hike along slickrock cliffs captures the essence of the Island in the Sky. A sheer mile below the trail, the gorges of the Colorado and Green Rivers join to form Cataract Canyon, while needles punctuate the skyline (page 64)

★ **See 2000-year-old Art:** The distinctive petroglyphs at **BLM Newspaper Rock Historical Monument** span centuries (page 68).

★ **Go Slickrock Hiking:** The **Cave Spring Trail** is a good introduction to slickrock hiking, with rock cairns that mark the way and ladders to assist with the steeper sections (page 72).

★ **Check out Chesler Park:** A trail winds through sand and slickrock before ascending to a lovely desert meadow that contrasts with the Needles District's characteristic red and white spires (page 76).

★ **Find Adventure in the Land of Standing Rocks:** Rock spires stand guard over myriad canyons in this remote section of the Maze District, accessible via a high-clearance 4WD vehicle (page 82).

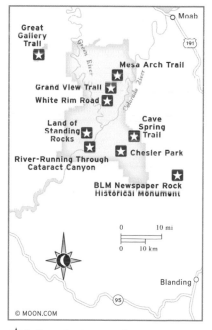

★ **Follow the Great Gallery Trail:** Ghostly life-size pictographs are located in remote Horseshoe Canyon. Hike through pleasant scenery and spring wildflowers to get there (page 85).

★ **Ride the Rapids:** The Colorado River picks up speed through **Cataract Canyon,** especially in spring, with 26 or more rapids guaranteeing a wild ride (page 87).

Canyonlands National Park

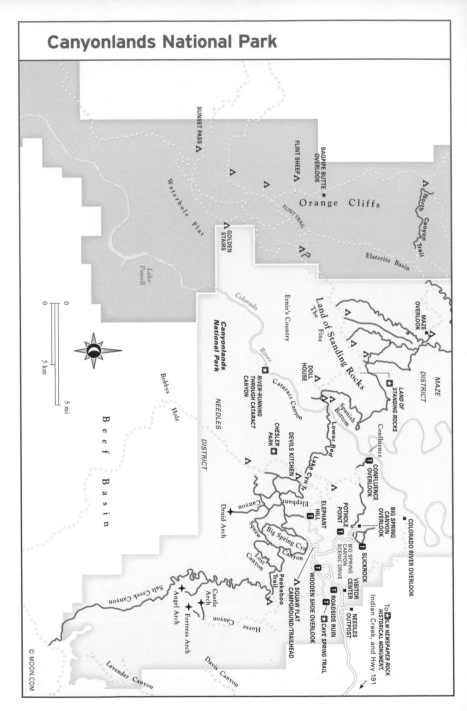

SUNSET PASS

FLINT SHEEP

BAGPIPE BUTTE OVERLOOK

Orange Cliffs

FLINT TRAIL

North Canyon Trail

Elaterite Basin

Waterhole Flat

GOLDEN STAIRS

Lake Powell

Colorado

Ernie's Country

The Fins

Land of Standing Rocks

MAZE OVERLOOK

MAZE DISTRICT

Canyonlands National Park

DOLL HOUSE

River

RIVER-RUNNING THROUGH CATARACT CANYON

LAND OF STANDING ROCKS

Bobby's Hole

NEEDLES

Cataract Canyon

Spanish Bottom

CHESLER PARK

DEVILS KITCHEN

Lower Red Lake Cyn

Confluence

CONFLUENCE OVERLOOK

COLORADO RIVER OVERLOOK

B e e f   B a s i n

DISTRICT

ELEPHANT HILL

POTHOLE POINT

BIG SPRING CANYON OVERLOOK

Druid Arch

Elephant Canyon

Big Spring Cyn

BIG SPRING CANYON SCENIC DRIVE

SLICKROCK

Squaw Canyon

Lost Canyon

VISITOR CENTER

Peekaboo Trail

WOODEN SHOE OVERLOOK

ROADSIDE RUIN

NEEDLES OUTPOST

Castle Arch

Angel Arch

Fortress Arch

Salt Creek Canyon

Horse Canyon

SQUAW FLAT CAMPGROUND/TRAILHEAD

CAVE SPRING TRAIL

To BLM NEWSPAPER ROCK HISTORICAL MONUMENT, Indian Creek, and Hwy 191

Lavender Canyon

Davis Canyon

0   5 km
0   5 mi

© MOON.COM

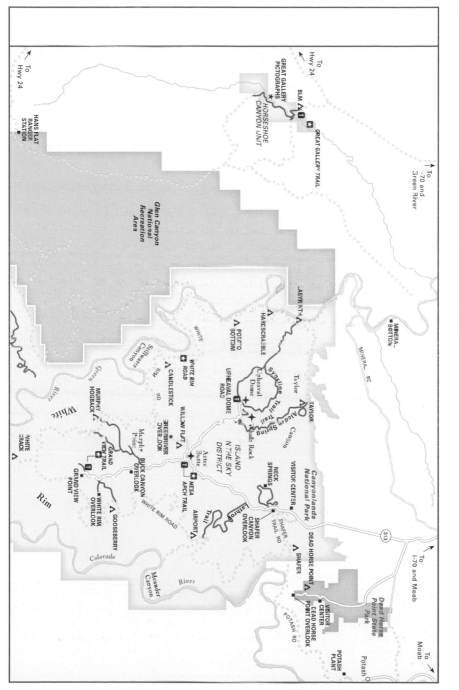

To Hwy 24

To Hwy 24

GREAT GALLERY PICTOGRAPHS

HORSESHOE CANYON UNIT

BLM

GREAT GALLERY TRAIL

HANS FLAT RANGER STATION

To I-70 and Green River

Glen Canyon National Recreation Area

LABYRINTH

HARDSCRABBLE

POTATO BOTTOM

WHITE RIM ROAD

UPHEAVAL DOME ROAD

Upheaval Dome

Syncline Trail

Taylor Canyon

MINERAL BOTTOM

MINERAL RD

Stillwater Canyon

WHITE RIM RD

CANDLESTICK

WILLOW FLAT

Murphy Point

GREEN RIVER OVERLOOK

MURPHY HOGBACK

TAYLOR

Alcove Spring Trail

Moab Run

GRAND VIEW TRAIL

BUCK CANYON OVERLOOK

Aztec Butte

ISLAND IN THE SKY DISTRICT

NECK SPRINGS

VISITOR CENTER

Canyonlands National Park

WHITE CRACK

Green River

GRAND VIEW POINT

WHITE RIM OVERLOOK

GOOSEBERRY

WHITE RIM ROAD

MESA ARCH TRAIL

AIRPORT

Lathrop Trail

SHAFER CANYON OVERLOOK

SHAFER TRAIL RD

DEAD HORSE POINT

SHAFER

313

To I-70 and Moab

White Rim

Colorado River

Meander Canyon

Potash Rd

DEAD HORSE POINT OVERLOOK

VISITOR CENTER

Dead Horse Point State Park

POTASH RD

POTASH PLANT

Potash

To Moab

Each district has its own distinct character. No bridges or roads directly connect the three land districts and the Horseshoe Canyon Unit, so most visitors have to leave the park to go from one region to another. The huge park can be seen in many ways and on many levels. Paved roads reach a few areas, 4WD roads go to more places, and hiking trails reach still more, but much of the land shows no trace of human passage. To get the big picture, you can fly over this incredible complex of canyons on an air tour; however, only a river trip or a hike lets you experience the solitude and detail of the land.

The park can be visited in any season of the year, with spring and autumn the best choices. Summer temperatures can climb past 100°F (38°C); carrying and drinking lots of water becomes critical then (bring at least one gallon per person per day). Arm yourself with insect repellent from late spring to midsummer. Winter days tend to be bright and sunny, although nighttime temperatures can dip into the teens or even below 0°F (-18°C). Winter visitors should inquire about travel conditions, as snow and ice occasionally close roads and trails at higher elevations.

PLANNING YOUR TIME

Unless you have a great deal of time, you can't really "do" the entire park in one trip. It's best to pick one section and concentrate on it.

Island in the Sky District

The mesa-top Island in the Sky District has paved roads to impressive belvederes such as Grand View Point and the strange Upheaval Dome. If you're short on time or don't want to make a rigorous backcountry trip, this district is the best choice. It is easily visited as a day trip from Moab. The "Island," which is actually a large mesa, is much like nearby Dead Horse Point on a giant scale; a narrow neck of land connects the north side with the "mainland."

If you're really on a tight schedule, it's possible to spend a few hours exploring Arches National Park, then head to Island in the Sky for a drive to the scenic Grand View overlook and a brief hike to Mesa Arch or the Upheaval Dome viewpoint. A one-day visit should include these elements, plus a hike along the Neck Springs Trail. For a longer visit, hikers, mountain bikers, and those with suitable high-clearance 4WD vehicles can drop off the Island in the Sky and descend about 1,300 feet (396 m) to White Rim Road, which follows the cliffs of the White Rim around most of the Island. Plan to spend at least two or three days exploring this 100-mile-long road.

Needles District

Colorful rock spires prompted the name of the Needles District, which is easily accessed from Highway 211 and U.S. 191 south of Moab. Splendid canyons contain many arches, strange rock formations, and archaeological sites. Overlooks and short nature trails can be enjoyed from the paved scenic drive in the park; if you are only here for a day, hike the Cave Spring and Pothole Point Trails. On a longer visit, make a loop of the Big Spring and Squaw Canyon Trails, and hike to Chesler Park. A 10-mile (16-km) round-trip hike will take you to the Confluence Overlook, a great view of the junction of the Green and Colorado Rivers.

Drivers with 4WD vehicles have their own challenging roads through canyons and other highly scenic areas.

Maze District

Few visitors make it over to the Maze District, which is some of the wildest country in the United States. Only the rivers and a handful of 4WD roads and hiking trails provide access. Experienced hikers can explore the maze of canyons on unmarked routes. Plan to spend at least two or three days in this area; even if you're only taking day hikes, it can take a long

---

Previous: Needles District hiking trails; rafters on the Colorado River; Mesa Arch.

Canyonlands in One Day

- Begin your day at the **Island in the Sky visitors center,** which overlooks an 800-foot-deep natural amphitheater.

- After a 6-mile (9.7 km) drive south, you'll find the trail for the easy walk to **Mesa Arch,** which rewards you with one of the most dramatic vistas in Utah: an arch on the edge of an 800-foot (244-m) cliff.

- For lunch, hit the picnic area at **Grand View Point,** another 6 miles (9.7 km) south, for astonishing views over red-rock canyons.

- After lunch, take a longer hike from a trailhead near the visitors center on the **Neck Springs Trail.**

- For dinner, the closest dining is in Moab, 32 miles (52 km) east of the visitors center, where you can quench your thirst and hunger at **Eddie McStiff's** brewpub.

time to get to any destination here. That said, a hike from the Maze Overlook to the Harvest Scene pictographs is a good bet if you don't have a lot of time. If you have more than one day, head to the Land of Standing Rocks area and hike north to the Chocolate Drops.

Horseshoe Canyon Unit
The Horseshoe Canyon Unit, a detached section of the park northwest of the Maze District, is equally remote. It protects the Great Gallery, a group of pictographs left by prehistoric Native Americans. This ancient artwork is reached at the end of a series of long unpaved roads and down a canyon on a

moderately challenging hiking trail. Plan to spend a full day exploring this area.

River District
The River District includes long stretches of the Green and the Colorado Rivers. River running is one of the best ways to experience the inner depths of the park. Boaters can obtain helpful literature and advice from park rangers. Groups planning their own trip through Cataract Canyon need a river-running permit. Flat-water permits are also required. River outfitters based in Moab offer trips ranging from half a day to several days in length.

Exploring the Park

There are four districts and a noncontiguous unit in **Canyonlands National Park** (425/719-2313, www.nps.gov/cany, $30 per vehicle, $25 motorcyclists, $15 bicyclists and pedestrians, good for one week in all districts, no fee to enter Maze or Horseshoe Canyon, $55 Southeast Utah Parks Pass good for Arches and Canyonlands National Parks and Hovenweep and Natural Bridges National Monuments), each affording great views, spectacular geology, a chance to see wildlife, and endless opportunities to explore. You

won't find crowds or elaborate park facilities because most of Canyonlands remains a primitive backcountry park. Indeed, bring along a lunch and any other food that you'll need during your stay. There are no restaurants and no accommodations in any unit of the park.

Front-country camping is allowed only in the established Island in the Sky Campground and Needles Campground.

Rock climbing is allowed in some areas of the park. Permits are not required unless the trip involves overnight camping; however, it's always a good idea to check in at district visitors centers for advice and information and to learn where climbing is restricted. Climbing is not allowed within 300 feet (91 m) of cultural sites.

Pets aren't allowed on trails and must be leashed in campgrounds. No firewood collecting is permitted in the park; backpackers must use gas stoves for cooking. Vehicle and boat campers can bring in firewood but must use grills or fire pans.

The best maps for the park are a series of topographic maps by National Geographic/Trails Illustrated; these have the latest trail and road information. For most day hikes, the simple maps issued at park visitors centers will suffice.

VISITORS CENTERS

Because Canyonlands covers so much far-flung territory, separate visitors centers serve each district. One website (www.nps.gov/cany) serves the whole park and is a good source for current information and permit applications. There are visitors centers at the entrances to the **Island in the Sky District** (435/259-4712, 8am-6pm daily late Apr.-late-Sept., 8am-5pm early spring and fall, closed late Dec.-early Mar.) and the **Needles District** (435/259-4711, 8am-6pm daily spring and fall, 8am-5pm daily July-Aug.). The **Hans Flat Ranger Station** (435/259-2652, 8am-4:30pm daily year-round) is on a remote plateau above the even more isolated canyons of the Maze District and the Horseshoe Canyon Unit. The River District is administered out of the **National Park Service Office** (2282 SW Resource Blvd., Moab, 435/719-2313, 8am-4pm Mon.-Fri.). This office can generally handle inquiries for all districts of the park. For backcountry information, or to make backcountry reservations, call 435/259-4351. Handouts from the ranger offices describe natural history, travel, and other aspects of the park.

If you are in Moab, it is most convenient to stop at the **Moab Information Center** (Main St. and Center St., 435/259-8825 or 800/635-6622, 8am-7pm Mon.-Sat., 9am-6pm Sun. mid-Mar.-Nov.), where a national park ranger or volunteers with the Canyonlands Natural History Association are often on duty. All visitors centers have brochures, maps, and books, as well as someone to answer your questions.

TOURS

Rangers lead interpretive programs (Apr.-Oct.) in the Island in the Sky and Needles Districts, and they guide hikers into Horseshoe Canyon (Sat.-Sun. spring and fall), weather permitting. Call the **Hans Flat Ranger Station** (435/259-2652) for details on these hikes.

OUTFITTERS

Outfitters must be authorized by the National Park Service to operate in Canyonlands. Most guides concentrate on river trips, but some can take you on mountain bike trips, including vehicle-supported tours of the White Rim 4WD Trail. Most of the guides operating in Canyonlands are based in Moab. For a complete list of authorized outfitters, visit the park website (www.nps.gov/cany).

Mountain Biking

- **Escape Adventures** (at Moab Cyclery, 391 S. Main St., Moab, 702/596-2953 or 800/596-2953, www.escapeadventures.com)
- **Rim Tours** (1233 S. U.S. 191, Moab, 435/259-5223, www.rimtours.com)
- **Western Spirit Cycling** (478 Mill Creek Dr., Moab, 435/259-8732 or 800/845-2453, www.westernspirit.com)

Rafting

- **Adrift Adventures** (378 N. Main St., Moab, 435/259-8594 or 800/874-4483, www.adrift.net)
- **Sheri Griffith Expeditions** (435/259-8229 or 800/332-2439, www.griffithexp.com)
- **Tag-A-Long Expeditions** (452 N. Main

St., Moab, 435/259-8594 or 800/453-3292, http://tagalong.com)

- **Western River Expeditions** (225 S. Main St., Moab, 801/942-6669 or 866/904-1163, www.westernriver.com)

BACKCOUNTRY EXPLORATION

A complex system of fees is charged for backcountry camping, 4WD exploration, and river rafting. Except for Island in the Sky Campground and Needles Campground, you'll need a **backcountry camping permit.** There is a $30 fee for a backpacking, biking, or 4WD overnight permit. **Day-use permits** (free, but limited in quantity) are required for vehicles, including motorcycles and bicycles on the White Rim Road, Elephant Hill, and a couple of other areas. Each of the three major districts has a different policy for backcountry vehicle camping, so it's a good idea to make sure that you understand the details. Backcountry permits are also needed for any trips with horses or stock; check with a ranger for details.

It's possible to reserve a backcountry permit in advance; for spring and fall travel to popular areas like Island in the Sky's White Rim Trail or the Needles backcountry, this is an extremely good idea. Find application forms on the Canyonlands website (https://canypermits.nps.gov). Forms should be completed and returned at least two weeks in advance of your planned trip. Telephone reservations are not accepted.

Back-road travel is a popular method of exploring the park. Canyonlands National Park offers hundreds of miles of exceptionally scenic jeep roads, favorites both with mountain bikers and 4WD enthusiasts. Park regulations require all motorized vehicles to have proper registration and licensing for highway use, and all-terrain vehicles are prohibited in the park; drivers must also be licensed. Normally you must have a vehicle with both 4WD and high clearance; it must also be maneuverable (large pickup trucks don't work for many places). It's essential for both motor vehicles and bicycles to stay on existing roads to prevent damage to the delicate desert vegetation. Carry tools, extra fuel, water, and food in case you break down in a remote area.

Before making a trip, drivers and cyclists should talk with a ranger to register and to check current road conditions, which can change drastically from one day to the next. The rangers can also tell you where to seek help if you get stuck. Primitive campgrounds are provided on most of the roads, but you'll need a backcountry permit from a ranger. Books on backcountry exploration include Charles Wells's *Guide to Moab, UT Backroads & 4-Wheel Drive Trails,* which includes Canyonlands, and Damian Fagan and David Williams's *A Naturalist's Guide to the White Rim Trail.*

One more thing about backcountry travel in Canyonlands: You may need to pack your poop out of the backcountry. Because of the abundance of slickrock and the desert conditions, it's not always possible to dig a hole, and you can't just leave your waste on a rock until it decomposes (decomposition is a very slow process in these conditions). Check with the ranger when you pick up your backcountry permit for more information.

Island in the Sky District

The main part of this district sits on a mesa high above the Colorado and Green Rivers. It is connected to points north by a narrow land bridge just wide enough for the road, known as "the neck," which forms the only vehicle access to the 40-square-mile (104-sq-km) Island in the Sky. Panoramic views from the "Island" can be enjoyed from any point along the rim; you'll see much of the park and southeastern Utah.

Short hiking trails lead to overlooks and to Mesa Arch, Aztec Butte, Whale Rock, Upheaval Dome, and other features. Longer trails make steep, strenuous descents from the Island to the White Rim Road below. Elevations on the Island average about 6,000 feet (1,829 m).

Although much of the rock within Canyonlands is not suitable for climbing, there are some routes in the Island in the Sky, including Taylor Canyon in the extreme northwest corner of the park, which is reached by lengthy and rugged 4WD roads.

Bring water for all hiking, camping, and travel in Island in the Sky. During the summer, water is available at the visitors center; otherwise, there is no water available in this district of the park.

GETTING THERE

From Moab, drive 10 miles (16 km) north on U.S. 191 and turn left (west) onto Highway 313. If you are coming in from I-70, drive 20 miles (32 km) south on U.S. 191 from exit 182 to reach the junction. Continue on this paved road for 22 miles (35 km) west then south to reach the park entrance. These aren't fast roads: From Moab, allow 45 minutes to reach the park. Note that GPS-based navigation systems don't always provide accurate positioning and mapping in remote areas like the Island in the Sky. Rely on maps and road signs to get you where you want to go, not your sat-nav system.

VISITORS CENTER

Stop here for information about Island in the Sky and to see exhibits on the geology and history of the area. Books and maps are available for purchase, and an audio tour of the park's scenic road is available for purchase or rental. The **visitors center** (435/259-4712, 8am-6pm daily late Apr.-late-Sept., 8:30am-5pm mid-Mar.-mid-April and Oct., 9am-4pm daily Nov.-Dec., 9am-4pm Fri.-Tues. Jan.-Feb., 8am-4pm daily Mar.1-Mar 16) is located just before the neck crosses to Island in the Sky. From Moab, go northwest 10 miles (16 km) on U.S. 191, then turn left and drive 15 miles (24 km) on Highway 313 to the junction for Dead Horse Point State Park. From here, continue straight for 7 miles (11.3 km).

SIGHTS
Shafer Canyon Overlook

Half a mile (0.8 km) past the visitors center is the Shafer Canyon Overlook (on the left, just before crossing the neck). The overlook has good views east down the canyon and onto the incredibly twisting **Shafer Trail Road.** Cattlemen Frank and John Schafer built the trail in the early 1900s to move stock between pastures (the *c* in their name was later dropped by mapmakers). Uranium prospectors upgraded the trail to a 4WD road during the 1950s so that they could reach their claims at the base of the cliffs. Today, Shafer Trail Road connects the mesa top with White Rim Road and Potash Road, 4 miles (6.4 km) and 1,200 vertical feet (366 m) below. High-clearance vehicles should be used on the Shafer. It's also fun to ride this road on a mountain bike. Road conditions can vary considerably, so contact a ranger before starting. Shafer Trail Viewpoint, across the neck,

---

1: Shafer Canyon Overlook **2:** Green River overlook **3:** The Island in the Sky is flanked by 800-foot cliffs.

provides another perspective 0.5 mile (0.8 km) farther on.

Back on top of the Island, the paved park road leads south from the neck 6 miles (9.7 km) across Gray's Pasture to a junction. The Grand View Point Overlook road continues south while the road to Upheaval Dome turns west.

Buck Canyon Overlook

As the park road continues south, a series of incredible vistas over the canyons of the Green and Colorado Rivers peek into view. The first viewpoint, 9 miles (14.5 km) south of the visitors center, is the wheelchair-accessible Buck Canyon Overlook, which looks east over the Colorado River canyon. Two miles (3.2 km) farther (11 mi/17.7 km south of the visitor center) is the **Grand View Picnic Area,** a handy lunch stop.

Grand View Point

At the end of the main road, 1 mile (1.6 km) past the Grand View Picnic Area (12 mi/19.3 km south of the visitors center), is the Grand View Point Overlook, perhaps the most spectacular panorama from Island in the Sky. Monument Basin lies directly below, and countless canyons, the Colorado River, the Needles, and mountain ranges are in the distance. The Grand View Point Overlook is wheelchair-accessible, and the easy 1-mile (1.6-km) **Grand View Trail** continues past the end of the road for other vistas from the point.

Return to the main road to explore more overlooks and geological curiosities in the western portion of Island in the Sky.

Green River Overlook

The Green River Overlook is just west of the main junction on a paved road. From this wheelchair-accessible overlook, Soda Springs Basin and a section of the Green River (deeply entrenched in Stillwater Canyon) can be seen below. Small Island in the Sky Campground is on the way to the overlook.

Upheaval Dome Road

At the end of the road, 5.3 miles (8.5 km) northwest of the junction (just over 11 mi/17.7 km from the visitors center), is **Upheaval Dome.** This geologic oddity is a fantastically deformed pile of rock sprawled across a crater about 3 miles (4.8 km) wide and 1,200 feet (366 m) deep. For many years, Upheaval Dome has kept geologists busy trying to figure out its origins. They once assumed that salt of the Paradox Formation pushed the rock layers upward to form the dome. Now, however, strong evidence suggests that a meteorite impact created the structure. The surrounding ring depression, caused by collapse, and the convergence of rock layers upward toward the center correspond precisely to known impact structures. Shatter cones and microscopic analysis also indicate an impact origin. When the meteorite struck, sometime in the last 150 million years, it formed a crater up to 5 miles (8 km) across. Erosion removed some of the overlying rock—perhaps as much as a vertical mile. The underlying salt may have played a role in uplifting the central section.

The easy **Crater View Trail** leads to overlooks on the rim of Upheaval Dome; the first viewpoint is 0.5 mile round-trip, and the second is 1 mile (1.6 km) round-trip. There's also a small **picnic area** here.

★ White Rim Road

This driving adventure follows the White Rim below the sheer cliffs of Island in the Sky. A close look at the light-colored surface reveals ripple marks and cross beds laid down near an ancient coastline. The plateau's east side is about 800 feet (244 m) above the Colorado River. On the west side, the plateau meets the bank of the Green River.

Travel along the winding road presents a constantly changing panorama of rock, canyons, river, and sky. Keep an eye out for desert bighorn sheep. You'll see all three levels of Island in the Sky District, from the high plateaus to the White Rim to the rivers.

Only 4WD vehicles with high clearance

Four-Wheeling in Canyonlands

Canyonlands is a tonic for people who think that just as a dog needs to run free every once in a while, jeeps need to occasionally escape the home-to-work loop.

Each of the park's three main districts has a focal point for 4WD travel. In the Island in the Sky, it's the 100-mile-long **White Rim Road.** Four-wheelers in the Needles head to **Elephant Rock** for the challenging climb to a network of roads. The Maze's **Flint Trail** traverses clay slopes that are extremely slippery when wet. Though all of the park's 4WD roads are rugged, those in the Maze are especially challenging, and this area is by far the most remote.

Drivers should note that ATVs are not permitted in national parks. All vehicles must be street-legal. The most commonly used vehicles are jeeps. Four-wheel drivers should be prepared to make basic road or vehicle repairs and should carry the following items:

Four-wheeling on White Rim Road

- at least one full-size spare tire
- extra gas
- extra water
- a shovel
- a high-lift jack
- chains for all four tires, especially October-April

Also note that towing from any backcountry area of Canyonlands is very expensive: It's not uncommon for bills to top $1,000.

Permits are required for overnight trips, camping is only in designated sites.

can make the trip. With the proper vehicle, driving is mostly easy but slow and winding; a few steep or rough sections have to be negotiated. The 100-mile (161-km) trip takes two or three days. Allow an extra day to travel all the road spurs.

Mountain bikers find this a great trip too; most cyclists arrange an accompanying 4WD vehicle to carry water and camping gear. Primitive campgrounds along the way provide convenient stopping places. Both cyclists and 4WD drivers must obtain **reservations** and a **backcountry permit** ($30) for the White Rim campsites from the Island in the Sky visitors center. Find application forms on the Canyonlands website (https://canypermits.

nps.gov); return the completed application at least two weeks in advance of your planned trip. Questions can be fielded via telephone (435/259-4351, 8am-noon Mon.-Fri.), but no telephone reservations are accepted. Demand exceeds supply during the popular spring and autumn seasons, when you should make reservations as far in advance as possible. No services or developed water sources exist anywhere on the drive, so be sure to have plenty of fuel and water with some to spare. Access points are Shafer Trail Road (from near Island in the Sky) and Potash Road (Hwy. 279 from Moab) on the east and Mineral Bottom Road on the west. White Rim sandstone forms the distinctive plateau crossed on the drive.

Island in the Sky Hikes

Trail	Effort	Distance	Duration
★ Mesa Arch Trail	easy	0.25 mi/0.4 km one-way	15 minutes
White Rim Overlook Trail	easy	0.75 mi/1.2 km one-way	1 hour
Upheaval Dome Viewpoint Trail	easy	1 mi/1.6 km one-way	1.5 hours
★ Grand View Trail	easy	1 mi/1.6 km one-way	1 hour
Whale Rock Trail	easy-moderate	0.5 mi/0.8 km one-way	1 hour
Aztec Butte Trail	moderate	1 mi/1.6 km one-way	1.5 hours
Neck Springs Trail	moderate	5.8-mi/9.3-km loop	3-4 hours
Gooseberry Trail	strenuous	2.5 mi/4 km one-way	5 hours
Syncline Loop Trail	strenuous	8-mi/12.9-km loop	5-7 hours
Murphy Point	strenuous	11-mi/17.7-km loop	5-7 hours
Alcove Spring Trail	strenuous	10 mi/16 km one-way	overnight
Lathrop Trail	strenuous	10.5 mi/16.9 km one-way	overnight

HIKING

Neck Springs Trail

Distance: 5.8-mile (9.3 km) loop
Duration: 3-4 hours
Elevation change: 300 feet (91 m)
Effort: moderate
Trailhead: Shafer Canyon Overlook

The trail begins near the Shafer Canyon Overlook and loops down Taylor Canyon to Neck and Cabin Springs, formerly used by ranchers (look for the remains of the old cowboy cabin near Cabin Springs). It then climbs back to Island in the Sky Road at a second trailhead 0.5 mile (0.8 km) south of the start. Water at the springs supports maidenhair fern and other plants. Also watch for birds and wildlife attracted to this spot. Bring water with you, as the springs are not potable.

Lathrop Trail

Distance: 10.5 miles (16.9 km) one-way to the Colorado River
Duration: overnight
Elevation change: 2,000 feet (610 m)
Effort: strenuous
Trailhead: on the left, 1.3 miles (2.1 km) past the neck

This is the only marked hiking route going all the way from Island in the Sky to the Colorado River. The first 3 miles (4.8 km) cross Gray's Pasture to the rim, which affords fantastic vistas over the Colorado. From here, the trail descends steeply, dropping 1,600 feet (488 m) over the next 2.5 miles (4 km) to White Rim Road, a little less than 7 miles (11.3 km) from the trailhead. Part of this section follows an old mining road past several abandoned mines, all relics of the uranium boom. Don't enter the shafts; they're in danger of collapse and may contain poisonous gases. From the mining area, the route descends through a wash to White Rim Road, follows the road a short distance south, then goes down Lathrop Canyon Road to the Colorado River, another 4 miles (6.4 km) and 500 vertical feet (152 m). The trail has little shade and can be very hot. Vehicular traffic may be encountered along the White Rim Road portion of the trail. For a long day hike (13.6 mi/21.9 km round-trip), turn around when you reach the White Rim Road and hike back up to the top of the mesa.

★ Mesa Arch Trail

Distance: 0.25 mile (0.4 km) one-way
Duration: 15 minutes
Elevation change: 80 feet (24 m)
Effort: easy
Trailhead: on the left, 5.5 miles (8.9 km) from the neck

This easy trail leads to a spectacular arch on the rim of the mesa. On the way, the trail crosses the arid grasslands and scattered juniper trees of Gray's Pasture. A trail brochure available at the start describes the ecology of the mesa. The rather barren, undramatic trail climbs gently until it suddenly reaches the edge of an 800-foot (244-m) precipice, topped by a sandstone arch. The arch frames views of rock formations below and the La Sal Mountains in the distance. Photographers come here to catch the sun (or moon) rising through the arch.

Murphy Point

Distance: 11-mile (17.7-km) loop
Duration: 5-7 hours
Elevation change: 1,100 feet (335 m)
Effort: strenuous
Trailhead: Murphy Point
Directions: From the Upheaval Dome junction on the main park road, head 3 miles (4.8 km) south. Turn right onto a rough dirt road and follow it 1.7 miles (2.7 km) to Murphy Point.

Murphy Trail starts as a jaunt across the mesa, then drops steeply from the rim down to White Rim Road. This strenuous route forks partway down; one branch follows Murphy Hogback (a ridge) to Murphy Campground on the 4WD road, and the other follows a wash to the road 1 mile (1.6 km) south of the campground.

White Rim Overlook Trail

Distance: 0.75 mile (1.2 km) one-way
Duration: 1 hour
Elevation change: 25 feet (8 m)
Effort: easy
Trailhead: Grand View Picnic Area

Hike east along a peninsula to an overlook of Monument Basin and beyond. There are also good views of White Rim Road and potholes,

Gooseberry Trail

Distance: 2.5 miles (4 km) one-way
Duration: 5 hours
Elevation change: 1,400 feet (427 m)
Effort: strenuous
Trailhead: Grand View Picnic Area

Mesa Arch spans the cliff's edge.

Gooseberry Trail drops off the mesa and makes an extremely steep descent to White Rim Road, just north of Gooseberry Campground. The La Sal Mountains are visible from the trail.

★ Grand View Trail

Distance: 1 mile (1.6 km) one-way
Duration: 1 hour
Elevation change: 50 feet (15 m)
Effort: easy
Trailhead: Grand View Point Overlook

At the overlook, Grand View Trail continues past the end of the road for other vistas from the point, which is the southernmost tip of Island in the Sky. This short hike across the slickrock will really give you a feel for the entire Canyonlands National Park. From the mesa-top trail, you'll see the gorges of the Colorado and Green Rivers come together; across the chasm is the Needles District. Look down to spot vehicles traveling along the White Rim Trail at the base of the mesa.

Aztec Butte Trail

Distance: 1 mile (1.6 km) one-way
Duration: 1.5 hours
Elevation change: 200 feet (61 m)
Effort: moderate
Trailhead: Aztec Butte parking area, 1 mile (1.6 km) northwest of road junction on Upheaval Dome Road

It's a bit of a haul up the slickrock to the top of this sandstone butte, but once you get here, you'll be rewarded with a good view of the Island and Taylor Canyon. Atop the butte a loop trail passes several Ancestral Puebloan granaries. Aztec Butte is one of the few areas in Island in the Sky with Native American ruins; the shortage of water in this area prevented permanent settlement.

Whale Rock Trail

Distance: 0.5 mile (0.8 km) one-way
Duration: 1 hour
Elevation change: 100 feet (30 m)
Effort: easy-moderate
Trailhead: Upheaval Dome Road, on the right, 4.4 miles (7.1 km) northwest of the road junction

A relatively easy trail climbs Whale Rock, a sandstone hump near the outer rim of Upheaval Dome. In a couple of places you'll have to do some scrambling up the slickrock, which is made easier and a bit less scary thanks to handrails. From the top of the rock, there are good views of the dome.

Watch your step along the Grand View Trail.

Grand View Trails

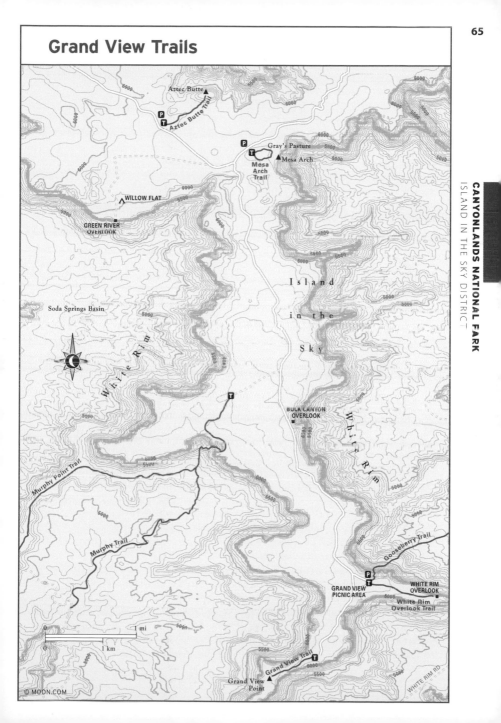

Aztec Butte

Aztec Butte Trail

Gray's Pasture

Mesa Arch

Mesa Arch Trail

WILLOW FLAT

GREEN RIVER OVERLOOK

Island

in the

Sky

Soda Springs Basin

White Rim

White Rim

BUCK CANYON OVERLOOK

Murphy Point Trail

Murphy Trail

Gooseberry Trail

GRAND VIEW PICNIC AREA

WHITE RIM OVERLOOK

White Rim Overlook Trail

Grand View Trail

Grand View Point

WHITE RIM RD.

0   1 mi

0   1 km

© MOON.COM

Upheaval Dome Viewpoint Trail

Distance: 1 mile (1.6 km) one-way
Duration: 1.5 hours
Elevation change: 150 feet (46 m)
Effort: easy
Trailhead: Upheaval Dome parking area

The trail leads to Upheaval Dome overviews; it's about 0.5 mile (0.8 km) to the first overlook and 1 mile (1.6 km) to the second. The shorter trail leads to the rim with a view about 1,000 feet (305 m) down into the jumble of rocks in the craterlike center of Upheaval Dome. The longer trail descends the slickrock and offers even better views. Energetic hikers can explore this formation in depth by circling it on the Syncline Loop Trail or from White Rim Road below.

Syncline Loop Trail

Distance: 8-mile (12.9-km) loop
Duration: 5-7 hours
Elevation change: 1,200 feet (366 m)
Effort: strenuous
Trailhead: Upheaval Dome parking area

Syncline Loop Trail makes a circuit completely around Upheaval Dome. The trail crosses Upheaval Dome Canyon about halfway around from the overlook; walk east 1.5 miles (2.4 km) up the canyon to enter the crater itself. This is the only nontechnical route into the center of the dome. A hike around Upheaval Dome with a side trip to the crater totals 11 miles (17.7 km), and it is best done as an overnight trip. Carry plenty of water for the entire trip; this dry country can be very hot in summer. The Green River is the only reliable source of water. An alternative approach is to start near Upheaval Campsite on White Rim Road; hike 4 miles (6.4 km) southeast on through Upheaval Canyon to a junction with the Syncline Loop Trail, then go another 1.5 miles (2.4 km) into the crater. The elevation gain is about 600 feet (183 m).

Alcove Spring Trail

Distance: 10 miles (16 km) one-way
Duration: overnight
Elevation change: 1,500 feet (457 m)
Effort: strenuous
Trailhead: 1.5 miles (2.4 km) southeast of the Upheaval Dome parking area

Alcove Spring Trail connects with White Rim Road in Taylor Canyon. Five miles (8 km) of the 10-mile (16-km) distance are on the steep trail down through Trail Canyon; the other 5 miles (8 km) are on a jeep road in Taylor Canyon. One downside of this trail is the 4WD traffic, which can be pretty heavy during the spring and fall. From the Taylor Canyon end of the trail, it is not far to the Upheaval Trail, which heads southeast to its junction with the Syncline Trail, which in turn leads to the Upheaval Dome parking area. Allow at least one overnight if you plan to hike this full loop. Day hikers should plan to turn around after the first 5-mile (8-km) section; this is still a very full day of hiking. Carry plenty of water—the trail is hot and dry.

CAMPGROUNDS

There is only one developed campground in the Island in the Sky District. **Island in the Sky Campground** on Murphy Point Road has only 12 sites ($15), available on a first-come, first-served basis; sites tend to fill up in all seasons except winter. There is one accessible campsite that is reserved for people with disabilities, and a paved path leading to the nearby pit-toilet. No water or services are available.

Camping is available just outside the park at **Dead Horse Point State Park** (reservations 800/322-3770, www.reserveamerica.com, $40 RV, $35 hike-in tent only, $140 yurt, plus $9 reservation fee), which is also very popular, so don't plan on getting a spot without reserving way ahead. There are also primitive Bureau of Land Management (BLM) campsites along Highway 313.

Upheaval Dome Trails

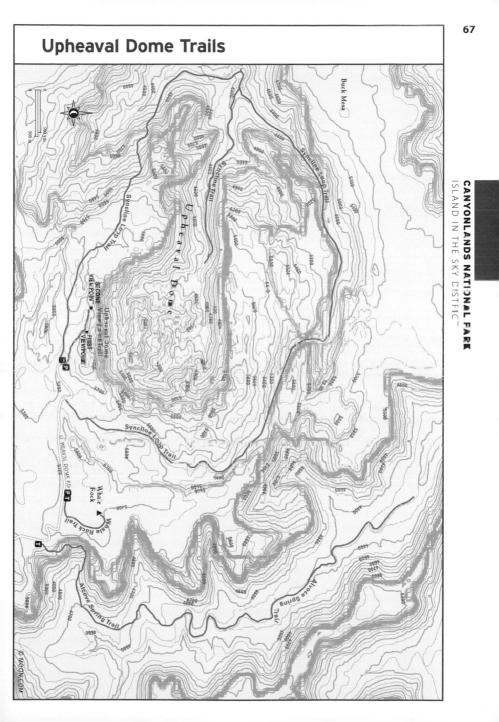

Buck Mesa

Syncline Loop Trail

Upheaval Dome

Syncline Loop Trail

Syncline Trail

CONE VIEWPOINT
Upheaval Dome Trail
FIRST VIEWPOINT

UPHEAVAL DOME RD.

Whale Rock

Whale Rock Trail

Alcove Spring Trail

Alcove Spring Trail

© MOON.COM

500 m
500 yds

Needles District

The Needles District, named for the area's distinctive sandstone spires, showcases some of the finest rock sculptures in Canyonlands National Park. Spires, arches, and monoliths appear in almost every direction. Prehistoric ruins and rock art exist in greater variety and quantity here than elsewhere in the park. Perennial springs and streams bring greenery to the desert.

While scenic paved Highway 211 leads to the district, this area of the park has only about a dozen miles of paved roads. Needles doesn't have a lot to offer travelers who are unwilling to get out of their vehicles and hike; however, it's the best section of the park for a wide variety of day hikes. Even a short hike opens up the landscape and leads to remarkable vistas and prehistoric sites.

The primary access road to Needles District, Highway 211, also passes through **Indian Creek National Monument,** designated in 2018 by President Donald Trump. Officials at this new monument are in the process of creating its management plan. For current recreational information, contact the BLM office in Monticello (365 N. Main, 435/587-1500).

GETTING THERE

To reach the Needles District, go 40 miles (64 km) south from Moab (or 14 mi/22.5 km north of Monticello) on U.S. 191, turn west onto Highway 211, and continue for 38 miles (61 km).

VISITORS CENTER

Stop at the **visitors center** (west end of Hwy. 211, 435/259-4711, 9am-4pm Fri.-Tues. Jan.-Feb., 8am-4pm daily Mar. 1-mid-Mar., 8am-6pm daily mid-Mar.-Sept., 8:30am-5pm daily Oct., 9am-4pm Nov.-Dec.) for information on hiking, back roads, and other aspects of travel in the Needles, as well as **backcountry permits** (required for all overnight stays in the backcountry) and maps, brochures, and books. Take about 15 minutes to watch the film on the region's geology. When the office isn't open, you'll find information posted outside.

SIGHTS
★ BLM Newspaper Rock Historical Monument

Although not in the park itself, Newspaper Rock lies just 150 feet (46 m) off Highway 211 on Bureau of Land Management (BLM) land on the way to the Needles District. At Newspaper Rock, a profusion of petroglyphs depict human figures, animals, birds, and abstract designs. These represent 2,000 years of human history during which prehistoric people and Ancestral Puebloan, Fremont, Paiute, Navajo, and Anglo travelers passed through Indian Creek Canyon. The patterns on the smooth sandstone rock face stand out clearly, thanks to a coating of dark desert varnish. A short nature trail introduces you to the area's desert and riparian vegetation.

From U.S. 191 between Moab and Monticello, turn west onto Highway 211 and travel 12 miles (19.3 km) to Newspaper Rock.

Indian Creek

The "splitter cracks" in the rock walls around **Indian Creek** offer world-class rock climbing, with close to 1,000 routes. Most routes here are tough, rating 5.10 and above. Fall climbing is best, followed by early spring; summer afternoons are way too hot, and it's dangerous to climb after a rainstorm.

Climbers should track down a copy of *Indian Creek: A Climbing Guide* by David Bloom, which has details and lots of pictures. **Moab Desert Adventures** (415

1: Big Spring Canyon Overlook **2:** Pothole Point Nature Trail **3:** Newspaper Rock **4:** camping at Needles Outpost

N. Main St., Moab, 804/814-3872, www. moabdesertadventures.com) offers guided climbing at Indian Creek.

Indian Creek's climbing walls start on Highway 211, about 15 miles (24 km) west of U.S. 191, and 3 miles (4.8 km) west of Newspaper Rock.

Needles and Anticline Overlooks

Although outside the park, these viewpoints atop the high mesa east of Canyonlands National Park offer magnificent panoramas of the surrounding area. Part of the BLM's **Canyon Rims Recreation Area** (www. blm.gov), these easily accessed overlooks provide the kind of awe-inspiring vistas over the Needles District that would otherwise require a hike in the park. The turnoff for both overlooks is at milepost 93 on U.S. 191, which is 32 miles (52 km) south of Moab and 7 miles (11.3 km) north of Highway 211. There are also two campgrounds along the access road.

For the **Needles Overlook,** follow the paved road 22 miles (35 km) west to its end (turn left at the junction 15 mi/24 km in). The BLM maintains a picnic area and interpretive exhibits here. A fence protects visitors from the sheer cliffs that drop off more than 1,000 feet (305 m). You can see much of Canyonlands National Park and southeastern Utah. Look south for the Six-Shooter Peaks and the high country of the Abajo Mountains; southwest for the Needles (thousands of spires reaching for the sky); west for the confluence area of the Green and Colorado Rivers, the Maze District, the Orange Cliffs, and the Henry Mountains; northwest for the lazy bends of the Colorado River canyon and the sheer-walled mesas of Island in the Sky and Dead Horse Point; north for the Book Cliffs; and northeast for the La Sal Mountains. The changing shadows and colors of the canyon country make for a continuous show throughout the day.

For the **Anticline Overlook,** from U.S. 191, head 15 miles (24 km) west to the junction with the Needles road, then turn right and drive 17 miles (27 km) north on a good gravel road to the fenced overlook at road's end. You'll be standing 1,600 feet (488 m) above the Colorado River. The sweeping panorama over the canyons, the river (and the bright blue evaporation ponds at the potash factory outside Moab), and the twisted rocks of the Kane Creek Anticline is nearly as spectacular as that from Dead Horse Point, only 5.5 miles (8.9 km) west as the crow flies. Salt and other minerals of the Paradox Formation pushed up overlying rocks into the dome visible below. Down-cutting by the Colorado River has revealed the twisted rock layers. Look carefully at the northeast horizon to see an arch in the Windows Section of Arches National Park, 16 miles (26 km) away.

The BLM operates two campgrounds in the Canyon Rims Recreation Area. **Hatch Point Campground** (10 sites, May-mid-Oct., $15) has a quiet and scenic mesa-top setting just off the road to the Anticline Overlook, about 9 miles (14.5 km) north of the road junction. Closer to the highway in a rock amphitheater is **Windwhistle Campground** (May-mid-Oct., $15); it's 6 miles (9.7 km) west of U.S. 191 on the Needles Overlook road. Although both of these campgrounds supposedly have water, it wasn't evident when we visited.

Needles Outpost

The **Needles Outpost campground** (435/979-4007, http://www.needlesoutpost. com, mid-Feb.-mid Dec., $20 tents or RVs, no hookups), just outside the park boundary, is a good place to stay if the campground in the park is full. A general store here has groceries, ice, gas, propane, showers ($3 campers, $6 noncampers), and basic camping supplies. Campsites have a fair amount of privacy and great views onto the park's spires. The turnoff from Highway 211 is one mile before the Needles visitors center.

SCENIC DRIVE

The main paved park road continues 6.5 miles (10.5 km) past the visitors center to **Big Spring Canyon Overlook**. On the way, you

Needles Hikes

Trail	Effort	Distance	Duration
Roadside Ruin Trail	easy	0.3 mi/0.5 km round-trip	15 minutes
★ Cave Spring Trail	easy	0.6 mi/1 km round-trip	45 minutes
Pothole Point Nature Trail	easy	0.6 mi/1 km round-trip	40 minutes
Slickrock Trail	easy-moderate	2.4 mi/3.9 km round-trip	2 hours
★ Chesler Park	moderate	3 mi/4.8 km one-way	3-4 hours
Squaw Canyon Trail	moderate	3.75 mi/6 km one-way	4 hours
Lost Canyon Trail	moderate-strenuous	3.25 mi/5.2 km one-way	4-5 hours
Big Spring Canyon Trail	moderate-strenuous	3.75 mi/6 km one-way	4 hours
Confluence Overlook Trail	moderate-strenuous	5.5 mi/8.9 km one-way	5 hours
Peekaboo Trail	strenuous	5 mi/8 km one-way	5-6 hours
Druid Arch	strenuous	5.5 mi/8.9 km one-way	5-7 hours
Lower Red Lake Canyon Trail	strenuous	9.5 mi/15.3 km one-way	2 days
Upper Salt Creek Trail	strenuous	12 mi/19.3 km one-way	2 days

can stop at several nature trails or turn onto 4WD roads. The overlook takes in a view of slickrock-edged canyons dropping away toward the Colorado River.

HIKING

The Needles District includes about 60 miles (97 km) of backcountry trails. Many interconnect to provide all sorts of day-hike and overnight opportunities. Cairns mark the trails, and signs point the way at junctions. You can normally find water in upper Elephant Canyon and canyons to the east in spring and early summer, although whatever remains is often stagnant by midsummer. Always ask the rangers about sources of water, and don't depend on its availability. Treat water from all sources, including springs, before drinking it. Chesler Park and other areas west of Elephant Canyon are very dry; you'll need to bring all your water. Mosquitoes, gnats, and deer flies can be pesky late spring to midsummer, especially in the wetter places, so be sure to bring insect repellent. To plan your trip, obtain the small hiking map available from the visitors center, the National Geographic/Trails Illustrated Needles District map, or USGS topographic maps. Overnight backcountry hiking requires a **permit** ($30 per group). Permits can be hard to get at the last minute during the busy spring hiking season, but you can apply for your permit any time after mid-July for the following spring. Find permit applications on the Canyonlands permitting website (https://canypermits.nps.gov). Note that campers at sites in Chesler Park, Elephant Canyon, and at Peekaboo will be required to pack out their human waste.

Roadside Ruin Trail

Distance: 0.3 mile (0.5 km) round-trip
Duration: 15 minutes
Elevation change: 20 feet (6 m)
Effort: easy
Trailhead: on the left, 0.4 mile (0.6 km) past the visitors center

This is one of two easy hikes near the visitors center. It passes near a well-preserved Ancestral Puebloan granary. A trail guide available at the start tells about the Ancestral Puebloans and the local plants.

★ Cave Spring Trail

Distance: 0.6 mile (1 km) round-trip
Duration: 45 minutes
Elevation change: 50 feet (15 m)
Effort: easy
Trailhead: Cave Spring
Directions: Turn left 0.7 mile (1.1 km) past the visitors center and follow signs about 1 mile (1.6 km) to the trailhead.

Don't miss the Cave Spring Trail, which introduces the geology and ecology of the park and leads to an old cowboy line camp. Pick up the brochure at the beginning. The loop goes clockwise, crossing some slickrock; two ladders assist hikers on the steep sections. Native Americans first used these rock overhangs for shelter, and faint pictographs still decorate the rock walls. Much later—from the late 1800s until the park was established in 1964—cowboys used these open caves as a line camp. The National Park Service has recreated the line camp, just 50 yards in from the trailhead, with period furnishings and equipment. If you're not up for the full hike, or would rather not climb ladders, the cowboy camp and the pictographs are just a five-minute walk from the trailhead.

This trail is a good introduction to hiking on slickrock and using rock cairns to find your way. Signs identify plants along the way.

Pothole Point Nature Trail

Distance: 0.6 mile (1 km) round-trip
Duration: 40 minutes
Elevation change: 20 feet (6 m)
Effort: easy
Trailhead: parking area on the left side of Big Spring Canyon Overlook Scenic Drive, 5 miles (8 km) past the visitors center

Highlights of this hike across the slickrock are the many potholes dissolved in the Cedar Mesa sandstone. A brochure illustrates the fairy shrimp, tadpole shrimp, horsehair worms, snails, and other creatures that spring to life when rain fills the potholes. Desert varnish rims the potholes; it forms when water evaporates, leaving mineral residues on the surface of the rocks. In addition to the potholes, you'll enjoy fine views of distant buttes from the trail.

Slickrock Trail

Distance: 2.4 miles (3.9 km) round-trip
Duration: 2 hours
Elevation change: 150 feet (46 m)
Effort: easy-moderate
Trailhead: parking area on the right side of Big Spring Canyon Overlook Scenic Drive, 6.2 miles (10 km) past the visitors center

The Slickrock Trail leads north to a series of four viewpoints, including a panoramic view over much of southeastern Utah, and overlooks of Big Spring and Little Spring Canyons. As its name indicates, much of the trail is across slickrock, but there are enough pockets of soil to support a good springtime display of wildflowers. The trailhead is almost at the end of the paved road, where **Big Spring Canyon Overlook,** 6.5 miles (10.5 km) past the visitors center, marks the end of the scenic drive but not the scenery.

Confluence Overlook Trail

Distance: 5.5 miles (8.9 km) one-way
Duration: 5 hours
Elevation change: 1,250 feet (381 m)
Effort: moderate-strenuous
Trailhead: Big Spring Canyon Overlook

The Confluence Overlook Trail begins at the

Big Spring Canyon Overlook Trails

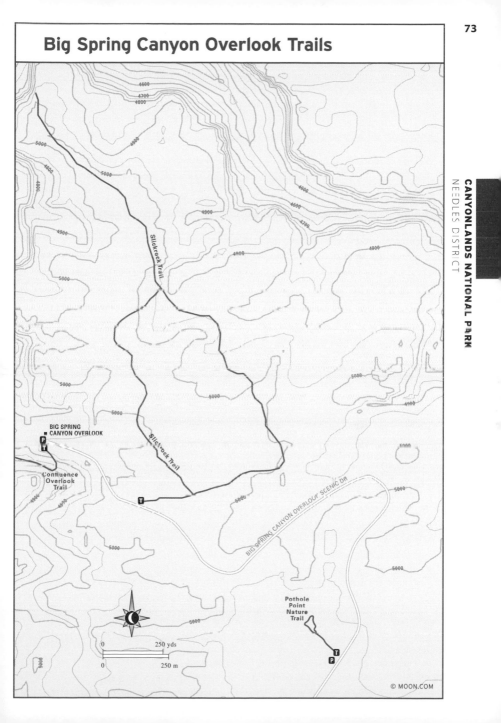

© MOON.COM

end of the paved road and winds west to an overlook of the Green and Colorado Rivers 1,000 feet (305 m) below; there's no trail down to the rivers. The trail starts with some ups and downs, crossing Big Spring and Elephant Canyons, and follows a jeep road for a short distance. Much of the trail is through open country, so it can get quite hot. Higher points have good views of the Needles to the south. You might see rafts in the water or bighorn sheep on the cliffs. Except for a few short steep sections, this trail is level and fairly easy; it's the length of this 11-mile (17.7-km) round-trip to the confluence as well as the hot sun that make it challenging. A very early start is recommended in summer because there's little shade. Carry water even if you don't plan to go all the way. This enchanting country has lured many a hiker beyond his or her original goal.

Peekaboo Trail

Distance: 5 miles (8 km) one-way
Duration: 5-6 hours
Elevation change: 550 feet (168 m)
Effort: strenuous
Trailhead: Squaw Flat trailhead
Directions: A road to Needles Campground and Elephant Hill turns left 2.7 miles (4.3 km) past the visitors center. The Squaw Flat trailhead is at the end of campground loop A.

Peekaboo Trail winds southeast over rugged up-and-down terrain, including some steep sections of slickrock (best avoided when wet, icy, or covered with snow) and a couple of ladders. There's little shade, so carry water. The trail follows Squaw Canyon, climbs over a pass to Lost Canyon, then crosses more slickrock before descending to Peekaboo Campground on Salt Creek Road (accessible by 4WD vehicles). Look for Ancestral Puebloan ruins on the way and rock art at the campground. A rockslide took out Peekaboo Spring, which is still shown on some maps. Options on this trail include a turnoff south through Squaw or Lost Canyon to make a loop of 8.75 miles (14.1 km) or more.

Squaw Canyon Trail

Distance: 3.75 miles (6 km) one-way
Duration: 4 hours
Elevation change: 700 feet (213 m)
Effort: moderate
Trailhead: Squaw Flat trailhead
Directions: A road to Needles Campground and Elephant Hill turns left 2.7 miles (4.3 km) past the visitors center. The Squaw Flat trailhead is at the end of campground loop A.

Squaw Canyon Trail follows the canyon south. Intermittent water can often be found until late spring, when there's plenty of greenery. Connect with the Big Spring Canyon Trail to make a great 7.5-mile (12-km) loop. Another possible loop is formed by linking the Squaw Canyon and Lost Canyon Trails, totaling 8.7 miles (14 km). Both of these loops require stiff climbs (with great views) to get over the slickrock hills separating the canyons.

Lost Canyon Trail

Distance: 3.25 miles (5.2 km) one-way
Duration: 4-5 hours
Elevation change: 360 feet (110 m)
Effort: moderate-strenuous
Trailhead: Squaw Flat trailhead
Directions: A road to Needles Campground and Elephant Hill turns left 2.7 miles (4.3 km) past the visitors center. The Squaw Flat trailhead is at the end of campground loop A.

Lost Canyon Trail is reached via Peekaboo or Squaw Canyon Trails and makes a loop with them. Lost Canyon is surprisingly lush, and you may be forced to wade through water. Most of the trail is in the wash bottom, except for a section of slickrock to Squaw Canyon.

Big Spring Canyon Trail

Distance: 3.75 miles (6 km) one-way
Duration: 4 hours
Elevation change: 370 feet (113 m)
Effort: moderate-strenuous
Trailhead: Squaw Flat trailhead

1: Slickrock Trail 2: Big Spring Canyon Trail

Directions: A road to Needles Campground and Elephant Hill turns left 2.7 miles (4.3 km) past the visitors center. The Squaw Flat trailhead is at the end of campground loop A.

Big Spring Canyon Trail crosses an outcrop of slickrock from the trailhead, then follows the canyon bottom to the head of the canyon. It's a lovely springtime hike with lots of flowers, including the fragrant cliffrose. Except in summer, you can usually find intermittent water along the way. At canyon's end, a steep slickrock climb leads to Squaw Canyon Trail and back to the trailhead for a 7.5-mile (12-km) loop. Another possibility is to turn southwest to the head of Squaw Canyon, then hike over a saddle to Elephant Canyon, for a 10.5-mile (16.9-km) loop.

★ Chesler Park

Distance: 3 miles (4.8 km) one-way
Duration: 3-4 hours
Elevation change: 920 feet (280 m)
Effort: moderate
Trailhead: Elephant Hill parking area or Squaw Flat trailhead—increases the round-trip distance by 2 miles/3.2 kilometers
Directions: Drive west 3 miles (4.8 km) past the Needles Campground turnoff (on passable dirt roads) to the Elephant Hill picnic area and trailhead at the base of Elephant Hill.

The Elephant Hill parking area doesn't always inspire confidence: Sounds of racing engines can often be heard from above as vehicles attempt the difficult 4WD road that begins just past the picnic area. However, the noise quickly fades as you hit the trail. Chesler Park is a favorite hiking destination. A lovely desert meadow contrasts with the red and white spires that give the Needles District its name. An old cowboy line camp is on the west side of the rock island in the center of the park. The trail winds through sand and slickrock before ascending a small pass through the Needles to Chesler Park. Once inside, you can take the Chesler Park Loop Trail (5 mi/8 km) completely around the park. The loop includes the unusual 0.5-mile (0.8-km) Joint Trail, which follows the bottom of a very narrow crack. Camping in Chesler Park is restricted to certain areas; check with a ranger.

Druid Arch

Distance: 5.5 miles (8.9 km) one-way
Duration: 5-7 hours
Elevation change: 1,000 feet (305 m)
Effort: strenuous
Trailhead: Elephant Hill parking area or Squaw Flat trailhead—increases the round-trip distance by 2 miles/3.2 kilometers

Chesler Park

Directions: Drive west 3 miles (4.8 km) past the Needles Campground turnoff (on passable dirt roads) to the Elephant Hill picnic area and trailhead at the base of Elephant Hill.

Druid Arch reminds many people of the massive slabs at Stonehenge in England, which are popularly associated with the druids. Follow the Chesler Park Trail 2 miles (3.2 km) to Elephant Canyon, turn up the canyon for 3.5 miles (5.6 km), and then make a steep 0.25-mile (0.4 km) climb, which includes a ladder and some scrambling, to the arch. Upper Elephant Canyon has seasonal water but is closed to camping.

Lower Red Lake Canyon Trail

Distance: 9.5 miles (15.3 km) one-way
Duration: 2 days
Elevation change: 1,000 feet (305 m)
Effort: strenuous
Trailhead: Elephant Hill parking area or Squaw Flat trailhead (increases the round-trip distance by 2 mi/3.2 km)
Directions: Drive west 3 miles (6.4 km) past the Needles Campground turnoff (on passable dirt roads) to the Elephant Hill picnic area and trailhead at the base of Elephant Hill.

Lower Red Lake Canyon Trail provides access to the Colorado River's Cataract Canyon. This long, strenuous trip is best suited for experienced hikers and is ideally completed in two days. Distance from the Elephant Hill trailhead is 19 miles (31 km) round-trip; you'll be walking on 4WD roads and trails. If you can drive Elephant Hill 4WD Road to the trail junction in Cyclone Canyon, the hike is only 8 miles (12.9 km) round-trip. The most difficult trail section is a steep talus slope that drops 700 feet (213 m) in 0.5 mile (0.8 km) into the lower canyon. The canyon has little shade and lacks any water source above the river. Summer heat can make the trip grueling; temperatures tend to be 5-10°F hotter than on other Needles trails. The river level drops between midsummer and autumn, allowing hikers to go along the shore both downstream to see the rapids and upstream to the confluence.

Undertows and strong currents make the river dangerous to cross.

Upper Salt Creek Trail

Distance: 12 miles (19.3 km) one-way
Duration: 2 days
Elevation change: 1,650 feet (503 m)
Effort: strenuous
Trailhead: end of Salt Creek Road
Directions: Drive to the end of the rugged 13.5-mile (21.7-km) 4WD road up Salt Creek to start this hike.

Several impressive arches and many inviting side canyons attract adventurous hikers to the extreme southeast corner of the Needles District. The trail goes south 12 miles (19.3 km) up-canyon to Cottonwood Canyon and Beef Basin Road near Cathedral Butte, just outside the park boundary. The trail is nearly level except for a steep climb at the end. Water can usually be found. Some wading and bushwhacking may be necessary. The famous "All-American Man" pictograph, shown on some topographic maps (or ask a ranger), is in a cave a short way off to the east at about the midpoint of the trail; follow your map and unsigned paths to the cave, but don't climb in—it's dangerous to you, the ruins, and the pictograph inside. Many more archaeological sites are near the trail, but they're all fragile, and great care should be taken when visiting them.

MOUNTAIN BIKING AND 4WD EXPLORATION

Visitors with bicycles or 4WD vehicles can explore the many backcountry roads that lead to the outback. More than 50 miles (81 km) of challenging roads link primitive campsites, remote trailheads, and sites with ancient cultural remnants. Some roads in the Needles District are rugged and require previous experience in handling 4WD vehicles on steep inclines and in deep sand. Be aware that towing charges from this area commonly run over $1,000.

The best route for mountain bikers is the 7-mile-long (11.3 km) Colorado Overlook Road, which starts near the visitors center.

Squaw Flat and Elephant Hill Trails

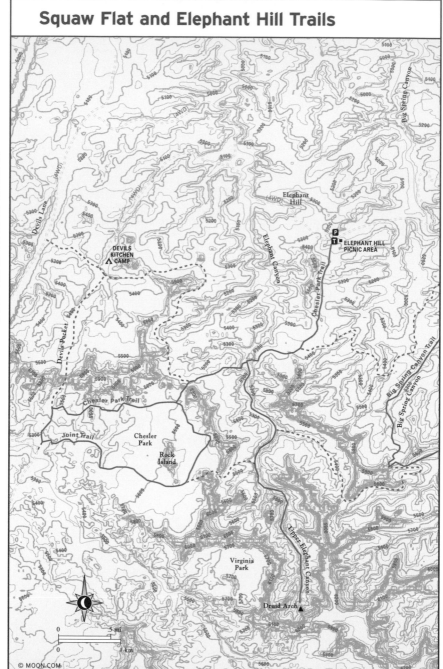

© MOON.COM

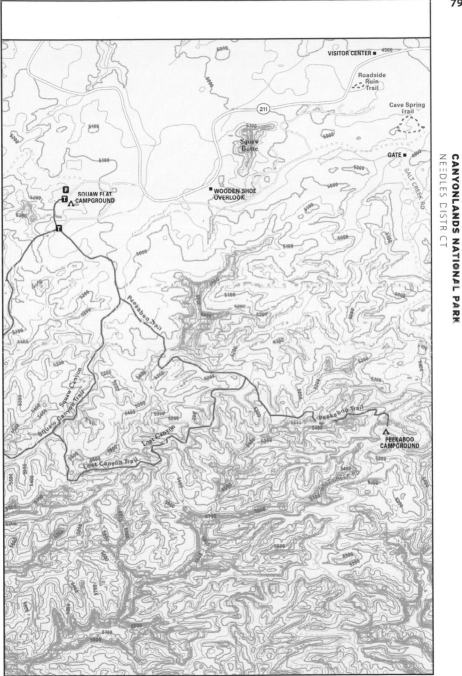

Although very steep for the first stretch and busy with 4WD vehicles spinning their wheels on the hill, Elephant Hill Road is another good bet, with just a few sandy parts. Start here and do a combination ride and hike to the Confluence Overlook. It's about 8 miles (12.9 km) from the Elephant Hill parking area to the confluence; the final 0.5 mile (0.8 km) is on a trail, so you'll have to lock up your bike and walk this last bit. Horse Canyon and Lavender Canyon are too sandy for pleasant biking.

All motor vehicles and bicycles must have a **day-use permit** and remain on designated roads. Overnight backcountry trips with bicycles or motor vehicles require a permit ($30 per group).

Salt Creek Canyon 4WD Road

This rugged route begins near Cave Spring Trail, crosses sage flats for the next 2.5 miles (4 km), and then terminates at Peekaboo Campground. Hikers can continue south into a spectacular canyon on Upper Salt Creek Trail.

Horse Canyon 4WD Road turns off to the left shortly before the mouth of Salt Canyon. The round-trip distance, including a side trip to Tower Ruin, is about 13 miles (21 km); other attractions include Paul Bunyan's Potty, Castle Arch, Fortress Arch, and side canyon hiking. Salt and Horse Canyons can easily be driven in 4WD vehicles. Salt Canyon is usually closed in summer because of quicksand after flash floods and in winter due to shelf ice.

Davis and Lavender Canyons

Both canyons are accessed via Davis Canyon Road off Highway 211; contain great scenery, arches, and Native American historic sites; and are easily visited with high-clearance vehicles. Davis is about 20 miles (32 km) round-trip, while sandy Lavender Canyon is about 26 miles (42 km) round-trip. Try to allow plenty of time in either canyon, because there is much to see and many inviting side canyons to

hike. You can camp on BLM land just outside the park boundaries, but not in the park itself.

Colorado Overlook 4WD Road

This popular route begins beside the visitors center and follows Salt Creek to Lower Jump Overlook. It then bounces across slickrock to a view of the Colorado River, upstream from the confluence. Driving, for the most part, is easy-moderate, although it's very rough for the last 1.5 miles (2.4 km). Round-trip distance is 14 miles (22.5 km). This is also a good mountain bike ride.

Elephant Hill 4WD Loop Road

This rugged backcountry road begins 3 miles (4.8 km) past the Needles Campground turnoff. Only experienced drivers with stout vehicles should attempt the extremely rough and steep climb up Elephant Hill (coming up the back side of Elephant Hill is even worse). The loop is about 10 miles (16 km) round-trip. Connecting roads go to the Confluence Overlook trailhead (the viewpoint is 1 mile/1.6 kilometers round-trip on foot), the Joint trailhead (Chesler Park is 2 miles/3.2 kilometers round-trip on foot), and several canyons. Some road sections on the loop are one-way. In addition to Elephant Hill, a few other difficult spots must be negotiated. The parallel canyons in this area are grabens caused by faulting, where a layer of salt has shifted deep underground.

This area can also be reached by a long route south of the park using Cottonwood Canyon and Beef Basin Road from Highway 211, about 60 miles (97 km) one-way. You'll enjoy spectacular vistas from the Abajo Highlands. Two very steep descents from Pappys Pasture into Bobbys Hole effectively make this section one-way; travel from Elephant Hill up Bobbys Hole is possible but much more difficult than going the other way, and it may require hours of road-building. The Bobbys Hole route may be impassable at times; ask about conditions at the BLM office in Monticello or at the Needles visitors center.

CAMPGROUNDS

The **Needles Campground** (year-round, reservations available and recommended for Loop B only Mar. 15-June 30 and Sept. 1-Oct. 31, $20), formerly known as Squaw Flat Campground, is about 6 miles (9.7 km) from the visitors center. It has water and 26 sites (two of which are accessible), with many snuggled under the slickrock. RVs must be less than 28 feet (8.5 m) long. Rangers present evening programs (spring-autumn) at the campfire circle on Loop A.

If you can't find a space at the Needles Campground—a common occurrence in spring and fall—the private campground at **Needles Outpost** (435/979-4007, https://needlesoutpost.com, Mar.-Nov., $22 tents or RVs, no hookups, showers $3), just outside the park entrance, is a good alternative.

Nearby BLM land also offers a number of places to camp. A string of campsites along **Lockhart Basin Road** are convenient and inexpensive. Lockhart Basin Road heads north from Highway 211 about 5 miles (8 km)

east of the entrance to the Needles District. **Hamburger Rock Campground** (no water, $6) is about 1 mile (1.6 km) up the road. North of Hamburger Rock, camping is dispersed, with many small (no water, free) campsites at turnoffs from the road. Not surprisingly, the road gets rougher the farther north you travel; beyond Indian Creek Falls, it's best to have 4WD. These campsites are very popular with climbers who are here to scale the walls at Indian Creek.

There are two first-come, first-served campgrounds ($15) in the Canyon Rims Special Recreation Management Area (www.blm.gov). **Windwhistle Campground,** backed by cliffs to the south, has fine views to the north and a nature trail; follow the main road from U.S. 191 for 6 miles (9.7 km) and turn left. At **Hatch Point Campground,** in a piñon-juniper woodland, you can enjoy views to the north. Go 24 miles (39 km) in on the paved and gravel roads toward Anticline Overlook, then turn right and continue for 1 mile (1.6 km). It's best to come supplied with water.

The Maze District

Only adventurous and experienced travelers will want to visit this rugged land west of the Green and Colorado Rivers. Vehicle access wasn't even possible until 1957, when mineral-exploration roads first entered what later became Canyonlands National Park. Today, you'll need a high-clearance, low gear-range 4WD vehicle, a horse, or your own two feet to get around, and most visitors spend at least three days in the district. The National Park Service plans to keep this district in its remote and primitive condition. If you can't come overland, an airplane flight provides the only easy way to see the scenic features.

The names of erosional forms describe the landscape—Orange Cliffs, Golden Stairs, the Fins, Land of Standing Rocks, Lizard Rock, the Doll House, Chocolate Drops, the Maze, and Jasper Canyon. The many-fingered

canyons of the Maze gave the district its name; although it is not a true maze, the canyons give that impression. It is extremely important to have a high-quality map before entering this part of Canyonlands. National Geographic/Trails Illustrated makes a good one, called *Canyonlands National Park Maze District, NE Glen Canyon NRA.*

GETTING THERE

Dirt roads to the **Hans Flat Ranger Station** (435/259-2652, 8am-4:30pm daily) and Maze District branch off from Highway 24 (across from the Goblin Valley State Park turnoff) and Highway 95 (take the usually unmarked Hite-Orange Cliffs Road between the Dirty Devil and Hite Bridges at Lake Powell). The easiest way in is the graded 46-mile (74-km) road from Highway 24; it's fast, although sometimes badly corrugated. The 4WD Hite-Orange Cliffs Road is longer, bumpier, and, for some drivers, tedious; it's 54 miles (87 km) from the turnoff at Highway 95 to the Hans Flat Ranger Station via the Flint Trail. All roads to the Maze District cross Glen Canyon National Recreation Area. From Highway 24, two-wheel-drive vehicles with good clearance can travel to Hans Flat Ranger Station and other areas near, but not actually in, the Maze District. From the ranger station it takes at least three hours of skillful four-wheeling to drive into the canyons of the Maze.

One other way of getting to the Maze District is by river. **Tex's Riverways** (435/259-5101 or 877/662-2839, www.texsriverways.com, about $150 pp) can arrange a jetboat shuttle on the Colorado River from Moab to Spanish Bottom. After the two-hour boat ride, it's 1,260 vertical feet (384 m) uphill in a little over 1 mile (1.6 km) to the Doll House via the Spanish Bottom Trail.

PLANNING AN EXPEDITION

Maze District explorers need a **backcountry permit** ($30) for overnight trips. Note that a backcountry permit in this district is not a reservation. You may have to share a site, especially in the popular spring months. As in the rest of the park, only designated sites can be used for vehicle camping. You don't need a permit to camp in the adjacent Glen Canyon National Recreation Area (NRA) or on BLM land.

There are no developed sources of water in the Maze District. Hikers can obtain water from springs in some canyons (check with a ranger to find out which are flowing) or from the rivers; purify all water before drinking. The Maze District has nine camping areas (two at Maze Overlook, six at Land of Standing Rocks), each with a 15-person, three-vehicle limit.

The National Geographic/Trails Illustrated topographic map of the Maze District describes and shows the few roads and trails here; some routes and springs are marked on

it too. Agile hikers experienced in desert and canyon travel may want to take off on cross-country routes, which are either unmarked or lightly cairned.

Extra care and preparation must be undertaken for travel in both Glen Canyon NRA and the Maze. Always ask rangers beforehand for current conditions. Be sure to leave an itinerary with someone reliable who can contact the rangers if you're overdue returning. Unless the rangers know where to look for you in case of breakdown or accident, a rescue could take weeks.

SIGHTS
★ Land of Standing Rocks

Here in the heart of the Maze District, strangely shaped rock spires stand guard over myriad canyons. Six camping areas offer scenic places to stay (**permit** required). Hikers have a choice of many ridge and canyon routes from the 4WD road, a trail to a confluence overlook, and a trail that descends to the Colorado River near Cataract Canyon.

Getting to the Land of Standing Rocks takes some careful driving, especially on a 3-mile (4.8-km) stretch above Teapot Canyon. The many washes and small canyon crossings here make for slow going. Short-wheelbase vehicles have the easiest time, of course. The turnoff for Land of Standing Rocks Road is 6.6 miles (10.6 km) from the junction at the bottom of the Flint Trail via a wash shortcut (add about 3 miles/4.8 kilometers if driving via the four-way intersection). The lower end of the Golden Stairs foot trail is 7.8 miles (12.6 km) in; the western end of the Ernies Country route trailhead is 8.6 miles (13.8 km) in; the Wall is 12.7 miles (20.4 km) in; Chimney Rock is 15.7 miles (25.2 km) in; and the Doll House is 19 miles (31 km) in, at the end of the road. If you drive from the south on Hite-Orange Cliffs Road, stop at the self-registration stand at the four-way intersection, about 31 miles (50 km) in from Highway 95; you can write your own permit for overnights in the park.

Tall, rounded rock spires near the end of the road reminded early visitors of dolls, hence the name Doll House. The Doll House is a great place to explore, or you can head out on nearby routes and trails.

North Point

Hans Flat Ranger Station and this peninsula, which reaches out to the east and north, are at an elevation of about 6,400 feet (1,950 m). Panoramas from North Point take in the vastness of Canyonlands, including the Maze, Needles, and Island in the Sky Districts. From **Millard Canyon Overlook,** just 0.9 mile (1.4 km) past the ranger station, you can see arches, Cleopatra's Chair, and features as distant as the La Sal Mountains and Book Cliffs. For the best views, drive out to Panorama Point, about 10.5 miles (16.9 km) one-way from the ranger station. A spur road to the left goes 2 miles (3.2 km) to Cleopatra's Chair, a massive sandstone monolith and area landmark.

HIKING
North Canyon Trail

Distance: 7 miles (11.3 km) one-way
Duration: overnight
Elevation change: 1,000 feet (305 m)
Effort: strenuous
Trailhead: on North Point Road
Directions: From Hans Flat Ranger Station, drive 2.5 miles (4 km) east, turn left onto North Point Road, and continue about 1 mile (1.6 km) to the trailhead.

This is just about the only trailhead in the Maze District that two-wheel-drive vehicles can usually reach. The trail leads down through the Orange Cliffs. At the eastern end of the trail, ambitious hikers can follow 4WD roads an additional 6 miles (9.7 km) to the Maze Overlook Trail, then 1 more mile (1.6 km) into a canyon of the Maze. Because North Point belongs to the Glen Canyon NRA, you can camp here without a permit.

Maze Overlook Trail

Distance: 3 miles (4.8 km) one-way (to Harvest Scene)
Duration: 3-4 hours
Elevation change: 550 feet (168 m)
Effort: strenuous

Trailhead: at the end of the road in the Maze District

Here, at the edge of the sinuous canyons of the Maze, the Maze Overlook Trail drops 1 mile (1.6 km) into the South Fork of Horse Canyon; bring a 25-foot-long rope to help lower backpacks through one difficult section. Once in the canyon, you can walk around the Harvest Scene, a group of prehistoric pictographs, or do a variety of day hikes or backpacking trips. These canyons have water in some places; check with the ranger when you get your permit. At least four routes connect with the 4WD road in the Land of Standing Rocks, shown on the Trails Illustrated map. Hikers can also climb Petes Mesa from the canyons or head downstream to explore Horse Canyon, but a dry fall blocks access to the Green River. You can stay at primitive camping areas **(backcountry permit required)** and enjoy the views.

The Golden Stairs

Distance: 2 miles (3.2 km) one-way
Duration: 3 hours
Elevation change: 800 feet (244 m)
Effort: moderate
Trailhead: bottom of Flint Trail, at Golden Stairs camping area
Directions: Drive the challenging Flint Trail, a 4WD route, to its bottom. The top of the Golden Stairs is 2 miles (3.2 km) east of the road junction at the bottom of the Flint Trail.

Hikers can descend this steep foot trail to the Land of Standing Rocks Road in a fraction of the time it takes for drivers to follow the roads. The trail offers good views of Ernies Country, the vast southern area of the Maze District, but it lacks shade or water. The eponymous stairs are not actual steps carved into the rock, but a series of natural ledges.

Chocolate Drops Trail

Distance: 4.5 miles (7.2 km) one-way
Duration: 5 hours
Elevation change: 550 feet (168 m)
Effort: strenuous
Trailhead: Chocolate Drops
Directions: The Land of Standing Rocks turnoff is

6.6 miles (10.6 km) from the junction at the bottom of the Flint Trail. The trailhead is just east of the Wall camping area.

The well-named Chocolate Drops can be reached by a trail from the Wall near the beginning of the Land of Standing Rocks. A good day hike makes a loop from Chimney Rock to the Harvest Scene pictographs; take the ridge route (toward Petes Mesa) in one direction and the canyon fork northwest of Chimney Rock in the other. Follow your topographic map through the canyons, and the cairns between the canyons and ridge. Other routes from Chimney Rock lead to lower Jasper Canyon (no river access) or into Shot and Water Canyons and on to the Green River.

Spanish Bottom Trail

Distance: 1.2 miles (1.9 km) one-way
Duration: 3 hours
Elevation change: 1,260 feet (384 m)
Effort: strenuous
Trailhead: Doll House, near Camp 1, just before the end of the Land of Standing Rocks Road

This trail drops steeply to Spanish Bottom beside the Colorado River; a thin trail leads downstream into Cataract Canyon and the first of a long series of rapids. **Surprise Valley Overlook Trail** branches to the right off the Spanish Bottom Trail after about 300 feet (91 m) and winds south past some dolls to a T junction (turn right for views of Surprise Valley, Cataract Canyon, and beyond); the trail ends at some well-preserved granaries, after 1.5 miles (2.4 km) one-way. From the same trailhead, the **Colorado-Green River Overlook Trail** heads north 5 miles (8 km) one-way from the Doll House to a viewpoint of the confluence. See the area's Trails Illustrated map for routes, trails, and roads.

4WD EXPLORATION
Flint Trail 4WD Road

This narrow, rough 4WD road connects the Hans Flat area with the Maze Overlook, Doll House, and other areas below. The road, driver, and vehicle should all be in good condition before attempting this route. Winter snow and mud close the road late December-March, as can rainstorms anytime. Check conditions with a ranger before you go. If you're starting from the top, stop at the signed overlook just before the descent to scout for vehicles headed up (the Flint Trail has very few places to pass). The top of the Flint Trail is 14 miles (22.5 km) south of Hans Flat Ranger Station; at the bottom, 2.8 nervous miles later, you can turn left and go 2 miles (3.2 km) to the Golden Stairs trailhead or 12.7 miles (20.4 km) to the Maze Overlook; keep straight 28 miles (45 km) to the Doll House or 39 miles (63 km) to Highway 95.

Horseshoe Canyon Unit

This canyon, a separate section of Canyonlands National Park, contains exceptional prehistoric rock art. Ghostly life-size pictographs in the Great Gallery provide an intriguing look into the past. Archaeologists think that the images had religious importance, although the meaning of the figures remains unknown. The Barrier Canyon Style of these drawings has been credited to an archaic culture beginning at least 8,000 years ago and lasting until about AD 450. Horseshoe Canyon also contains rock art left by the subsequent Fremont and Ancestral Puebloan people. The relationship between the earlier and later prehistoric groups hasn't been determined.

Call the **Hans Flat Ranger Station** (435/259-2652) to inquire about ranger-led hikes to the Great Gallery (Sat.-Sun. spring, summer, and fall); when staff are available, additional walks may be scheduled. In-shape hikers will have no trouble making the hike on their own, however.

GETTING THERE

Horseshoe Canyon is a noncontiguous unit of Canyonlands and requires quite a bit of driving to reach. It is northwest of the Maze District. The access road turns east from Highway 24 between Hanksville (14 mi/22.5 km south) and I-70 exit 149 (19 mi/31 km north). The access road is signed, but it's also handy to note that the turn is across the road from the entrance to Goblin Valley State Park. Once on this graded dirt road, travel 30 miles (48 km) east to Horseshoe Canyon, keeping left at the Hans Flat Ranger Station and Horseshoe Canyon turnoff 25 miles (40 km) in. In good weather, the road is passable to most passenger cars, though the road has many washboard sections and blowing sand can be a hazard. If you have questions, call Hans Flat Ranger Station (435/259-2652) or another of the park's visitors centers. Allow an hour to make the journey in from Highway 24 to the canyon and the Great Gallery trailhead.

HIKING
★ Great Gallery Trail

Distance: 3.5 miles (5.6 km) one-way
Duration: 4-6 hours
Elevation change: 800 feet (244 m)
Effort: moderate-strenuous
Trailhead: parking area on the canyon's west rim

From the rim and parking area, the trail descends 800 feet (244 m) in 1 mile (1.6 km) on an old jeep road, which is now closed to vehicles. At the canyon bottom, turn right and go 2 miles (3.2 km) upstream to the Great Gallery. The sandy canyon floor is mostly level; trees provide shade in some areas.

Look for other rock art along the canyon walls on the way to the Great Gallery. Take care not to touch any of the drawings, because they're fragile and irreplaceable—the oil from your hands will remove the paints. Horseshoe Canyon also offers pleasant scenery and spring wildflowers. Carry plenty of water. Neither camping nor pets are allowed in the canyon, although horses are OK. Camping is permitted on the rim. Contact the Hans Flat Ranger Station (435/259-2652) or the Moab Information Center (435/259-8825 or 800/635-6622) for road and trail conditions.

Horseshoe Canyon can also be reached via primitive roads from the east. A 4WD road runs north 21 miles (34 km) from Hans Flat Ranger Station and drops steeply into the canyon from the east side. The descent on this road is so rough that most people prefer to park on the rim and hike the last mile of road. A vehicle barricade prevents driving right up to the rock-art panel, but the 1.5-mile (2.4-km) walk is easy.

The River District

The River District is the name of the administrative unit of the park that oversees conservation and recreation for the Green and Colorado Rivers.

Generally speaking, there are two boating experiences on offer in the park's River District. First are the relatively gentle paddling and rafting experiences on the Colorado and Green Rivers above their confluence. After these rivers meet, deep in the park, the resulting Colorado River then tumbles into Cataract Canyon, a white-water destination par excellence with abundant Class III-V rapids.

While rafting and canoeing enthusiasts can plan their own trips to any section of these rivers, by far the vast majority of people sign on with outfitters, often located in Moab, and let them do the planning and work. Do-it-yourselfers must start with the knowledge that permits are required for most trips but are not always easily procured; because these rivers flow through rugged and remote canyons, most trips require multiple days and can be challenging to plan.

No matter how you execute a trip through the River District, there are several issues to think about beforehand. There are no designated campsites along the rivers in Canyonlands. During periods of high water, camps can be difficult to find, especially for large groups. During late summer and fall, sandbars are usually plentiful and make ideal camps. There is no access to potable water along the river, so river runners either need to bring along their own water or be prepared to purify river water.

While it's possible to fish in the Green and Colorado Rivers, these desert rivers don't offer much in the way of species that most people consider edible. You'll need to bring along all your foodstuffs.

The park requires all river runners to pack out their solid human waste. Specially designed portable toilets that fit into rafts and canoes can be rented from most outfitters in Moab.

RIVER-RUNNING ABOVE THE CONFLUENCE

The Green and Colorado Rivers flow smoothly through their canyons above the confluence of the two rivers. Almost any shallow-draft boat can navigate these waters: Canoes, kayaks, rafts, and powerboats are commonly used. Any travel requires advance planning because of the remoteness of the canyons and the scarcity of river access points. No campgrounds, supplies, or other facilities exist past Moab on the Colorado River or the town of Green River on the Green River. All river runners must follow park regulations, which include carrying life jackets, using a fire pan for fires, and packing out all garbage and solid human waste. The river flow on both the Colorado and the Green Rivers averages a gentle 2-4 mph (7-10 mph at high water). Boaters typically do 20 miles (32 km) per day in canoes and 15 miles (24 km) per day on rafts.

The Colorado has one modest rapid, called the Slide (1.5 mi/2.4 km above the confluence), where rocks constrict the river to one-third of its normal width; the rapid is roughest during high water levels in May-June. This is the only difficulty on the 64 river miles (103

km) from Moab. Inexperienced canoeists and rafters may wish to portage around it. The most popular launch points on the Colorado are the Moab Dock (just upstream from the U.S. 191 bridge near town) and the Potash Dock (17 mi/27 km downriver on Potash Rd./Hwy. 279).

On the Green River, boaters at low water need to watch for rocky areas at the mouth of Millard Canyon (33.5 mi/54 km above the confluence, where a rock bar extends across the river) and at the mouth of Horse Canyon (14.5 mi/23.3 km above the confluence, where a rock and gravel bar on the right leaves only a narrow channel on the left side). The trip from the town of Green River through Labyrinth and Stillwater Canyons is 120 miles (193 km). Launch points include Green River State Park (in the town of Green River) and Mineral Canyon (52 mi/84 km above the confluence and reached on a fair-weather road from Hwy. 313). Boaters who launch at Green River State Park pass through Labyrinth Canyon; a free interagency permit is required for travel along this stretch of the river. **Permits** are available from the BLM office (82 Dogwood Ave., Moab, 435/259-2100, 7:45am-4:30pm Mon.-Fri.), the Canyonlands National Park headquarters (2282 SW Resource Blvd., Moab, 435/719-2313, 8am-4pm Mon.-Fri.), Green River State Park in Green River, or the John Wesley Powell River History Museum (1765 E. Main St., Green River, 435/564-3427, 9am-5pm Mon.-Sat.). A permit can also be downloaded from the BLM website (www.blm.gov).

No roads go to the confluence. The easiest return to civilization for nonmotorized craft is a pickup by jet boat from Moab by **Tex's Riverways** (435/259-5101, www.texsriverways.com) or **Tag-A-Long Tours** (800/453-3292, www.tagalong.com). A far more difficult way out is hiking either of two trails just above the Cataract Canyon Rapids to 4WD roads on the rim. Don't plan to attempt this unless you're a very strong hiker and have a packable watercraft.

National park rangers require that boaters above the confluence obtain a backcountry permit ($30) from the **Moab National Park Service office** (2282 SW Resource Blvd., Moab, 435/719-2313, 8am-4pm Mon.-Fri.).

Notes on boating the Green and Colorado Rivers are available on request from the National Park Service's Moab office (435/259-3911). Bill and Buzz Belknap's *Canyonlands River Guide* has river logs and maps pointing out items of interest on the Green River below the town of Green River and all of the Colorado River from the upper end of Westwater Canyon to Lake Powell.

★ RIVER-RUNNING THROUGH CATARACT CANYON

The Colorado River enters Cataract Canyon at the confluence and picks up speed. The rapids begin 1 mile (6.1 km) downstream and extend for the next 14 miles (22.5 km) to Lake Powell. Especially in spring, the 26 or more rapids give a wild ride equal to the best in the Grand Canyon. The current zips along at up to 16 mph and forms waves more than 7 feet (2.1 m) high. When the excitement dies down, boaters have a 34-mile (55-km) trip across Lake Powell to Hite Marina; most people either carry a motor or arrange for a powerboat to pick them up. Depending on water levels, which can vary wildly from year to year, the dynamics of this trip and the optimal take-out point can change. Depending on how much motoring is done, the trip through Cataract Canyon takes 2-5 days.

Because of the real hazards of running the rapids, the National Park Service requires boaters to have proper equipment and a **permit** ($30). Many people go on commercial trips with Moab outfitters on which everything has been taken care of. Private groups must contact the **Canyonlands River Unit of the National Park Service** (435/259-3911, www.nps.gov/cany) far in advance for permit details.

Moab

Located near the Colorado River in a green valley enclosed by high red sandstone cliffs, Moab makes an excellent base for exploring the surrounding canyon country. The biblical Moab was a kingdom at the edge of Zion; early settlers must have felt themselves at the edge of their world too.

Today, Moab (pop. 5,000, elev. 4,025 ft/1,225 m) is the largest town in southeastern Utah. Its existence on the fringe of Mormon culture and its sizable young non-Mormon population give it a unique character. The town's first boom came during the 1950s, when vast deposits of uranium, important fuel for the atomic age, were discovered. By the 1970s the uranium mines were largely abandoned, but all the rough roads that had been built to access the mines set the stage for exploration with

Highlights

Look for ★ to find recommended sights, activities, dining, and lodging.

★ **Camp at Dead Horse Point State Park:** Set up camp on this peninsula of land perched 2,000 feet (610 m) above the Colorado River to enjoy spectacular views and mountain bike trails for the whole family (page 94).

★ **Hike Corona Arch and Bowtie Arch Trail:** Three arches are visible from this short, easy trail, including 140-foot wide Corona Arch (page 103).

★ **Wander through Fisher Towers:** These thin rock columns reach nearly 1,000 feet (305 m) into the desert sky. Hiking trails loop through the unworldly landscape, leading to views of rugged Onion Creek Canyon (page 105).

★ **Bike down the Gemini Bridges Trail:** Skip the pros and poseurs at the Slickrock Trail and have some real fun on this mostly downhill ride (page 107).

★ **Go high:** You really grasp the scale of Moab's canyon country by getting an eagle's eye view on an **air tour** (page 113).

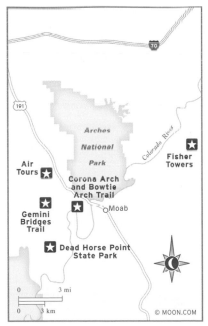

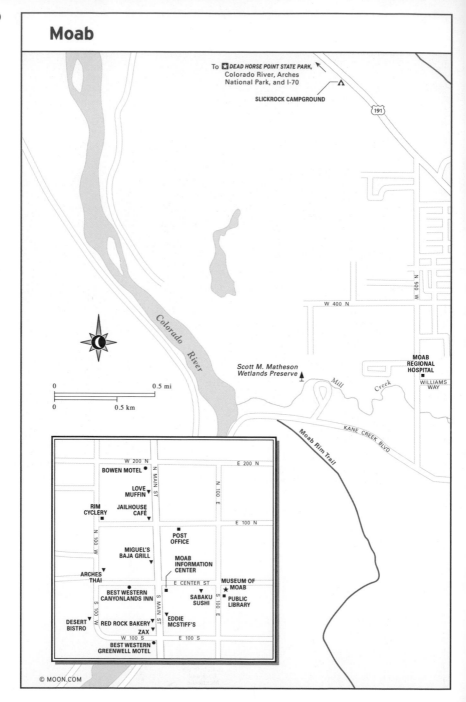

Moab

To ✚ *DEAD HORSE POINT STATE PARK,*
Colorado River, Arches
National Park, and I-70

SLICKROCK CAMPGROUND

191

Colorado River

W 400 N

N 500 W

MOAB
REGIONAL
HOSPITAL

WILLIAMS
WAY

*Scott M. Matheson
Wetlands Preserve*

Mill Creek

KANE CREEK BLVD

Moab Rim Trail

0   0.5 mi
0   0.5 km

W 200 N   E 200 N

BOWEN MOTEL

N MAIN ST

N 100 E

LOVE
MUFFIN

RIM
CYCLERY

JAILHOUSE
CAFÉ

E 100 N

N 100 W

POST
OFFICE

MIGUEL'S
BAJA GRILL

MOAB
INFORMATION
CENTER

ARCHES
THAI

E CENTER ST

MUSEUM OF
MOAB

S MAIN ST

S 100 E

BEST WESTERN
CANYONLANDS INN

SABAKU
SUSHI

PUBLIC
LIBRARY

DESERT
BISTRO

S 100 W

RED ROCK BAKERY
ZAX

EDDIE
MCSTIFF'S

W 100 S   E 100 S

BEST WESTERN
GREENWELL MOTEL

© MOON.COM

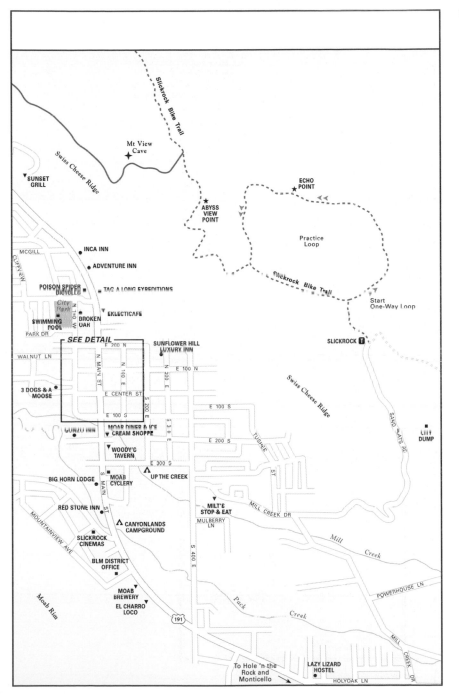

jeeps, ATVs, and mountain bikes. Another legacy of the uranium boom can be seen along the highway at the north end of town, where the area around the Colorado River bridge is the site of a massive environmental cleanup, slated to take years to complete.

In recent years Moab has become nearly synonymous with mountain biking. The slickrock canyon country seems made for exploration by bike, and people come from all over the world to pedal the backcountry. River trips on the Colorado River are nearly as popular, and a host of other outdoor recreational diversions—from horseback riding to 4WD jeep exploring to skydiving—combine to make Moab one of the most popular destinations in Utah.

As Moab's popularity has grown, so have concerns that the town and the surrounding countryside are simply getting loved to death. On a busy day, hundreds of mountain bikers form queues to negotiate the trickier sections of the famed Slickrock Trail, and more than 20,000 people crowd into town on peak-season weekends to bike, hike, float, and party. As noted in an article in *Details* magazine, "Moab is pretty much the Fort Lauderdale of the intermountain West."

Whether this old Mormon town and the delicate desert environment can endure such an onslaught of popularity is a question of increasing concern.

PLANNING YOUR TIME

While many people come to Moab because of what it's near, there's certainly enough to do in the town to justify adding a day or two to a park-focused itinerary just for exploring Moab and environs. The hiking trails around town are varied and beautiful (and you can hike with your pooch). Or pay a few bucks to take a jet-boat tour on the Colorado River, a horseback ride in Castle Valley, or a jeep tour into the backcountry.

Moab is the most hospitable town in this part of Utah, so don't blow right through. Spend a hot afternoon shopping for books, crafts, and outdoor gear. The quality of the food and beer has its own appeal, particularly after several days of hiking or driving the Utah outback. Take time to stop and enjoy Moab's quirky charms. However, be forewarned that the adrenaline (or is it testosterone?) level reaches a fever pitch here during spring break, so don't plan a quiet weekend in Moab anytime around Easter.

Sights

It's fair to say that Moab doesn't tempt travelers with a lot of traditional tourism establishments, but all you have to do is raise your eyes to the horizon. The locale is so striking that you'll want to get outdoors and explore, and the astonishing sights of Canyonlands and Arches National Parks are just minutes from town. And there's nothing wrong with just enjoying the enthusiastic vibe of the town.

MUSEUM OF MOAB

The regional **Museum of Moab** (118 E. Center St., 435/259-7985, www.moabmuseum.org, 10am-6pm Mon.-Sat. Apr. 15-Oct. 15, noon-5pm Mon.-Sat. Oct. 16-Apr. 14, $10 adults, $7.50 seniors, $5 ages 5-14) tells the story of Moab and Grand County's past, from prehistoric and Ute artifacts to the explorations of Spanish missionaries. Photos and tools show pioneer Moab life, much

---

of which centered on ranching or mining. You'll also find displays of rocks and minerals as well as the bones of huge dinosaurs, including the backbone of a sauropod found by a rancher just outside town.

HOLE 'N THE ROCK

Twelve miles (19.3 km) south of Moab, Albert Christensen worked 12 years to excavate his dream home within a sandstone monolith. When he died in 1957, his wife, Gladys, worked another eight years to complete the 5,000-square-foot house, called **Hole 'n the Rock** (11037 S. U.S. 191, 435/686 2250, www.theholeintherock.com, 9am-5pm daily, House tours $6.50 6 and older, exotic zoo $4.25 2 and older). It's now a full-on roadside attraction. The interior has notable touches like a 65-foot chimney drilled through the rock ceiling, paintings, taxidermy exhibits, and a lapidary room. The 14-room home is open for 12-minute-long guided tours and offers a gift shop, a petting zoo, exotic animals, a picnic area, and a snack bar.

MILL CANYON DINOSAUR TRAIL

The 0.5-mile (0.8-km) **Mill Canyon Dinosaur Trail,** with numbered stops,

identifies the bones of dinosaurs that lived in the wet climate that existed here 150 million years ago. You'll see fossilized wood and dinosaur footprints too. Pick up the brochure from the **Moab Information Center** (25 E. Center St., at Main St., 435/259-8825, www.discovermoab.com) or at the trailhead.

To reach the dinosaur bone site, drive 15 miles (24 km) north of Moab on U.S. 191, then turn left (west) at an intersection just north of milepost 141. Cross the railroad tracks; after 0.6 mile (1 km), turn left at the Y intersection; after another 0.5 mile (0.8 km), turn right and proceed 0.6 mile (1 km) on a rough dirt road (impassable when wet) to the trailhead. On the way to the trailhead, you'll pass another trailhead, where a short trail leads to dinosaur tracks.

You'll find many other points of interest nearby. A copper mill and tailings dating from the late 1800s are across the canyon. The ruins of Halfway Stage Station, where travelers once stopped on the Thompson-Moab run, are a short distance down the other road fork. Jeepers and mountain bikers explore the nearby Monitor and Merrimac Buttes; a sign just off U.S. 191 has a map and details.

Hole 'n the Rock is a popular roadside attraction

COPPER RIDGE DINOSAUR TRACKWAYS

Apatosaurus, aka brontosaurus, and theropod tracks crisscross an ancient riverbed at the **Copper Ridge Dinosaur Trackways** site. It's easy to make out the two-foot-wide hind footprints of the brontosaurus, but its small front feet didn't leave much of a dent in the sand. Three-toed tracks of the carnivorous theropods, possibly *Allosaurus*, are 8-15 inches long, and some show an irregular gait—perhaps indicating a limp.

The Copper Ridge tracks are 23 miles (37 km) north of Moab on U.S. 191; turn right (east) 0.75 mile (1.2 km) north of milepost 148. Cross the railroad tracks and turn south onto the dirt road, following signs 2 miles (3.2 km) to the tracks. It's a short walk to the trackway. A network of mountain bike trails, the "Dino-Flow" trails, can also be accessed from the parking area.

MOAB GIANTS

If you (or your kids) want a more commercial take on the local dinosaurs, visit **Moab Giants** (112 W. Hwy. 313, 435/355-0228, www.moabgiants.com, 10am-6pm Thurs.-Tues.) There are two experiences and ticket prices. The outdoor Dino Pass ($16 adults, $12 ages 4-15, $50 family) lets you walk a well-executed 0.5-mile (0.8-km) outdoor trail flanked by more than 100 life-size dinosaur replicas. The Discovery Pass ($22 adult, $16 ages 4-15, $70 family) includes the outdoor dino exhibits plus a museum with a focus on fossil footprints and a movie theater with two 3-D films on ancient local life. This large complex is at the corner of U.S. 191 and the road to Dead Horse Point.

★ DEAD HORSE POINT STATE PARK

Just east of Canyonlands National Park's Island in the Sky District and a short drive northwest of Moab is one of Utah's most spectacular state parks. At **Dead Horse Point** (435/259-2614, www.stateparks.utah.gov,

day use $20 per vehicle), the land drops away in sheer cliffs, and 2,000 feet (610 m) below, the Colorado River twists through a gooseneck on its long journey to the sea. The river and its tributaries have carved canyons that reveal a geologic layer cake of colorful rock formations. Even in a region with impressive views around nearly every corner, Dead Horse Point stands out for its exceptionally breathtaking panorama. You'll also see below you, along the Colorado River, the result of powerful underground forces: Salt, under pressure, has pushed up overlying rock layers into an anticline. This formation, the Shafer Dome, contains potash that is being processed by the Moab Salt Plant. You can see the mine buildings, processing plant, and evaporation ponds, which are tinted blue to hasten evaporation.

A narrow neck of land only 30 yards wide connects the point with the rest of the plateau. Cowboys once herded wild horses onto the point, then placed a fence across the neck to make a 40-acre corral. They chose the desirable animals from the herd and let the rest go. According to one tale, a group of horses left behind after such a roundup became confused by the geography of the point. They couldn't find their way off and circled repeatedly until they died of thirst within sight of the river below. You may also hear other stories of how the point got its name.

Besides the awe-inspiring views, the park also has a **visitors center** (9am-5pm daily), a very popular campground, a picnic area, a group area, a nature trail, hiking trails, and great mountain biking on the **Intrepid Trail System.** Spectacularly scenic hiking trails run along the east and west rims of the park; hikers are also allowed to use the Intrepid trails. Rangers lead hikes during the busy spring season and on some evenings during the summer, including monthly full-moon hikes. Whether you're visiting for the day or camping at Dead Horse Point, it's best to bring

---

1: walk in the footsteps of dinosaurs at the Copper Ridge Dinosaur Trackways **2:** Fremont style of rock art at Sego Canyon **3:** Dead Horse Point State Park

Moab's Mining Boom and Bust

Moab is within the Paradox Salt Basin, a geologic formation responsible for the area's famous arch formations and accumulations of valuable minerals relatively near the surface. In addition to significant mineral wealth, mining and oil exploration have provided the region with some of its liveliest history and most colorful characters. French scientist Marie Curie, who discovered the element radium in uranium ore in 1898, visited the Moab area in 1899 to inspect a uranium-processing operation near the Dolores River.

Oil exploration in the 1920s caused some excitement in Moab, but nothing like that of the uranium boom that began in 1952. A down-on-his-luck geologist from Texas named Charles Steen struck it rich at his Mi Vida claim southeast of Moab. Steen's timing was exquisite: Uranium was highly sought-after by the federal government, primarily for use in Cold War-era atomic weapons and in nuclear power plants. An instant multimillionaire, Steen built a large mansion overlooking Moab and hosted lavish parties attended by Hollywood celebrities (his home is now the Sunset Grill restaurant). The Mi Vida mine alone would ultimately be worth more than $100 million, and it put Moab on the map.

By the end of 1956, Moab was dubbed "The Richest Town in the USA" and "The Uranium Capital of the World." In the wake of Steen's discovery, thousands of prospectors, miners, laborers, and others descended on the area, hoping to cash in on the mother lode. Moab's population tripled in just three years as eager prospectors swarmed into the canyons.

By the mid-1960s, the boom had died out. As the uranium played out, however, mining operations began in 1965 in one of the largest potash deposits in the world, on the Colorado River between Moab and Dead Horse Point, and work continues there today. Other valuable materials mined in the Moab area over the years include vanadium (used in steel processing), lead, gold, copper, and silver, along with helium, natural gas, and oil.

Cleanup of 16 million tons of uranium tailings is now underway near the U.S. 191 Colorado River crossing. The toxic tailings are being hauled 30 miles (48 km) north to a disposal site near I-70. As of April 2019, 9.5 million tons of radioactive tailings had been transported from the former uranium mill site, with roughly 6.5 million tons remaining.

plenty of water. Although water is available here, it is trucked in.

Dead Horse Point is easily reached by paved road, either as a destination itself or as a side trip on the way to the Island in the Sky District of Canyonlands National Park. From Moab, head northwest 10 miles (16 km) on U.S. 191, then turn left and travel 22 miles (35 km) on Highway 313. The drive along Highway 313 climbs through a scenic canyon and tops out on a ridge with panoramas of distant mesas, buttes, mountains, and canyons. There are several rest areas along the road.

SCENIC DRIVES

Each of the following routes is at least partly accessible to standard low-clearance highway vehicles. If you have a 4WD vehicle, you have the option of additional off-road exploring.

You'll find detailed travel information on these and other places in Charles Wells's *Guide to Moab, UT Backroads & 4-Wheel Drive Trails,* which, along with a good selection of maps, is available at the **Moab Information Center** (25 E. Center St., at Main St., 435/259-8825 or 800/635-6622, www.discovermoab.com). Staff at the info center usually know current road and trail conditions.

Utah Scenic Byway 279

Highway 279 goes downstream along the west side of the Colorado River Canyon, across the river from Moab. Pavement extends 16 miles (26 km) past fine views, prehistoric rock art, arches, and hiking trails. A potash plant marks the end of the highway; a rough dirt road continues to Canyonlands National Park. From Moab, head north 3.5 miles (5.6 km) on U.S. 191, then turn left onto

Highway 279. The highway enters the canyon at the "portal," 2.7 miles (4.3 km) from the turnoff. Towering sandstone cliffs rise on the right, and the Colorado River drifts along just below on the left.

Stop at a signed pullout on the left, 0.6 mile (1 km) past the canyon entrance, to see **Indian Ruins Viewpoint,** small prehistoric Native American ruins tucked under a ledge across the river. The stone structure was probably used for food storage.

Groups of **petroglyphs** cover cliffs along the highway 5.2 miles (8.4 km) from U.S. 191, which is 0.7 mile (1.1 km) beyond milepost 11. Look across the river to see the Fickle Finger of Fate among the sandstone fins of Behind the Rocks. A petroglyph of a bear is 0.2 mile (0.3 km) farther down the highway. Archaeologists think that the Fremont people and the later Utes did most of the artwork in this area.

A signed pullout on the right, 6.2 miles (10 km) from U.S. 191, points out **dinosaur tracks** and petroglyphs visible on rocks above. Sighting tubes help locate the features. It's possible to hike up the steep hillside for a closer look.

Ten miles (16 km) west of the highway turnoff is the trailhead for the **Corona Arch Trail** (3 mi/4.8 km round trip).

The aptly named **Jug Handle Arch,** with an opening 46 feet (14 m) high and 3 feet (1 m) wide, is close to the road on the right, 13.6 miles (21.9 km) from U.S. 191. Ahead the canyon opens up where underground pressure from salt and potash has folded the rock layers into an anticline.

At the **Moab Salt Plant,** mining operations inject water underground to dissolve potash and other chemicals, then pump the solution to evaporation ponds. The ponds are dyed blue to hasten evaporation, which takes about a year. You can see these colorful ponds from Dead Horse Point and Anticline Overlook on the canyon rims.

High-clearance vehicles can continue on the unpaved road beyond the plant. The road passes through varied canyon country, with views overlooking the Colorado River. At a road junction in Canyonlands National Park's Island in the Sky District, you have a choice of turning left for the 100-mile (161-km) White Rim Trail (4WD vehicles only past Musselman Arch), continuing up the steep switchbacks of the Shafer Trail Road (4WD recommended) to the paved park road, or returning the way you came.

Utah Scenic Byway 128

Highway 128 turns northeast from U.S. 191 just south of the Colorado River bridge, 2 miles (3.2 km) north of Moab. This exceptionally scenic canyon route follows the Colorado for 30 miles (48 km) upstream before crossing at Dewey Bridge and turning north to I-70. The entire highway is paved and passes many campsites and trailheads. The Lions Park picnic area at the turnoff from U.S. 191 is a pleasant stopping place. Big Bend Recreation Site is another good spot 7.5 miles (12 km) up Highway 128.

The rugged scenery along this stretch of the Colorado River has been featured in many films—mostly Westerns, but also *Thelma & Louise*—and commercials. If you're intrigued, stop by the free **Film Museum** at Red Cliffs Ranch, a resort near milepost 14.

The paved and scenic **La Sal Mountains Loop Road,** with viewpoints overlooking Castle Valley, Arches and Canyonlands National Parks, Moab Rim, and other scenic features, has its northern terminus at Castle Valley. From here, this route climbs high into the La Sals, and then loops back to Moab. Vegetation along the drive runs the whole range from the cottonwoods, sage, and rabbitbrush of the desert to forests of aspen, fir, and spruce. The 62-mile (100-km) loop road can easily take a full day with stops for scenic overlooks, a picnic, and a bit of hiking or fishing. Because of the high elevations, the loop's season usually lasts May to October. Before venturing off the Loop Road, it's a good idea to check current back-road conditions with the **Moab Ranger District** (62 E. 100 N., 435/259-7155, www.fs.usda.gov/mantilasal).

Rock Art Around Moab

The fertile valley around Moab has been home to humans for thousands of years. Prehistoric Fremont and Ancestral Puebloan people once lived and farmed in the bottoms of the canyons around Moab. Their rock art, granaries, and dwellings can still be seen here. Nomadic Utes had replaced the earlier groups by the time the first nonnative settlers arrived. They left fewer signs of settlement but added their artistry to the area's rock-art panels. You don't need to travel far to see excellent examples of Native American pictographs and petroglyphs.

Sego Canyon: If you approach Moab along I-70, consider a side trip to one of the premier rock-art galleries in Utah. Sego Canyon is about 5 miles (8 km) north of I-70; take exit 187, the Thompson Springs exit. Drive through the slumbering little town and continue up the canyon behind it (BLM signs also point the way). A side road leads to a parking area where the canyon walls close in. Sego Canyon is a showcase of prehistoric rock art—it preserves rock drawings and images that are thousands of years old. The Barrier Canyon Style drawings may be 8,000 years old; the more recent Fremont Style images were created in the last 1,000 years. Compared to these ancient pictures, the Ute etchings are relatively recent: Experts speculate that they may have been drawn in the 1800s, when Ute villages still lined Sego Canyon. The newer petroglyphs and pictographs are more representational than the older ones. The ancient Barrier Canyon figures are typically horned ghostlike beings that look like aliens from early Hollywood sci-fi thrillers. The Fremont Style images depict stylized human figures made from geometric shapes; the crudest figures are the most recent. The Ute images are of bison and hunters on horseback.

Potash Road (Hwy. 279): From U.S. 191 just north of the Colorado River bridge, take Highway 279 west along the river 5.2 miles (8.4 km) to these easily accessed petroglyphs. There's even a sign ("Indian Writing") to guide you to them.

Golf Course Rock Art: Take U.S. 191 south to the Moab Golf Course, which is about 4 miles (6.4 km) from the corner of Main and Center Streets in downtown Moab. Turn left and proceed to Spanish Trail Road. Approximately 1 mile (1.6 km) past the fire station, turn right onto Westwater Drive. Proceed 0.5 mile (0.8 km) to a small pullout on the left side of the road. An area approximately 30 feet by 90 feet (9 m by 27 m) is covered with human and animal figures, including "Moab Man" and what is popularly referred to as the "reindeer and sled."

Kane Creek Boulevard: Kane Creek Boulevard (south of downtown Moab; watch for the McDonald's) follows the Colorado River and leads to a number of excellent rock-art sites.

You can also ask at the **Moab Information Center** (25 E. Center St., at Main St., 435/259-8825, www.discovermoab.com, 8am-4pm daily) for a road log of sights and side roads. The turnoff from Highway 128 is 15.5 miles (25 km) up from U.S. 191.

A graded county road, **Onion Creek Road,** turns southeast off Highway 128 about 20 miles (32 km) from U.S. 191 and heads up Onion Creek, crossing it many times. Avoid this route if storms threaten. The unpleasant-smelling creek contains poisonous arsenic and selenium. Colorful rock formations of dark red sandstone line the creek. After about 8 miles (12.9 km), the road climbs steeply out of Onion Creek to upper Fisher Valley and a junction with Kokopelli's Trail, which follows a jeep road over this part of its route.

Some of the area's most striking sights are the gothic spires of **Fisher Towers,** which soar as high as 900 feet (275 m) above Professor Valley. Supposedly, the name Fisher is not that of a pioneer but a corruption of the geologic term *fissure* (a narrow crack). In 1962, three climbers from Colorado made the first ascent of Titan Tower, the tallest of the three towers. The almost vertical rock faces, overhanging bulges, and sections of rotten rock made for an exhausting 3.5 days of climbing; the party descended to the base for two of the nights. Their final descent from the summit took only six hours. More recently, slackliners have walked a rope strung between

From the junction with U.S. 191, turn west and proceed 0.8 mile (1.3 km) to the intersection of Kane Creek Drive and 500 West. Keep left and continue along Kane Creek Drive approximately 2.3 miles (3.7 km) to the mouth of Moon Flower Canyon. Along the rock cliff just beyond the canyon, you will see a rock-art panel behind a fence. Continue another 1.2 miles/1.9 kilometers (3.5 mi/5.6 km from 500 West) to another rock-art panel, where a huge rock surface streaked with desert varnish is covered with images of bighorn sheep, snakes, and human forms. For a unique rock-art image, continue on Kane Creek Boulevard past the cattle guard, where the road turns from pavement to graded gravel road. About 1.4 miles (2.3 km) from the cattle guard, just past the second sign for the Amasa Back trail, 5.5 miles (8.9 km) from the intersection of Kane Creek Drive and 500 West, watch for two small pullouts. Down the slope from the road is a large boulder with rock art on all four sides. The most amazing image is of a woman giving birth.

One of the Kane Creek petroglyphs depicts a woman giving birth.

Courthouse Wash: Although this site is located within Arches National Park, it is accessed from a parking lot off U.S. 191 just north of the Colorado River bridge, 1 mile (1.6 km) north of Moab. A 0.5-mile (0.8-km) hike leads to the panel, which is almost 19 feet (5.8 m) high and 52 feet (15.9 m) long. It has both pictographs and petroglyphs, with figures resembling ghostly humans, bighorn sheep, scorpions, and a large beaked bird. This panel, which was vandalized in 1980, was restored by the National Park Service; restoration work revealed older images underneath the vandalized layer.

A Rock Art Auto Tour brochure is available at the **Moab Information Center** (25 E. Center St., at Main St., Moab, 435/259-8825, www.discovermoab.com, 8am–4pm daily).

the two tallest towers, and visitors to the towers can frequently see climbers. The Bureau of Land Management (BLM) has a small campground and picnic area nearby, and a hiking trail skirts the base of the three main towers. An unpaved road turns southeast off Highway 128 near milepost 21, which is 21 miles (34 km) from U.S. 191, and continues 2 miles (3.2 km) to the picnic area.

The existing **Dewey Bridge,** 30 miles (48 km) up the highway, replaced a picturesque wood-and-steel suspension bridge built in 1916, which burned in 2008. Here, the BLM has built the Dewey Bridge Recreation Site, with a picnic area, a trailhead, a boat launch, and a small campground.

Upstream from Dewey Bridge are the wild rapids of **Westwater Canyon.** The Colorado River cut this narrow gorge into dark metamorphic rock. You can raft or kayak down the river in one day or a more leisurely two days; many local outfitters offer trips. Camping is limited to a single night. Unlike most desert rivers, this section of the Colorado River also offers good river-running at low water levels in late summer and autumn. Westwater Canyon's inner gorge, where boaters face their greatest challenge, is only about 3.5 miles (5.6 km) long; however, you can enjoy scenic sandstone canyons both upstream and downstream.

The rough 4WD **Top-of-the-World Road** climbs to an overlook with outstanding views of Fisher Towers, Fisher Valley, Onion Creek, and beyond. Pick up a map at the **Moab Information Center** (25 E. Center St., at Main St., 435/259-8825, www.discovermoab.com) to guide you to the rim. The elevation here is 6,800 feet (2,073 m), nearly 3,000 feet (915 m) higher than the Colorado River.

Kane Creek Scenic Drive

Kane Creek Road heads downstream along the Colorado River on the same side as Moab. The 4 miles (6.4 km) through the Colorado River Canyon are paved, followed by 6 miles (9.7 km) of good dirt road through Kane Springs Canyon. This route also leads to the **Matheson Wetland Preserve** (934 W. Kane Creek Blvd.), which is a Nature Conservancy site, as well as great rock art, several hiking trails and campgrounds, and some modern-day **cave dwellings.** People with high-clearance vehicles or mountain bikes can continue across Kane Springs Creek to Hurrah Pass and an extensive network of 4WD trails. From Moab, drive south on Main Street (U.S. 191) for 1 mile (1.6 km) and then turn right onto Kane Creek Boulevard, which becomes Kane Creek Road.

Recreation

Moab is at the center of some of the most picturesque landscapes in North America. Even the least outdoorsy visitor will want to explore the river canyons, natural arches, and mesas. Mountain biking, four-wheeling, and river tours are the recreational activities that get the most attention in the Moab area, although hikers, climbers, and horseback riders also find plenty to do. If you're less physically adventurous, you can explore the landscape on scenic flights or follow old mining roads in a jeep to remote backcountry destinations.

It's easy to find outfitters and sporting goods rental operations in Moab; it's the largest business segment in town. There's a remarkable cohesion to the town's operations: It seems that everyone markets everyone else's excursions and services, so just ask the closest outfitter for whatever service you need, and chances are excellent you'll get hooked up with what you want.

Make the **Moab Information Center** (25 E. Center St., at Main St., 435/259-8825, www.discovermoab.com, 8am-4pm daily) your first stop in town. It's an excellent source for information about the area's recreational options. The center is staffed by representatives of the National Park Service, the BLM, the U.S. Forest Service, and the Canyonlands Field Institute; they can direct you to the adventure of your liking. The center also has literature, books, and maps for sale. BLM officials can point you to the developed and undeveloped designated campsites near the Moab Slickrock Bike Trail, up Kane Creek, and along the Colorado River; you must use the designated sites in these areas.

To reach most of Moab's prime hiking trails requires a short drive to trailheads. For more options, head to nearby Arches and Canyonlands National Parks. For small groups, **Canyonlands Field Institute** (435/259-7750 or 800/860-5262, http://cfi-moab.org) leads day hikes (mid-Apr.-mid-Oct., $480 for up to six people, includes transportation and park admission) at various locations near Moab; join one to really learn about the area's natural history. The institute also offers rafting trips down the Colorado and multiday trips with an archaeological and natural history focus.

HIKING KANE CREEK SCENIC DRIVE AND U.S. 191 SOUTH

The high cliffs just southwest of town provide fine views of the Moab Valley, the highlands of Arches National Park, and the La Sal Mountains.

Vicinity of Moab

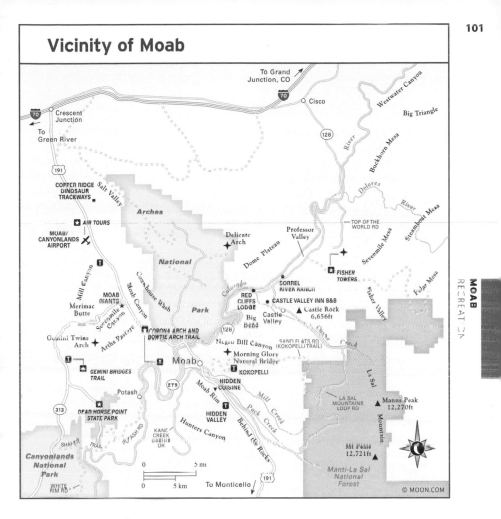

© MOON.COM

Moab Rim Trail

Distance: 6 miles (9.7 km) round-trip
Duration: 4 hours
Elevation change: 940 feet (287 m)
Effort: moderate
Trailhead: Kane Creek Boulevard, 2.6 miles (4.2 km) northwest of its intersection with U.S. 191 in Moab

If you're hiking, expect to share this route with mountain bikers and 4WD enthusiasts. The trail climbs northeast 1.5 miles (2.4 km) along tilted rock strata of the Kayenta Formation to the top of the plateau west of Moab, with the first of several great views over town and the Spanish Valley. Once on top, hikers can follow jeep roads southeast to Hidden Valley Trail, which descends to U.S. 191 south of Moab—a 5.5-mile (8.9-km) trip one-way. Experienced hikers can also head south from the rim to Behind the Rocks, a fantastic maze of sandstone fins.

Hidden Valley Trail

Distance: 2.3 miles (3.7 km) round-trip to Behind the Rocks overlook
Duration: 3 hours
Elevation change: 680 feet (207 m)

Odd Formations Behind the Rocks

the Behind the Rocks formations

A look at a topographic map will show that something strange is going on in the area called **Behind the Rocks.** Massive fins of Navajo sandstone, 100-500 feet (30-152 m) high, 50-200 feet (15-61 m) thick, and up to 0.5 mile (0.8 km) long cover a large area. Narrow vertical cracks, sometimes only a few feet wide, separate the fins. The concentration of arches in the area is similar to that in Arches National Park, with more than 20 major named arches. Where canyon drainages penetrate the sandstone, pour-offs form into 400-1,000-foot-deep sheer-walled canyons, often exposing perennial springs at the bottom. Behind the Rocks was inhabited extensively by the Ancestral Puebloan and Fremont peoples, the two cultures apparently overlapping here. Petroglyph panels, habitation caves, stone ruins, and middens abound throughout the area.

No maintained trails exist, and some routes require technical climbing skills. The maze offers endless routes for exploration. If you get lost, which is very easy to do, remember that the fins are oriented east-west; the rim of the Colorado River canyon is reached by going west, and Spanish Valley is reached by going east. Bring plenty of water, a topographic map (Moab 7.5-minute), and a compass. Access routes are the **Moab Rim** and **Hidden Valley Trails** (from the north and east) and **Pritchett Canyon** (from the west and south). Although it is only a couple of miles from Moab, Behind the Rocks seems a world away.

Effort: moderate

Trailhead: 3 miles (4.8 km) south of Moab on U.S. 191. Turn right onto Angel Rock Road. After two blocks, turn right onto Rimrock Road and drive to the parking area.

You'll see not only a hidden valley from this trail, but also panoramas of the Moab area and the Behind the Rocks area. The trail ascends a series of steep switchbacks to a broad shelf below the Moab Rim, then follows the shelf (hidden valley) to the northwest. It then crosses a low pass and follows a second shelf in the same direction. Near the end of the second shelf, the trail turns left to a divide, where you can see a portion of the remarkable fins of Behind the Rocks. The trail continues 0.3 mile (0.5 km) from the divide down to the end of the Moab Rim Trail, with the possibility of hiking on loop trails. Instead of turning left to the divide, you can make a short side trip (no trail) to the right for views of Moab.

Hunter Canyon

Distance: 4 miles (6.4 km) round-trip
Duration: 4 hours
Elevation change: 240 feet (73 m)
Effort: moderate
Trailhead: on Kane Creek Scenic Drive, 7.5 miles (12 km) west of its intersection with U.S. 191. Hunters Canyon is on the left, 1 mile (1.6 km) beyond the switchbacks.
Directions: To reach the trailhead from Moab, drive 8 miles (12.9 km) on Kane Creek Boulevard along the Colorado River and up Kane Creek Canyon. The road is asphalted where it fords Hunter Creek, but the asphalt is usually covered with dirt washed over it by the creek.

A rock arch and other rock formations in the canyon walls and the lush vegetation along the creek are highlights of a Hunter Canyon hike. Off-road vehicles have made tracks a short way up; you'll be walking mostly along the creek bed. Short sections of trail lead around thickets of tamarisk and other water-loving plants. Look for Hunter Arch on the right, about 0.5 mile (0.8 km) up. Most of the water in Hunter Canyon comes from a deep pool surrounded by hanging gardens of maidenhair ferns. A dry fall and a small natural bridge are above the pool. This pretty spot marks the hike's turnaround point and an elevation gain of 240 feet (73 m).

HIKING HIGHWAY 279
Portal Overlook Trail

Distance: 4 miles (6.4 km) round-trip
Duration: 3 hours
Elevation change: 980 feet (300 m)
Effort: moderate
Trailhead: JayCee Park Recreation Site, Highway 279, 4.2 miles (6.8 km) west of the Highway 279-U.S. 191 junction

The Portal Overlook Trail switchbacks up a slope, then follows a sloping sandstone ledge of the Kayenta Formation for 2 miles (3.2 km) to an overlook. A panorama (the "portal") takes in the Colorado River, Moab Valley, Arches National Park, and the La Sal Mountains. This trail is a twin of the Moab Rim Trail across the river. Expect to share it with mountain bikers.

★ Corona Arch and Bowtie Arch Trail

Distance: 3 miles (4.8 km) round-trip
Duration: 2 hours
Elevation change: 200 feet (61 m)
Effort: moderate
Trailhead: Highway 279, 10 miles (16 km) west of the Highway 279-U.S. 191 Junction

If you have time for only one hike in the Moab area, this one is especially recommended. The trail leads across slickrock country to two impressive arches. You can't see them from the road, although a third arch—Pinto—is visible. The trail climbs 1.5 miles (2.4 km) from the parking area, crosses railroad tracks, and follows a jeep road and a small wash to an ancient gravel bar. Pinto Arch, also called Gold Bar Arch, stands to the left, but there's no trail to it. Follow rock cairns to Corona and Bowtie Arches. Handrails and a ladder help in the few steep spots.

Despite being only a few hundred yards apart, each arch has a completely different character and history. Bowtie formed when a pothole in the cliffs above met a cave underneath. It used to be called Paul Bunyan's Potty before that name was appropriated for an arch in Canyonlands National Park. The hole is about 30 feet (9 m) in diameter. Corona Arch, reminiscent of the larger Rainbow Bridge, eroded out of a sandstone fin. The graceful span is 140 feet (43 m) long and 105 feet (32 m) high. Both arches are composed of Navajo sandstone.

HIKING HIGHWAY 128
Grandstaff Canyon

Distance: 4 miles (6.4 km) round-trip
Duration: 3-4 hours
Elevation change: 330 feet (100 m)
Effort: easy-moderate
Trailhead: Highway 128, 3 miles (4.8 km) east of the Highway 128-U.S. 191 junction

One of the most popular hiking destinations in the Moab area, the Grandstaff Canyon trail follows a lively stream dammed by beavers and surrounded by abundant greenery and sheer cliffs. The high point of the hike is

Morning Glory Natural Bridge, the sixth-longest natural rock span in the country at 243 feet (74 m).

The trail is named after William Grandstaff, the first African American to live in the area from about 1877 to 1881. The trailhead and a large parking area are on the right just after crossing a concrete bridge 3 miles (4.8 km) from U.S. 191. The Grandstaff Campground, run by the BLM, is on the banks of the Colorado River just across the road from the trailhead.

The trail follows the creek up the canyon, with numerous stream crossings. Although the crossings are not difficult, hikers must be comfortable with stepping from rock to rock.

To see Morning Glory Natural Bridge, head 2 miles (3.2 km) up the main canyon to the second side canyon on the right, then follow a good but fairly steep side trail for 0.5 mile (0.8 km) up to the long, slender bridge. The spring and small pool underneath keep the air cool even in summer; ferns, columbines, and abundant poison ivy grow here.

★ Fisher Towers

Distance: 4.4 miles (7.1 km) round-trip
Duration: 4 hours
Elevation change: 670 feet (204 m)
Effort: moderate
Trailhead: off Highway 128; 21 miles (34 km) east of the Highway 128-U.S. 191 junction, turn right and go 2.2 miles (3.5 km) on an improved dirt road to a parking lot

These spires of dark red sandstone rise 900 feet (274 m) above Professor Valley. You can hike around the base of these needle rocks on a trail accessed by a short flight of stairs from the BLM picnic area. The trail follows a small slickrock-covered ridge leading away from the main cliffs; when the ridge narrows, go left into the ravine through a small cut in the ridge. From the bottom of the ravine, the trail heads steeply up and then begins to wind directly beneath the Fisher Towers. After

skirting around the largest tower, the Titan, the trail ascends and ends after 2.2 miles (3.5 km) on a ridge with a panoramic view. The Fisher Towers attract many very good rock climbers, and hikers may find that they linger along the trail to watch some spectacular climbing exploits. Carry plenty of water, as much of the trail is exposed and is frequently quite hot.

BIKING

The first mountain bikes came to Moab in 1982, when they were used to herd cattle. That didn't work out so well, but within a decade or so, Moab had become the West's most noted mountain bike destination. In addition to riding the famed and challenging slickrock trails (slickrock is the exposed sandstone that composes much of the land's surface here, and despite its name, bike tires grab it quite nicely) that wind through astonishing desert landscapes, cyclists can pedal through alpine meadows in the La Sal Mountains or take nearly abandoned 4WD tracks into the surrounding backcountry. Beware: The most famous trails—like the Slickrock Bike Trail—are not for beginners. Other trails are better matched to the skills of novices. A good online resource for trails and advice is the Moab Bike Patrol (www.moabbikepatrol.com).

It's a good idea to read up on Moab-area trails before planning a trip; heaps of books and pamphlets are available. You can also hire an outfitter to teach you about the special skills needed to mountain bike in slickrock country, or join a guided tour. The Moab Information Center's website (www.discovermoab.com) also has good information about bike trails.

Most people come to Moab to mountain bike mid-March to late May, and then again in the fall mid-September to the end of October. Unless you are an early riser, summer is simply too hot for extended bike touring in these desert canyons. Be prepared for crowds, especially in mid-March during spring break. The Slickrock Trail alone has been known to attract more than 150,000 riders per year.

1: Bowtie Arch 2: Morning Glory Natural Bridge
3: the trail up Grandstaff Canyon 4: Fisher Towers

Mountain Bike Etiquette

When mountain biking in the Moab area, don't expect an instant wilderness experience. Because of the popularity of the routes, the fragile desert environment is under quite a bit of stress, and you'll need to be considerate of the thousands of other people who share the trails. By keeping these rules in mind, you'll help keep Moab from being loved to death.

- **Ride only on open roads and trails.** Much of the desert consists of extremely fragile plant and animal ecosystems, and riding recklessly through cryptobiotic soils can destroy desert life and lead to erosion. If you pioneer a trail, chances are someone else will follow the tracks, leading to ever more destruction. When riding on slickrock, brake carefully to avoid leaving skid marks on the rocks.

- **Protect and conserve scarce water sources.** Don't wash, swim, walk, or bike through potholes, and camp well away from isolated streams and water holes. The addition of your insect repellent, body oils, suntan lotion, or bike lubrication can destroy the thriving life of a pothole. Camping right next to a remote stream can deprive shy desert wildlife of life-giving water access.

- **Leave all Native American sites and artifacts as you find them.** First, it's against the law to disturb antiquities; second, it's stupid. Enjoy looking at rock art, but don't touch the images—body oils hasten their deterioration. Don't even think about taking potsherds, arrowheads, or artifacts from where you find them. Leave them for others to enjoy or for archaeologists to interpret.

- **Dispose of solid human waste thoughtfully.** The desert can't easily absorb human fecal matter. Desert soils have few microorganisms to break down organic material, and, simply put, mummified turds can last for years. Be sure to bury solid waste at least 6 to 12 inches deep in sand and at least 200 feet (61 m) away from streams and water sources. Pack out toilet paper in plastic bags. Check regulations; in some areas human waste disposal bags are required.

- **Check before riding power-assisted bikes on trails.** At the current moment, pedal-assist or e-bikes are prohibited on some singletrack bike paths and trails in Moab, while other trails, even the famed Slickrock Trail, are now open to e-bike riders. Check the status of your trail at the Moab Information Center before heading out.

If you've never biked on slickrock or in the desert, here are a few basic guidelines. Take care if venturing off a trail—it's a long way down some of the sheer cliff faces. A trail's steep slopes and sharp turns can be tricky, so a helmet is a must. Knee pads and riding gloves also protect from scrapes and bruises. Fat bald tires work best on the rock; partially deflated knobby tires do almost as well. Carry plenty of water—one gallon in summer, half a gallon in cooler months. Tiny plant associations, which live in fragile cryptobiotic soil, don't want you tearing through their homes; stay on the rock and avoid the crusty black cryptobiotic soil.

Dozens of trails thread through the Moab area; one good place for beginners to start is on the **Intrepid Trail System** at Dead Horse Point State Park. Descriptions of several local trails follow.

MOAB Brand Trails

The interconnected loops and spur trails (named for cattle brands that spell out M-O-A-B) form a trail system with several options that are especially good for beginners or riders who are new to slickrock. The 7-mile (11.3-km) **Bar-M** loop is easy and makes a good family ride, although you might share the packed-dirt trail with motor vehicles; try **Circle O** (no motor vehicles) for a good 3-mile (4.8-km) initiation to slickrock riding. More experienced slickrock cyclists can find some challenges on the **Deadman's Ridge, Long Branch,** and **Killer-B** routes at the southern end of the trail system.

To reach the trailhead for all these rides, head about 8 miles (12.9 km) north of town on U.S. 191 to the parking lot for the Bar M Chuckwagon (now closed), and park at the south end of the lot.

Slickrock Bike Trail

Undulating slickrock in the Sand Flats Recreation Area just east of Moab challenges even the best mountain bike riders; this is not an area in which to learn riding skills. Originally, motorcyclists laid out this route, although now most riders rely on leg and lung power. The 2-mile (3.2 km) practice loop near the trail's beginning allows first-time visitors a chance to get a feel for the slickrock. The "trail" consists only of painted white lines. Riders following it have less chance of getting lost or finding themselves in hazardous areas. Plan on about five hours to do the 10.5-mile (16.9-km) main loop, and expect to do some walking.

Side trails lead to viewpoints overlooking Moab, the Colorado River, and arms of Grandstaff Canyon. Panoramas of the surrounding canyon country and the La Sal Mountains add to the pleasure of biking.

To reach the trailhead from Main Street in Moab, turn east and go 0.4 mile (0.6 km) on 300 South, turn right and go 0.1 mile (0.2 km) on 400 East, turn left (east) and go 0.5 mile (0.8 km) on Mill Creek Drive, then turn left and go 2.5 miles (4 km) on Sand Flats Road. The Sand Flats Recreation Area, where the trail is located, charges $5 for an automobile day pass, $2 for a bicycle or motorcycle. Camping ($15) is available, but there is no water—bring plenty with you!

Farther up Sand Flats Road, the quite challenging, often rock-strewn **Porcupine Rim Trail** draws motorcyclists, jeeps, and mountain bikers; after about 11 miles (17.7 km), the trail becomes single-track, and four-wheelers drop out. The whole trail is about 15 miles (24 km) long.

★ Gemini Bridges Trail

This 14-mile (22.5-km) one-way trail passes tremendous twin rock arches (the bridges) and the slickrock fins of the Wingate Formation, making this one of the most scenic of the trails in the Moab area; it's also one of the more moderate trails in terms of necessary skill and fitness. The trail begins 12.5 miles (20.1 km) up Highway 313, just before the turnoff to Dead Horse Point State Park. It's a stiff 21-mile (33.8-km) uphill ride from Moab to reach the trailhead; consider shortening the ride by parking at the MOAB Brand parking area or taking a shuttle from town. Several companies, including **Coyote Shuttle** (435/260-2097, www.coyoteshuttle.com, $25), provide this service, enabling cyclists to concentrate on the fun, mostly downhill ride back toward Moab. The Gemini Bridges Trail, which is shared with motorcycles and 4WD vehicles, ends on U.S. 191 just north of town.

Intrepid Trail System

Mountain bikers, including novices, should bring their rides to Dead Horse Point, where the Intrepid Trail System offers about 15 miles (24 km) of slickrock and sand single-track trails in three loops that range from a 1-mile (1.6-km) beginner's loop to a more challenging 9-mile (14.5-km) loop. All routes start at the visitors center and have great views into the canyon country. To reach Dead Horse Point State Park (435/259-2614, $20) from Moab, take U.S. 191 north 9 miles (14.5 km), then turn west onto Highway 313 and follow it 23 miles (37 km) to the park entrance.

Lower Monitor and Merrimac Trail

A good introduction to the varied terrains of the Moab area, the 7.5-mile (12-km) Lower Monitor and Merrimac Trail includes lots of slickrock riding and a bit of sand. Reach the trailhead by traveling 15 miles (24 km) north of Moab on U.S. 191 and turning west (left) onto Mill Canyon Road, just past milepost 141. Make sure to go on the lower trail, not the Monitor and Merrimac Jeep Trail. After your ride, explore the nearby Mill Canyon Dinosaur Trail (foot traffic only).

Sovereign Single Track

Not every bike trail here is over slickrock; the challenging single-track Sovereign Trail is good to ride in hot weather. The trail, which contains rocky technical sections, a bit of slickrock, and more flowing single-track, is shared with motorcycles. Several trailheads access this trail; a popular one is from Willow Springs Road. From Moab, travel 11 miles (17.7 km) north on U.S. 191 and turn right onto Willow Springs Road, following this sandy road 2.5 miles (4 km) to the trailhead. To best see the options, pick up a map at a local bike store.

Kokopelli's Trail

Mountain bikers have linked a 142-mile (229-km) series of back roads, paved roads, and bike trails through the magical canyons of eastern Utah and western Colorado. The trail is usually ridden from east to west, starting in Loma, Colorado, and passing Rabbit Valley, Cisco Boat Landing, Dewey Bridge, Fisher Valley, and Castle Valley before landing on Sand Flats Road in Moab. Lots of optional routes, access points, and campsites allow for many possibilities. This multiday trip requires a significant amount of advance planning; **Bikerpelli Sports** (www.bikerpelli.com) is a good place to start this process.

Moab Canyon Pathway (Road Biking)

Although the Moab area is great for biking, riding along busy U.S. 191 is no fun. The Moab Canyon Pathway starts at the pedestrian and bike bridge over the Colorado River on Highway 128 at the north end of town and closely parallels the highway north to Arches National Park. From the entrance to the park, the path, which is separated from the road, continues north, climbing to the junction of U.S. 191 and Highway 313, the road to Dead Horse Point State Park and Canyonlands' Island in the Sky District.

From this intersection, the bike path is on a relatively wide shoulder; it's a 35-mile (56-km) ride to Canyonlands' Grand View Point, or a mere 24-mile (39-km) uphill chug to Dead Horse Point.

The paved route provides easy cycling access to the MOAB Brand mountain bike trails just off U.S. 191 and a more challenging ride to the Intrepid trails in Dead Horse Point State Park and the Gemini Bridges Trail, which starts just outside the park.

Bike Tours

Most of the bicycle rental shops in Moab offer daylong mountain bike excursions, while outfitters offer multiday tours that vary in price depending on the difficulty of the trail and the degree of comfort involved. The charge for these trips is usually around $200-250 per day, including food and shuttles. Be sure to inquire whether rates include bike rental.

Rim Tours (1233 S. U.S. 191, 435/259-5223 or 800/626-7335, https://rimtours.com) is a well-established local company offering several half-day (around $105-135 pp for 2-3 cyclists), full-day (around $150-165 pp for 2-3 cyclists), and multiday trips, including a five-day bike camping trip in Canyonlands' Maze District ($1,250). **Magpie Cycling** (800/546-4245, http://magpieadventures.com) is a small local business that runs day trips, which include instruction on mountain biking techniques and overnight rides, mostly in Canyonlands, including a three-day tour of the White Rim Trail ($875).

Western Spirit Cycling (478 Mill Creek Dr., 435/259-8732, www.westernspirit.com) offers mountain and road bike tours in the western United States, with about one-third of them in Utah. Moab-area trips include the White Rim, the Maze, and Kokopelli's Trail (5 days, $1,260). Another Moab-based company with tours all over the West is **Escape Adventures** (local base at Moab Cyclery, 391 S. Main St., 435/259-7423 or 800/596-2953, www.escapeadventures.com), which leads multiday mountain bike trips, including a five-day "Best of Moab" tour of mountain bike trails ($1,195 camping, $1,995 inn accommodations); some of the tours combine cycling with rafting, climbing, hiking, or plane rides.

Rentals and Repairs

Rim Cyclery (94 W. 100 N., 435/259-5333, www.rimcyclery.com, 8am-6pm daily) is Moab's oldest bike and outdoor gear store, offering both road and mountain bike sales, rentals, and service. Mountain bike rentals are also available at **Poison Spider Bicycles** (497 N. Main St., 435/259-7882 or 800/635-1792, www.poisonspiderbicycles.com, 8am-7pm daily spring and fall, 9am-6pm daily winter and summer) and **Chile Pepper** (702 S. Main St., 435/259-4688 or 888/677-4688, www.chilebikes.com, 8am-5pm daily). **Moab Cyclery** (391 S. Main St., 435/259-7423 or 800/559-1978, www.moabcyclery.com, 8am-6pm daily) offers rentals, tours, shuttles, and gear. Expect to pay about $60-80 per day to rent a mountain bike, a little less for a road bike; e-bike rentals are around $100 a day. If you just want to tool around a bit, rent a basic townie ($35) at **Bike Fiend** (69 E. Center St., 435/315-0002, www.moabbikefiend.com, 8am-6pm daily).

Shuttle Services

Several of the Moab area's best mountain bike trails are essentially one-way, and unless you want to cycle back the way you came, you'll need to arrange a shuttle service to pick you up and bring you back to Moab or your vehicle. Also, if you don't have a vehicle or a bike rack (available at most shops when you rent a bike), you will need to use a shuttle service to get to more distant trailheads. **Coyote Shuttle** (435/260-2097, www.coyoteshuttle.com) and **Whole Enchilada Shuttle** (435/260-2534, https://wholeenchiladashuttles.com) both operate shuttle services; depending on distance, the usual fare is $15-30 per person. Both companies also shuttle hikers to trailheads and pick up rafters.

Even a visitor with a tight schedule can get out and enjoy the canyon country on rafts and other watercraft. Outfitters offer both laid-back and exhilarating day trips, which usually require little advance planning. Longer multiday trips include gentle canoe paddles along the placid Green River and thrilling expeditions down the Colorado River.

You'll need to reserve well in advance for most of the longer trips. The BLM and the National Park Service limit trips through the backcountry, and space, especially in high season, is at a premium. Experienced rafters can also plan their own unguided trips, although you'll need a **permit** for all areas except for the daylong Fisher Towers float upstream from Moab.

The rafting season runs April to September, and jet-boat tours run February to November. Most do-it-yourself river-runners obtain their permits by applying in January-February for a March drawing; the Moab Information Center's BLM ranger (25 E. Center St., at Main St., 435/259-8825) can advise on this process and provide the latest information about available cancellations.

Rafting and Kayaking Trips

For most of the following trips, full-day rates include lunch and beverages, while part-day trips include just lemonade and soft drinks. On overnight trips, you'll sleep in tents in backcountry campgrounds.

The **Colorado River** offers several exciting options. The most popular day run near Moab starts upstream near Fisher Towers and bounces through several moderate rapids on the way back to town. Full-day raft trips ($85-110 pp adults) run from Fisher Towers to near Moab. Half-day trips ($60-75 pp adults) run over much the same stretch of river but don't usually include lunch.

Several outfitters offer guided **stand-up paddling** trips (half day about $75-85) on quiet stretches of the Colorado River near the border of Arches National Park.

For a more adventurous rafting trip, the

Colorado's rugged **Westwater Canyon** offers lots of white water and several Class III-IV rapids near the Utah-Colorado border. These long day trips are more expensive, typically around $180-200 per day. The Westwater Canyon is also often offered as part of multiday adventure packages.

The **Cataract Canyon** section of the Colorado River, which begins south of the river's confluence with the Green River and extends to the backwater of Lake Powell, usually requires four days of rafting to complete. However, if you're in a hurry, some outfitters offer time-saving trips that motor rather than float through placid water and slow down only to shoot rapids, enabling these trips to conclude in as little as one day. This is the wildest white water in the Moab area, with big boiling Class III-IV rapids. Costs range $485-1,650, depending on what kind of craft, the number of days, and whether you fly, hike, or drive out at the end of the trip.

The **Green River** also offers Class II-III rafting and canoeing or kayaking opportunities, although they are milder than those on the Colorado. Trips on the Green make good family outings. Most trips require five days, leaving from the town of Green River, paddling through **Labyrinth Canyon** and taking out at Mineral Bottom, just before Canyonlands National Park. Costs range $950-1,750 for a five-day rafting trip.

Rafting or Kayaking on Your Own

The Class II-III **Fisher Towers** section of the Colorado River is gentle enough for amateur rafters to negotiate on their own. A popular one-day raft trip with mild rapids begins from the Hittle Bottom Recreation Site (Hwy. 128, 23.5 mi/38 km north of Moab, near Fisher Towers) and ends 14 river miles (22.5 km) downstream at Take-Out Beach (Hwy. 128, 10.3 mi/16.6 km north of U.S. 191). You can rent rafts and the mandatory life jackets in Moab, and you won't need a permit on this section of river.

Experienced white-water rafters can run the Whitewater Canyon of the Colorado River on their own. Obtain **permits** ($10) by calling 435/259-7012 up to two months prior to launch date; it's important to plan well in advance. The usual put-in is at the Westwater Ranger Station 9 miles (14.5 km) south of I-70 exit 227; another option is the Loma boat launch in Colorado. A start at Loma adds a day or two to the trip along with the sights of Horsethief and Ruby Canyons. Normal takeout is at Cisco, although it's possible to continue 16 miles (26 km) on slow-moving water through open country to Dewey Bridge.

Wild West Voyages (422 Kane Creek Blvd., 435/35-0776 or 866/390-3994, www.canyonvoyages.com) and **Navtec Expeditions** (321 N. Main St., 435/259-7983 or 800/833-1278, www.navtec.com) are two local rafting companies that rent rafts (from $120-140 per day). Both companies also rent kayaks ($40-65 per day) and stand-up paddleboards ($55-65) for those who would rather organize their own river adventures.

Rafting Outfitters

Moab is full of river-trip companies, and most offer a variety of day and multiday trips; in addition, many will combine raft trips with biking, horseback riding, hiking, or 4WD excursions. Check out the many websites at www.discovermoab.com. The following list includes major outfitters offering a variety of rafting options. Most lead trips to the main river destinations on the Colorado and Green Rivers as well as other rivers in Utah and the West. Red River Adventures runs trips in smaller self-paddled rafts and inflatable kayaks. Inquire about natural history or petroglyph tours if these specialty trips interest you.

- **Adrift Adventures** (378 N. Main St., 435/259-8594 or 800/874-4483, www.adrift.net)

- **Canyonlands Field Institute** (1320 S. Hwy. 191, 435/259-7750 or 800/860-5262, http://cfimoab.org)

1: mountain biker riding on slickrock **2:** paddling into the Labyrinth Canyon

- **Wild West Voyages** (422 Kane Creek Blvd., 435/355-0776, www.wildwestvoyages.com)
- **Moab Adventure Center** (225 S. Main St., 435/259-7019 or 866/904-1163, www.moabadventurecenter.com)
- **Navtec Expeditions** (321 N. Main St., 435/259-7983 or 800/833-1278, www.navtec.com)
- **Red River Adventures** (1140 S. Main St., 435/259-4046 or 877/259-4046, www.redriveradventures.com)
- **Sheri Griffith Expeditions** (2231 S. Hwy. 191, 503/259-8229 or 800/332-2439, www.griffithexp.com)
- **Tag-A-Long Expeditions** (378 N. Main St., 435/259-8594 or 800/874-4483, www.tagalong.com)

Canoeing

Canoeists can also sample the calm waters of the Green River on multiday excursions with **Moab Rafting and Canoe Company** (420 Kane Creek Blvd., 435/259-7722, www.moabrafting.com), which runs scheduled guided trips ($999 for a four-day trip) to four sections of the Green and to calmer stretches of the Colorado River. They also rent canoes ($40-50 per day), including the necessary equipment.

Another good source for DIY canoe and kayak trips on the Green River is **Tex's Riverways** (691 N. 500 West, 435/259-5101 or 877/662-2839, www.texsriverways.com), which specializes in rentals, shuttles, and support for self-guided trips.

Jet Boats and Motorboats

Canyonlands by Night & Day (435/259-5261 or 800/394-9978, www.canyonlandsbynight.com, Apr.-mid-Oct., $79 adults, $69 ages 4-12, includes dinner, $69 adult, $59 ages 4-12 boat only) tours leave at sunset in an open tour boat and go several miles upstream on the Colorado River; a guide points out canyon features. The sound and light show begins on the way back. Music and historical narration

accompany the play of lights on the canyon walls. Reservations are a good idea because the boat fills up fast. This company also offers a selection of daytime jet-boat tours, including a three-hour trip ($109 adults, $99 children) to the Colorado River canyon downstream from Moab. Trips depart from the Spanish mission-style office just north of Moab, across the Colorado River.

4WD EXPLORATION

Road tours offer visitors a special opportunity to view unique canyon-country arches and spires, Indigenous rock art, and wildlife. An interpretive brochure and map at the **Moab Information Center** (25 E. Center St., at Main St., 435/259-8825, www.discovermoab.com) outlines Moab-area 4WD trails: four rugged 15-54-mile (24-87-km) loop routes through the desert that take 2.5-4 hours to drive. Those who left their trusty four-by-fours and off-road-driving skills at home can take an off-road jeep tour with a private operator. Most Moab outfitters offer jeep or Hummer tours, often in combination with rafting or hiking options. The **Moab Adventure Center** (452 N. Main St., 435/259-7019 or 866/404-1163, www.moabadventurecenter.com) runs two-hour ($89 adults, $59 youths) and half-day ($185 adults, $135 youths) guided Hummer safaris. The Adventure Center, which can book you on any number of trips, can also arrange jeep rentals (from $260 per day).

Jeep and other 4WD-vehicle rentals are also available at a multitude of other Moab outfits, including **Twisted Jeep Rentals** (446 S. Main St., 435/259-0335, www.twistedjeeps.com) and **Cliffhanger Jeep Rentals** (40 W. Center St., 435/259-0889, www.cliffhangerjeeprental.com). Expect to pay at least $225 per day.

ATVS AND DIRT BIKES

As an alternative to four-by-four touring in the backcountry, there's all-terrain vehicle (ATV) and motorcycle "dirt biking," typically but not exclusively geared toward youngsters and families. Although youths ages 8-15 may operate an ATV, provided they possess an Education Certificate issued by Utah State Parks and Recreation or an equivalent certificate from their home state, parents should research ATV safety before agreeing to such an outing. Much of the public land surrounding Moab is open to ATV exploration, with many miles of unpaved roads and existing trails on which ATVs can travel. However, ATV and dirt bike riding is not allowed within either Arches or Canyonlands National Parks.

One particularly popular area for ATVs is **White Wash Sand Dunes,** with many miles of dirt roads in a strikingly scenic location. It is 48 miles (77 km) northwest of Moab, reached by driving 13 miles (21 km) south from I-70 exit 175, just east of Green River. The dunes are interspersed with large cottonwood trees and bordered by red sandstone cliffs. In addition to the dunes, White Wash is a popular route around three sides of the dunes.

ATVs and dirt bikes are available from a number of Moab-area outfitters, including **High Point Hummer** (281 N. Main St., 435/259-2972 or 877/486-6833, www.highpointhummer.com) and **Moab Tour Company** (427 N. Main St., 435/259-4080 or 877/725-7317, www.moabtourcompany.com). A half-day dirt bike or ATV rental starts at around $299.

★ AIR TOURS

You'll have a bird's-eye view of southeastern Utah's incredible landscape from Moab's Canyonlands Field with **Redtail Aviation** (435/259-7421, https://flyredtail.com). A 30-minute flight over Arches National Park is $109 per person; add Canyonlands and the rate is $229 per person. Longer tours are also available, and flights operate year-round.

SKYDIVING

If you think the Arches and Canyonlands area looks dramatic from an airplane, imagine the excitement of parachuting into the desert landscape. **Skydive Moab** (Canyonlands Fields Airport, U.S. 191, 16 miles (26 km) north of Moab, 435/259-5867, www.skydivemoab.com) offers jumps for both first-time and experienced skydivers. First-timers receive 30 minutes of ground schooling, followed by a half-hour flight before a tandem parachute jump with an instructor from 10,000 feet (3,048 m). Tandem skydives, including instruction and equipment, start at $169; equipment and parachutes are available for rent.

ATV rentals aren't hard to find in Moab.

CLIMBING

Just outside town, the cliffs along Highway 279 and Fisher Towers attract rock climbers. For world-class crack climbing, head south to Indian Creek, near the Needles District of Canyonlands National Park.

Moab Desert Adventures (39 E. Center St., 804/814-3872 or 877/765-6622, www.moabdesertadventures.com) offers rock-climbing and canyoneering lessons, both for beginners and experienced climbers; families are welcome. A half-day of basic climbing instruction is $185 for a private lesson; rates are lower for groups of two to four students. Head out for a climbing or canyoneering trip with **Moab Cliffs & Canyons** (253 N. Main St., 435/259-3317 or 877/641-5271, www.cliffsandcanyons.com). A day of climbing rock crags will cost $250 for one person, $195 per person for two.

Moab has a couple of stores with rock climbing gear and informative staff: **Gearheads** (1040 S. Main St., 435/259-4327, 8am-8pm daily) and **Pagan Mountaineering** (59 S. Main St., 435/259-1117, www.paganclimber.com, 9am-8pm daily).

HORSEBACK RIDING

Head up the Colorado River to the Fisher Towers area, where **Moab Horses** (Hauer Ranch, Hwy. 128, milepost 21, 435/259-8015, www.moabhorses.com, half-day $90 for two or more riders) runs guided trail rides. Also along Highway 128, **Red Cliffs Lodge** (Hwy. 128, milepost 14, 435/259-2002 or 866/812-2002, www.redcliffslodge.com) and **Sorrel River Ranch** (Hwy. 128, milepost 17, 435/259-4642 or 877/317-8244, www.sorrelriver.com) both offer trail rides.

GOLF

The **Moab Golf Club** (2705 E. Bench Rd., 435/259-6488, https://moabgolfcourse.com, $42-58) is an 18-hole par-72 public course in a well-watered oasis amid stunning red-rock formations. To get here from Moab, go south 5 miles (8 km) on U.S. 191, turn left onto Spanish Trail Road and follow it 2 miles (3.2 km), then go right on Murphy Lane and follow it to Bench Road and the golf course.

LOCAL PARKS

The **City Park** (181 W. 400 N.) has shaded picnic tables and a playground. It's also home to the **Moab Recreation and Aquatic Center** (374 Park Ave., 435/259-8226), a very nice community center with indoor and outdoor swimming pools, a weight room, and group exercise classes.

Two miles (3.2 km) north of town, **Lions Park** (U.S. 191 and Hwy. 128) offers picnicking along the Colorado River. **Rotary Park** (Mill Creek Dr.) is family-oriented and has lots of activities for kids.

Entertainment and Events

For a town of its size, Moab puts on a pretty good nightlife show, with lots of hikers, bikers, and rafters reliving their daily conquests in bars and brewpubs. There are also notable seasonal music events, ranging from folk to classical.

NIGHTLIFE

A lot of Moab's nightlife focuses on the well-loved **Eddie McStiff's** (57 S. Main St., 435/259-2337, www.eddiemcstiffs.com, 11:30am-close daily), right downtown, with abundant beers on draft, cocktails, two outdoor seating areas, and live music on a regular basis.

Woody's Tavern (221 S. Main St., 435/259-9323, www.woodystavernmoab.com, 2pm-1am Mon.-Sat., 11am-1am Sun.), a classic dive bar, has pool and live bands on the weekend—you might hear bluegrass, rock, or jam bands. Come for some barbecue and stay for the blues (or vice versa; both are good) at **Blu Pig** (811 S. Main St., 435/259-3333, 11:30am-10pm daily).

For a more family-friendly evening out, cruise the Colorado with **Canyonlands by Night** (435/259-5261, www.canyonlandsby-night.com, Apr.-mid-Oct., $79 adults, $69 ages 4-12, includes dinner). The evening cruise ends with a sound-and-light presentation along the sandstone cliffs. Dinner packages are available; children under age four are not permitted, per Coast Guard regulations.

EVENTS

To find out about local happenings, contact the Moab Information Center (25 E. Center St., at Main St., 435/259-8825, www.discovermoab.com) or browse *Moab Happenings*, available free around town or online (www.moabhappenings.com). Unsurprisingly, Moab offers quite a few annual biking events. The **Moab Skinny Tire Festival**, held in mid-March, and the **Moab Century Tour**, held in late September or early October, are both sponsored road bike events that benefit the fight against cancer. For information on both, visit www.skinnytireevents.com or call 435/260-8889. The bike demo event **OuterBike** (www.outerbike.com) is held in early October, and the **Moab Ho-Down Mountain Bike and Film Festival** (http://moabhodown.com) in late October offers silly competitions, endurance races, jump contests, skills camps and other fun events (costume party!), plus an evening of bike-themed films.

Other major annual athletic events include a number of running events organized by **Mad Moose Events** (www.madmooseevents.com). These include the **Canyonlands Half Marathon and Five Mile Run,** held the third Saturday in March, and a women's half marathon held in early June, the **Thelma and Louise Half Marathon.**

Moab's most popular annual event, more popular than anything celebrating two wheels, is the **Easter Jeep Safari** (www.rr4w.com), which is the Sturgis or Daytona Beach of recreational four-wheeling. Upward of 2,500 4WD vehicles (it's not exclusively for jeeps, although ATVs are not allowed) converge on Moab for ten days' worth of organized backcountry trail rides. "Big Saturday" (the day before Easter) is the climax of the event, when all participating vehicles parade through Moab. Plan well ahead for lodging if you are planning to visit Moab during this event, as hotel rooms are often booked a year in advance.

Memorial Day weekend brings artists, musicians, and art cars to the city park for the **Moab Arts Festival** (435/259-2742, www.moabartsfestival.org).

The dust gets kicked up at the Spanish Trail Arena (3641 S. U.S. 191, just south of Moab) with the professional **Canyonlands PRCA Rodeo** (www.moabcanyonlandsrodeo.com), held the last weekend in May or first weekend in June, with a rodeo, a parade, a dance, horse racing, and a 4-H gymkhana.

The **Moab Music Festival** (435/259-7003, www.moabmusicfest.org) is first and foremost a classical chamber music festival, but every year a few jazz, bluegrass, or folk artists are included in the lineup. More than 30 artists are currently involved in the festival, held in late August and early September. Many of the concerts are held in dramatic outdoor settings. The **Moab Folk Festival** (www.moabfolkfestival.com) is the town's other big annual musical event, attracting top-notch acoustic performers to Moab the first weekend of November.

SHOPPING

Main Street, between 200 North and 200 South, has nearly a dozen galleries and gift shops with T-shirts, outdoor apparel, Native American art, and other gifts. **Back of Beyond Books** (83 N. Main St., 435/259-5154, 9am-10pm daily) features an excellent selection of regional books and maps. Pick up those missing camping items at **Gearheads**

(1040 S. Main St., 435/259-4327, 8am-8pm daily), an amazingly well-stocked outdoor store. If you're heading out to camp or hike in the desert, Gearheads is a good place to fill your water jugs with free filtered water.

Moab's largest grocery store, **City Market** (425 S. Main St., 435/259-5181, 6am-11pm daily), is a good place to pick up supplies; it has a pharmacy and a gas station.

Stop by the **Moonflower Community Cooperative** (39 E. 100 N., 435/259-5712, 8am-8pm daily) for natural-food groceries.

Food

Moab has the largest concentration of good restaurants in Southern Utah. No matter what else the recreational craze has produced, it has certainly improved the food. Several Moab-area restaurants are closed for vacation in February, so call ahead if you're visiting in winter.

CASUAL DINING

Food isn't limited to muffins at ★ **Love Muffin** (139 N. Main St., 435/259-6833, http://lovemuffincafe.com, 6:30am-1pm daily, $7-9), but if you decide to skip the breakfast burritos or tasty rainbow quinoa, the Shake Yo Peaches muffin may be just what you need. While you're eating breakfast, order a Cubano sandwich to pack along for lunch.

Another good option for a tasty but healthy breakfast or lunch is ★ **Eklectica Coffee and Collectables** (352 N. Main St., 435/259-6896, 7am-2:30pm daily, $5-10), a charming and busy little café serving delicious organic and vegetarian dishes. For a more traditional breakfast, try the **Jailhouse Café** (101 N. Main St., 435/259-3900, 7am-noon Wed.-Mon., $8-11), a Moab classic.

Dense, chewy bagels and good sandwiches make the **Red Rock Bakery** (74 S. Main St., 435/259-5941, 7am-noon daily, $3-7) worth a visit.

Two Moab diners have an old-fashioned ambience and really good food. At the **Moab Diner & Ice Cream Shoppe** (189 S. Main St., 435/259-4006, http://moabdiner.com, 6am-9pm daily, $7-15), the breakfasts are large, with a Southwestern green chili edge to much of the food. The house-made ice cream is delicious. Another spot with great burgers and shakes is ★ **Milt's Stop & Eat** (356 Millcreek Dr., 435/259-7424, www.miltsstopandeat.com, 11am-8pm Tues.-Sun., $5-8)—it's a local classic, and just the place to stop and sprawl under the big tree out front after a day of biking or hiking.

For good Mexican food in a friendly, unfussy strip-mall setting, head south of downtown to tiny **El Charro Loco** (812 S. Main St., 435/355-0854, 11am-10pm daily, $7-20). Don't miss the pastries here—they're a special treat. No alcohol is served. A more upscale Mexican restaurant is **Miguel's Baja Grill** (51 N. Main St., 435/259-6546, www.miguelsbajagrill.net, 5pm-10pm daily, $10-26), with well-prepared Baja-style seafood, including good fish tacos. It's a busy place, so make a reservation or be prepared to wait.

Zax (96 S. Main St., 435/259-6555, www.zaxmoab.com, 11am-10pm daily, $10-15) is a busy restaurant in the heart of downtown with something for everyone. If you're with fussy eaters, this might be the ticket for sandwiches, steaks, pasta, pizza, or salad, and there's an all-you-can-eat pizza, soup, and salad bar ($15).

Get away from high-volume assembly-line restaurants at **Sabaku Sushi** (90 E. Center St., 435/259-4455, www.sabakusushi.com, 5pm-9:30pm Tues.-Sun., rolls $6-16), which offers surprisingly good sushi with a few innovations (seared elk meat is featured in one roll).

In a pretty building a block off the main drag, **Arches Thai** (60 N. 100 W., 435/355-0533, http://archesthai.com, 11am-10pm daily,

Moab Wineries

Southern Utah is not exactly the first place you think of when you envision fine wine, but for a handful of wine pioneers, the Moab area is the *terroir* of choice. Actually, conditions around Moab are similar to parts of Spain and the eastern Mediterranean, where wine grapes have flourished for millennia. The area's first wine grapes were planted in the 1970s through the efforts of the University of Arizona and the Four Corners Regional Economic Development Commission. The results were positive, as the hot days, cool nights, and deep sandy soil produced grapes of exceptional quality and flavor. A fruit-growing cooperative was formed in Moab to grow wine grapes, and by the 1980s the co-op was producing wine under the Arches Winery label. As teetotal Utah's first winery, Arches Winery was more than a novelty—its wines were good enough to accumulate nearly 40 prizes at national wine exhibitions.

Arches Winery was a true pioneer, and now two wineries produce wine in the Moab area, both open for wine tasting. In addition, many of Moab's fine restaurants offer wine from these local wineries.

Castle Creek Winery (Red Cliffs Lodge, Hwy. 128, 14 miles (22.5 km) east of Moab, 435/259-3332, www.castlecreekwinery.com, 11am-6pm Mon.-Sat.), formerly Arches Winery, produces merlot, cabernet sauvignon, chenin blanc, chardonnay, and a number of blended wines.

Spanish Valley Vineyards and Winery (4710 Zimmerman Lane, 6 mi/9.7 km south of Moab, 435/259-8134, www.moab-utah.com/spanishvalleywinery, noon-6pm Mon.-Sat. Mar.-Oct., noon-5pm Mon.-Sat. Feb. and Nov.) produces riesling, gewürztraminer, cabernet sauvignon, and syrah.

MOAB
FOOD

$13-21) has surprisingly good Thai food. It's a pleasant place if you're not in a hurry.

The **Broken Oar** (53 W. 400 N., 435/259-3127, 5pm-10pm Mon.-Sat., closed Dec., $11-29) is just north of downtown in a large log building that looks like a ski lodge. In addition to burgers, pasta, and steaks, the restaurant offers a selection of meats from its smoker. The beer and wine menu veers toward local producers.

About 3 miles (4.9 km) south of downtown, ★ **Hidden Cuisine** (2740 S. Hwy. 191, 425/259-7711, www.hidden-cuisine. com, 8am-2pm Tues.-Wed., 8am-2pm and 5:30pm-9:30pm Thurs.-Sun., $13-27) is that rare thing in Utah: a restaurant specializing in South African food. While you can get a good burger here, try the delicious South-African-style ribs or the *babotie* (a ground beef stew baked with savory custard) for a meal out of the ordinary. For lunch, the citrus quinoa salad is especially tasty.

BREWPUBS

After a hot day out on the trail, who can blame you for thinking about a cold brew and a hearty meal? Luckily, Moab has two excellent pubs to fill the bill. ★ **Eddie McStiff's** (57 S. Main St., 435/259-2337, www.eddiemcstiffs.com, 11:30am-close daily, $9-19) is an extremely popular place to sip a cool beer or a mojito, eat standard pub food (the pizza is a good bet), and meet other travelers in good weather there's seating in a nice courtyard. You'd have to try hard not to have fun here.

There's more good beer and perhaps better food at the **Moab Brewery** (686 S. Main St., 435/259-6333, www.themoabbrewery. com, 11:30am-10pm Sun.-Thurs., 11:30am-11pm Fri.-Sat., $8-21), although it doesn't attract the kind of scene you'll find at Eddie McStiff's. The atmosphere is light and airy, and the food is good—steaks, sandwiches, burgers, and a wide selection of salads. Try the spinach salad with smoked salmon ($13) or the smoked tri-tip beef ($19). There's deck seating when weather permits. Immediately next door, the same folks operate the Moab Distillery; though there's no tasting room, you can sample their gin and vodka in the brewery.

FINE DINING

Just off Main Street, the ★ **Desert Bistro** (36 S. 100 W., 435/259-0756, www.desertbistro.com, reservations recommended, 5pm-10pm daily, $22-50) is housed in a lovely renovated building that was, when it was built in 1892, Moab's first dance hall. Today, it's a longtime favorite for regional fine dining. Its seasonal, sophisticated Southwest-meets-continental cuisine features local meats and game plus fresh fish and seafood. The patio dining is some of the nicest in Moab, and the indoor dining rooms are pretty and peaceful.

The **River Grill** (Sorrel River Ranch, Hwy. 128, 17 mi/27 km northeast of Moab, 435/259-4642, www.sorrelriver.com, 7am-2pm and 6pm-9pm daily Apr.-Oct., 7am-10am and 6pm-9pm daily Nov.-Mar., $34-48) has a lovely dining room and riverside patio that overlooks spires of red rock and the dramatic cliffs of the Colorado River. The scenery is hard to top, and the food is good, with a focus on prime beef and continental specialties. Dinner reservations are strongly recommended.

The **Sunset Grill** (900 N. U.S. 191, 435/259-7146, www.moab-utah.com/sunsetgrill, 5pm-9:30pm Mon.-Sat., $14-35) is in uranium king Charlie Steen's mansion, situated high above Moab, with sweeping million-dollar views of the valley. Choose from steaks, fresh seafood, and a selection of pasta dishes—what you'll remember is the road up here and the view. The grill now offers a free shuttle from most Moab locations; call 435/259-7777 to request a ride during regular restaurant hours.

Accommodations

Moab has been a tourism destination for generations and offers a wide variety of lodging choices, ranging from older motels to new upscale resorts. U.S. 191 is lined with all the usual chain motels, but we tend to go for the smaller local operations that are within walking distance of downtown restaurants and shopping, and that's mostly what you'll find listed here. Check with hotel booking sites for chain motel rooms farther out of town.

Moab Property Management (435/259-5125 or 800/505-5343, www.moabutahlodging.com) can make bookings at area vacation homes, which include some relatively inexpensive apartments. Another handy tool is www.moab-utah.com, which has a complete listing of lodging websites for the Moab area.

The only time Moab isn't busy is in the dead of winter, November to February. At all other times, be sure to make reservations well in advance. Summer room rates are listed here; in winter rates typically drop 40 percent, and in the busy spring break season, they tend to rise, especially during Easter weekend, when jeepers fill the town.

UNDER $50

The **Lazy Lizard Hostel** (1213 S. U.S. 191, 435/259-6057, www.lazylizardhostel.com) costs just $16 (cash preferred) for simple dorm-style accommodations. You won't need a hostel membership to stay at this casual classic Moab lodging. All guests share access to a hot tub, kitchen, barbecue, coin-operated laundry, and a common room with cable TV. Showers for nonguests ($3) and private guest rooms ($39 for 2 people) are also offered. Log cabins can sleep two ($45-47) to six ($62) people. If you're traveling in a large group, the hostel also offers a number of group houses that can sleep from 12 to 30 people under one roof. The Lazy Lizard is 1 mile (1.6 km) south of town, behind A-1 Storage; the turnoff is about 200 yards south of Moab Lanes.

$50-100

A couple of older but well-cared-for motels just north of downtown have clean, unfussy guest rooms starting at about $75-90: the **Adventure Inn** (512 N. Main St., 435/662-2466 or 866/662-2466, www.

adventureinnmoab.com) and the **Inca Inn** (570 N. Main St., 435/259-7261 or 866/462-2466, www.incainn.com), with a pool.

In the heart of town but off the main drag, the **Rustic Inn** (120 E. 100 S., 435/259-6477, www.moabrusticinn.com, $90-100) offers basic motel rooms, a guest laundry room, and a pool. If you want something more spacious, there are also apartments ($149-169). They have two bedrooms, a living room, and a kitchen. The apartments are popular, so book well in advance.

$100-150

Another simple but quite adequate place is the **Bowen Motel** (169 N. Main St., 435/259-7132 or 800/874-5439, www.bowenmotel.com, $118-152), a homey motel with an outdoor pool. The Bowen offers a variety of room types, including three-bedroom family suites and an 1,800-square-foot three-bedroom house with a full kitchen.

A few blocks south of downtown, the **Red Stone Inn** (535 S. Main St., 435/259-3500 or 800/772-1972, www.moabredstone.com, $139-149) is a one-story knotty-pine-sided motel; all guest rooms have efficiency kitchens. Other amenities include a bicycle maintenance area, a covered patio with a gas barbecue grill, a hot tub, and guest laundry. Motel guests have free access to the hotel pool next door at the Red Stone's sister property, the sprawling **Big Horn Lodge** (550 S. Main St., 435/259-6171 or 800/325-6171, www.moabbighorn.com, $109-119), which has similar knotty-pine guest rooms equipped with microwaves and fridges as well as a pool and a steak restaurant. If you want seclusion in a quiet community 18 miles (29 km) east of Moab, stay at the **Castle Valley Inn** (424 Amber Lane, Castle Valley, 435/259-6012 or 888/466-6012, www.castlevalleyinn.com, $145-235). The B&B-style inn adjoins a wildlife refuge in a stunning landscape of red-rock mesas and needle-pointed buttes. You can stay in one of the main house's four guest rooms, in a cabin, or in one of the three bungalows that have kitchens. Facilities include a hot tub. To reach Castle Valley Inn,

follow Highway 128 east from Moab for 16 miles (26 km), turn south, and continue 2.3 miles (3.7 km) toward Castle Valley.

OVER $150

The ★ **Best Western Canyonlands Inn** (16 S. Main St., 435/259-2300 or 800/649-5191, www.canyonlandsinn.com, $257-299) is at the heart of Moab, with suites, a pool, a fitness room and spa, a better-than-average complimentary breakfast, and a bike storage area. This is the best address in the downtown area if you're looking for upscale amenities.

At the heart of downtown Moab, **Best Western Greenwell Motel** (105 S. Main St., 435/259-6151 or 800/528-1234, www.bestwesternmoab.com, $175-224) has a pool, fitness facilities, an on-premises restaurant, and some kitchenettes.

One of the most interesting accommodations options in Moab is the ★ **Gonzo Inn** (100 W. 200 S., 435/259-2515 or 800/791-4044, www.gonzoinn.com, $203-249). With a look somewhere between an adobe inn and a postmodern warehouse, the Gonzo doesn't try to appear anything but hip. Expect large guest rooms with vibrant colors and modern decor, a pool, and a friendly welcome.

Located in a lovely and quiet residential area, the ★ **Sunflower Hill Luxury Inn** (185 N. 300 E., 435/259-2974 or 800/662-2786, www.sunflowerhill.com, $257-337) offers high-quality accommodations. Choose from a guest room in one of Moab's original farmhouses, a historic ranch house, or a garden cottage. All 12 guest rooms have private baths, air-conditioning, and queen beds; there are also two suites. Guests share access to an outdoor swimming pool and a hot tub, bike storage, patios, and large gardens. Children over age seven are welcome, and the inn is open year-round.

Families or groups might want to rent a condo at **Moab Springs Ranch** (1266 N. U.S. 191, 435/259-7891 or 888/259-5759, www.moabspringsranch.com, $225-365, 2-night minimum), located on the north end of town on the site of Moab's oldest ranch.

The townhomes have a parklike setting with a swimming pool and a hot tub, and they sleep up to 10. Book well in advance.

A cluster of four charming and pet-friendly cottages dubbed **3 Dogs & a Moose** (171 and 173 W. Center St., 435/260-1692, www.3dogsandamoosecottages.com) is just off the main drag. The two smaller cottages ($140-205) are perfect for couples, and the larger cottages ($320-330) sleep up to six. Booking is through Airbnb; follow links from the website.

A short drive from Moab along the Colorado River's red-rock canyon is the region's most upscale resort, the **Sorrel River Ranch** (Hwy. 128, 17 mi/27 km northeast of Moab, 435/259-4642 or 877/317-8244, www.sorrelriver.com, $770-1,069, minimum two-night stay required). The ranch sits on 240 acres in one of the most dramatic landscapes in the Moab area—just across the river from Arches National Park and beneath the soaring mesas of Castle Valley. Accommodations are in a series of beautifully furnished wooden lodges, all tastefully fitted with Old West-style furniture and kitchenettes. Horseback rides are offered into the arroyos behind the ranch, and kayaks and bicycles are available for rent. The ranch's restaurant, the **River Grill** (435/259-4642, 7am-2pm and 6pm-9pm daily Apr.-Oct., 7am-10am and 6pm-9pm daily Nov.-Mar., $34-48), has some of the best views in Utah.

Sharing a similar view of the Colorado River and Castle Valley but 3 miles (4.8 km) closer to Moab is the sprawling **Red Cliffs Lodge** (Hwy. 128, milepost 14, 435/259-2002 or 866/812-2002, www.redcliffslodge.com, $289), which houses guests in "mini suites" in the main lodge building and in a number of riverside cabins that can sleep up to six ($379). The lodge offers the Cowboy Grill bar and restaurant, horseback rides, and mountain bike rentals and will arrange river raft trips. The lodge is also the headquarters for Castle Creek Winery and the site of the free **Moab Museum of Film & Western Heritage,** which displays a collection of movie memorabilia from Westerns filmed in the area.

CAMPGROUNDS
Moab Campgrounds

It's really easy and comfy to camp at ★ **Up the Creek** (210 E. 300 S., 435/260-1888, www.moabupthecreek.com, mid-Mar.-Oct., $26 for 1 person, $33 for 2, $40 for 3), a walk-in, tents-only campground tucked into a residential neighborhood near downtown Moab. The shady campground, with a bathhouse and showers, picnic tables, and a few propane grills (campfires are prohibited), is right alongside a bike path.

RV parks cluster at the north and south ends of town. **Moab Valley RV Resort** (1773 N. U.S. 191, at Hwy. 128, 2 mi /3.2 km north of Moab, 435/259-4469, www.moabvalleyrv.com, $37-48 tents, from $58 RVs) is open year-round; it has showers, a pool, a playground, and free wireless Internet access. Pets are allowed only in RVs. Although this place is convenient to town and Arches, it is pretty close to a large ongoing environmental cleanup project involving removal of radioactive mine tailings (according to the Environmental Protection Agency, it's safe to camp here). **Moab KOA** (3225 S. U.S. 191, 435/259-6682 or 800/562-0372, http://moab-koa.com, Mar.-Nov., $50-57 tents, from $56 RVs with hookups, $109-189 cabins), barely off the highway 4 miles (6.4 km) south of town, has showers, a laundry room, a store, miniature golf, and a pool.

More convenient to downtown, **Canyonlands RV Resort and Campground** (555 S. Main St., 435/259-6848 or 800/522-6848, www.sunrvresorts.com, $39-44 tents, $52-57 RVs, $99 cabins) is open year-round; it has showers, a laundry room, a store, a pool, and two-person air-conditioned cabins—bring your own bedding. One mile (1.6 km) north of Moab, **Slickrock Campground** (1301½ N. U.S. 191, 435/259-7660 or 800/448-8873, http://slickrockcampground.com, $39-49 tents or RVs without hookups, $62-72 with hookups, $79 cabins

---

1: Up the Creek campground **2:** BLM campground near Moab

with air-conditioning and heat but no bath or kitchen) remains open year-round; it has nice sites with some shade as well as showers, a store, an outdoor café, and a pool.

You'll also find campgrounds farther out at Arches and Canyonlands National Parks, Dead Horse Point State Park, Canyon Rims Recreation Area, and east of town in the cool La Sal Mountains.

For something a little less rugged, **Under Canvas Moab** (13748 N. U.S. 191, 801/895-3213, www.undercanvas.com/camps/moab, open mid-Mar.-Oct.) offers a luxury safari tent experience on 40 acres near the entrance to Arches National Park. Lodging is in a variety of large wall tents, some with private en suite bathrooms, and all fitted with fine bedding and furniture. In other words, this isn't exactly roughing it. Tent accommodations that sleep four start at $219 per night, with modern plumbing and bathroom facilities in group shower houses. Adventure packages are also available that customize outdoor activities to your preferences, and also include three camp-cooked meals a day.

BLM Campgrounds

There are 26 BLM campgrounds (most $10-15) in the Moab area. Although these spots can't be reserved, sites are abundant enough that campers are rarely unable to find a spot.

The campgrounds are concentrated on the banks of the Colorado River—along Highway 128 toward Castle Valley, along Highway 279 toward the potash factory, and along Kane Creek Road—and at the Sand Flats Recreation Area near the Slickrock Trail. Only a few of these campgrounds can handle large RVs, none have hookups, and few have piped water. For a full list of BLM campground and facilities, visit www.discovermoab.com.

Dead Horse Point State Park Campground

Soak in Dead Horse Point's spectacular scenery at the park's **Kayenta Campground** (reservations 800/322-3770, www.reserveamerica.com, $35 hike-in tent camping, $40 RVs, $140 yurts, plus $10 reservations fee), just past the visitors center, which offers sites with water and electric hookups but no showers. The campground nearly always fills up during the main season, so it's almost essential to reserve well in advance. Winter visitors may camp at the park; no hookups are available, but the restrooms have water.

If you aren't able to secure a spot inside the park, try the BLM's **Horsethief Campground** (no drinking water, $15) on Highway 313 a few miles east of the state park entrance. It has nearly 60 sites, all first come, first served, so it's usually possible to find a site.

Information and Services

Moab is a small town, and people are generally friendly. Between the excellent Moab Information Center and the county library—and the friendly advice of people in the street—you'll find it easy to assemble all the information you need to have a fine stay.

INFORMATION

The **Moab Information Center** (25 E. Center St., at Main St., 435/259-8825, www.discovermoab.com, 8am-4pm daily) is the place to start for nearly all local and area information. The

National Park Service, the BLM, the U.S. Forest Service, the Grand County Travel Council, and the Canyonlands Natural History Association are all represented here. Visitors who need help from any of these agencies should start at the information center rather than at the agency offices. Free literature is available, the selection of books and maps for sale is large, and the staff is knowledgeable. The center's website is also well organized and packed with information. In addition, the center screens a high-definition 4K film, *Welcome to Moab,* which introduces visitors to the wonders of the surrounding area.

The **BLM district office** (82 E. Dogwood Ave., 435/259-2100, 7:45am-4:30pm Mon.-Fri.) is on the south side of town behind Comfort Suites. Some land-use maps are sold here, and this is the place to pick up **river-running permits.**

SERVICES

The **Grand County Public Library** (257 E. Center St., 435/259-1111, 9am-8pm Mon.-Fri., 9am-5pm Sat.) is a good place for local history and general reading.

The **post office** (50 E. 100 N., 435/259-7427) is downtown. **Moab Regional Hospital** (450 W. Williams Way, 435/719-3500) provides medical care. For ambulance, sheriff, police, or fire emergencies, dial 911.

Dogs can spend a day or board at **Karen's Canine Campground** (435/259-7922, https://karensk9campground.wordpress.com) while their people hike the no-dog trails in Arches and Canyonlands.

Getting There

SkyWest, associated with United Airlines (800/335-2247, www.united.com), provides daily scheduled air service between **Canyonlands Field** (CNY, U.S. 191, 16 miles (26 km) north of Moab, 435/259-4849, www.moabairport.com) and Denver. Grand Junction, Colorado, is 120 miles (193 km) east of Moab via I-70 and has better air service; Salt Lake City is 240 miles (385 km) northwest of Moab.

Moab Express (435/260-9289, https://moabexpress.com) runs shuttles between Moab and Canyonlands Field ($25 pp, must book in advance). Moab Express shuttles also link to the Grand Junction airport in Colorado.

Enterprise (711 S. Main St., 435/259-8505, www.enterprise.com) rents cars at the airport.

The Southeastern Corner

Although Arches and Canyonlands capture more attention, Utah's southeastern corner contains an incredible wealth of scenic and culturally significant sites. Round out your trip to this part of Utah with a tour of Ancestral Puebloan ruins, remote desert washes, soaring natural bridges, snowy mountain peaks, and a vast reservoir in a red-rock desert.

U.S. 191 runs south from Moab between Canyonlands National Park and the surprisingly tall Abajo Mountains to the west and the La Sal Mountains to the east. In the heat of the summer, these mountains are cool refuges. Also east of the highway, near the Colorado border, is Hovenweep National Monument, an Ancestral Puebloan site with an astounding collection of masonry buildings. Here the Ancestral Puebloans

Highlights

Look for ★ to find recommended sights, activities, dining, and lodging.

★ **Visit Edge of the Cedars State Park Museum:** Archaeological exhibits provide a good introduction to Ancestral Puebloan, Ute, Navajo, and Anglo history (page 129)

★ **Float the San Juan River:** Ignore the rest of the world by paddling through deep canyons and down Class III rapids (page 131)

★ **Go back in Time:** An impressive collection of masonry dwellings can be found at **Hovenweep National Monument** (page 133).

★ **Hike in Natural Bridges National Monument:** Three spectacular natural bridges are your reward on this 8.6-mile (13.8-km) loop hike. A 9-mile (14.5-km) drive with short hikes to each bridge will also do the trick (page 142).

★ **Roam Goblin Valley State Park:** Wander amid sandstone oddities—big mushroom-shaped rock formations, some with eroded "eyes" (page 151).

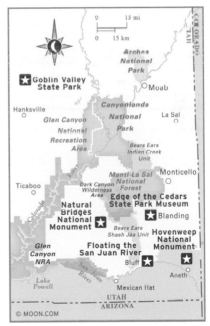

The Southeastern Corner

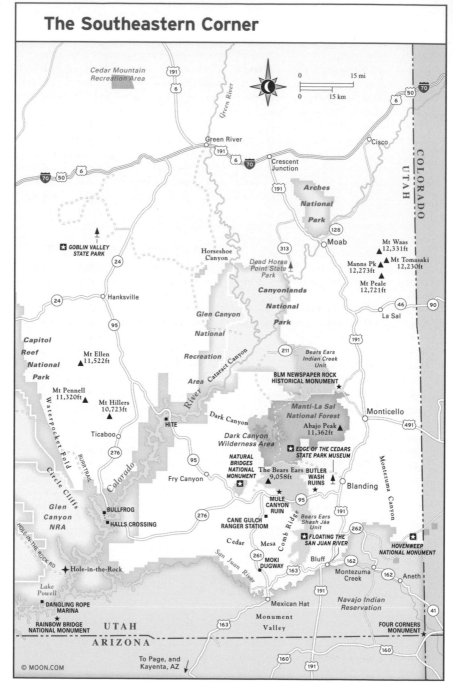

Cedar Mountain
Recreation Area

Green River

Green River

Cisco

COLORADO
UTAH

Crescent
Junction

Arches

National

Park

Moab

Mt Waas
12,331ft

GOBLIN VALLEY
STATE PARK

Horseshoe
Canyon

Dead Horse
Point State
Park

Manns Pk
12,273ft

Mt Tomasaki
12,230ft

Mt Peale
12,721ft

Hanksville

Canyonlands

National

Park

La Sal

Capitol

Reef

National

Park

Glen Canyon

National

Recreation

Area

Mt Ellen
11,522ft

Bears Ears
Indian Creek
Unit

BLM NEWSPAPER ROCK
HISTORICAL MONUMENT

Cataract Canyon

Manti-La Sal
National Forest

Monticello

Mt Pennell
11,320ft

River

Mt Hillers
10,723ft

Dark Canyon

Abajo Peak
11,362ft

HITE

Ticaboo

Dark Canyon
Wilderness Area

EDGE OF THE CEDARS
STATE PARK MUSEUM

Colorado

NATURAL
BRIDGES
NATIONAL
MONUMENT

The Bears Ears
9,058ft

BUTLER
WASH
RUINS

Waterpocket Fold

Fry Canyon

Blanding

Circle Cliffs

BURR TRAIL

MULE
CANYON
RUIN

Bears Ears
Shash Jáa
Unit

Montezuma Canyon

BULLFROG

CANE GULCH
RANGER STATION

Glen

Canyon

NRA

HALLS CROSSING

Cedar

Mesa

Comb Ridge

FLOATING THE
SAN JUAN RIVER

HOVENWEEP
NATIONAL MONUMENT

HOLE-IN-THE-ROCK RD

MOKI
DUGWAY

Bluff

San Juan River

Montezuma
Creek

Aneth

Hole-in-the-Rock

Lake
Powell

DANGLING ROPE
MARINA

Mexican Hat

Navajo Indian
Reservation

RAINBOW BRIDGE
NATIONAL MONUMENT

UTAH

Monument

Valley

FOUR CORNERS
MONUMENT

ARIZONA

© MOON.COM

To Page, and
Kayenta, AZ

0   15 mi
0   15 km

lived in what was more or less a city until they suddenly departed about 900 years ago.

The San Juan River runs across the south ern tier of the region, with Cedar Mesa to the north and Monument Valley and Navajo Nation land to the south. Bluff, a charming village that's the put-in for many river trips on the San Juan, was settled in 1880 by Mormon pioneers who made the incredible wagon train trip from Escalante through steep canyons, including Hole-in-the-Rock.

Cedar Mesa is a place to explore on foot; canyons here often shelter Ancestral Puebloan ruins. To the west of the mesa, Natural Bridges National Monument is often overlooked, probably because it's rather remote. But its soaring stone bridges (carved by streams and spanning a streambed) are beautiful, even elegant, and a night in the campground will allow you to see stars in one of the nation's darkest places.

At Lake Powell the Colorado River is backed up by the Glen Canyon Dam. Lake Powell draws boaters—including visitors who rent houseboats to motor to the huge reservoir's remote inlets and canyons—but for a quick look, the car ferry across the lake is far less expensive. The surrounding Glen Canyon National Recreation Area encompasses the rugged canyons that drop down toward Lake Powell, before the dam was built, Glen Canyon was considered the equal of the Grand Canyon for drama and beauty, and in low-water years, a few peeks into the past are possible. A popular side trip—usually visited via tour boats from one of the lake's marinas—is to Rainbow Bridge National Monument, where the enormous stone bridge spans an arm of the lake.

On the northwestern edge of the region, about 25 miles (40 km) south of I-70, Goblin Valley State Park has rock formations that would be worthy of national park status if they weren't so close to Arches. Here you can hike among hoodoos, spires, and balancing rocks, many with wind-carved "eyes" that explain the area's supernatural moniker.

Remember that this is remote country: Fill your gas tank when you have the opportunity. Hanksville and Blanding are good places to check your gauge; if it's showing less than half a tank, definitely fill up. Likewise, pack a lunch and plenty of water when exploring remote areas such as Cedar Mesa, Hovenweep, or Glen Canyon.

PLANNING YOUR TIME

Although it's possible to spend many days exploring the backcountry of Cedar Mesa, floating the San Juan River, houseboating to remote reaches of Lake Powell, or really getting to understand the ancient dwellings at Hovenweep National Monument, most travelers will, at least initially, just pass through. Be sure to allow a day to visit Hovenweep and the Edge of the Cedars Museum in Blanding. From there, if you are short on time, head west across Cedar Mesa to Natural Bridges National Monument and north through Hanksville to Goblin Valley State Park.

Although there are motels in all the towns included in this chapter, you'll have more flexibility if you are camping. There are many campgrounds and even more de facto primitive campsites where you can make your own camp; however, be certain that you have the necessary permits before camping in the Cedar Mesa area.

South of Moab

U.S. 191 runs south out of Moab, with the La Sal Mountains to the east and Canyonlands National Park to the west. A string of small towns—Monticello, Blanding, and Bluff—offer places to stop for a meal or a motel room as well as opportunities to explore mountains, desert, rivers, and archaeological sites.

MONTICELLO

This small Mormon town (pop. 2,000) is about 50 miles (81 km) south of Moab and pretty much its polar opposite. Quiet and relatively untouristed, it's the best place to stay if you're visiting the Needles District of Canyonlands National Park and don't want to camp. Monticello (mon-tuh-SELL-o) is at an elevation of 7,069 feet (2,155 m), just east of the Abajo Mountains. It is 46 miles (74 km) east of the entrance to the Needles District.

Food

A great addition to otherwise sleepy Monticello, the ★ **Granary Bar and Grill** (64 S. 300 W., 435/587/2597, www.granarybargrill.com, 7am-10pm, 11am-4pm, and 5pm-10pm daily, dinner $9-27) offers good food and craft cocktails in a converted grain silo with a Prohibition-era speakeasy atmosphere. The Granary is part of the Grist Mill Inn, and with a wide menu of pasta, burgers, steaks and other well-prepared main courses, this is the best place to eat within miles.

Accommodations

Monticello has a number of comfortable and affordable motels. The **Inn at the Canyons** (533 N. Main St., 435/587-2458, www.monticellocanyonlandsinn.com, $115-125) is nicely renovated and has an indoor pool, a pretty basic continental breakfast, and microwaves and fridges in the guest rooms. The **Monticello Inn** (164 E. Central St.,

435/587-2274, www.themonticelloinn.com, $75-89) is a well-maintained older motel with a pleasant in-town setting.

The local B&B, the **Grist Mill Inn** (64 S. 300 E., 435/587-2597, www.oldgristmillinn.com, $119-149), is indeed housed in an old flour mill. But rest assured, you won't be sleeping under an old millstone: The seven guest rooms are all furnished in typical B&B fashion, and all have private baths and TVs. An additional four rooms are found in the Cottage, a separate but adjacent building; the inn also rents two large homes for groups. The adjacent Granary Bar and Grill is the best place to eat in Monticello.

CAMPING

Campgrounds in the nearby Manti-La Sal National Forest include **Buckboard** and **Dalton Springs** (435/587-2041, $10). Buckboard, 7 miles (11.3 km) west of town on Blue Mountain Road (Forest Rd. 105), is at 8,600 feet (2,621 m) elevation, so it's not your best bet early in the spring. But when the rest of southeastern Utah swelters in the summer, this shady campground is perfect. Dalton Springs is along the same road, a couple of miles closer to town, at 8,200 feet (2,500 m). An abandoned ski area nearby is a good place for mountain biking.

Information and Services

Stop at the **Southeastern Utah Welcome Center** (216 S. Main St., 435/587-3401, www.monticelloutah.org, 9am-6pm daily Mar.-Oct., 9am-3pm Wed.-Sun. Nov.-Feb.) for information about southeastern Utah, including Canyonlands National Park.

The **San Juan Hospital** (364 W. 100 N., 435/587-2116) is friendly and small, and it's a good place to have any camping-related injuries repaired.

BLANDING

The largest town in San Juan County, Blanding (pop. 3,500, elev. 6,105 ft/1,860 m) is also a handy, if not exactly compelling, stop for travelers. The restaurant scene here is especially dire; if you're staying here, you might opt to picnic. Blanding is one the few "dry" towns in Utah, meaning alcohol cannot be sold inside the municipality. In 2017, locals had a chance to vote for the first time in more than 80 years to allow beer and wine sales in town. Blanding overwhelmingly voted to keep the anti-alcohol restrictions in place. In this environment, few restaurants of note take root.

If you're heading east toward Hovenweep or west into the Cedar Mesa area, check your gas gauge. Blanding is a good place to gas up—it's a long way between gas stations in this corner of Utah.

TOP EXPERIENCE

★ Edge of the Cedars State Park Museum

One mile (1.6 km) north of present-day Blanding, Ancestral Puebloan people built at least six groups of pueblo structures between AD 700 and 1220. The **Edge of the Cedars State Park Museum** (660 W. 400 N., 435/678-2238, www.stateparks.utah.gov, 10am-4pm Mon.-Sat., $5 adults, $3 children) features an excellent array of pottery, baskets, sandals, jewelry, and stone tools. The pottery collection on the second floor stands out for its rich variety of styles and decorative designs. This is the top museum in Utah if you're interested in the history and art of the Ancestral Puebloans, and it serves as a marvelous introduction to the ruins at nearby Hovenweep National Monument. The museum also has exhibits and artifacts of the people who followed the Ancestral Puebloans—the Utes and Navajo and the early Anglo pioneers.

A short trail behind the museum leads past a ruin that has been excavated and partly restored to suggest the village's appearance when the Ancestral Puebloans lived here.

You may enter the kiva by descending a ladder through the restored roof; the walls and interior features are original.

The Dinosaur Museum

The Dinosaur Museum (754 S. 200 W., 435/678-3454, www.dinosaur-museum.org, 9am-1pm Mon.-Sat. Apr. 15-Oct. 15, $4.50 adults, $3.50 seniors, $3 children) showcases the prehistoric plant and animal life of this corner of Utah. Exhibits include life-size models of dinosaurs (including the dino model used in the original King Kong movie) as well as fossils and skeletons. Don't miss the models of feathered dinosaurs.

Food

Blanding is not a center of gastronomy. In fact, restaurants seem to have trouble even staying open in this alcohol-free town. Only the fast-food joints are open on Sunday. Though **The Patio Drive In** (95 Grayson Pkwy., 435/678-2177, 11am-8pm Mon.-Thurs., 11am-9pm Fri.-Sat., $7-10) has a big local reputation as a drive-in restaurant, there are also a handful of tables and booths in the diner. **The Homestead** (121 E. Center St., 435/678-3456, 11am-9pm Mon.-Fri., 4pm-9pm Sat., $11-30) is the local steak house, with typical American fare and pizza, plus Navajo tacos.

Accommodations

With one exception, Blanding's motels are all pretty generic. That exception is ★ **Stone Lizard Lodge** (88 W. Center St., 435/678-3323, www.stonelizardlodging.com, $124-175), an older motel with remodeled but homey guest rooms, including a two-bedroom suite ($149). There's also a good breakfast. The motel also offers a pleasant garden area in the back with comfortable seating. The **Four Corners Inn** (131 E. Center St., 435/678-3257 or 800/574-3150, www.fourcornersinnblanding.com, $76-90), which has a restaurant next door, a simple continental breakfast, and several pet-friendly rooms, is a fine enough place to spend a night.

CAMPGROUNDS

At the south edge of town, **Blue Mountain RV Park** (1930 S. Main St., 435/678-7840, www.bluemountainrvpark.com, $26 tents, $35 RVs) is also home to a trading post with some high-quality Native American rugs, jewelry, and baskets. Although tent campers are welcome at the RV park, **Devil's Canyon Campground** (reservations 877/444-6777, www.recreation.gov, $10, plus $9 reservation fee), at an elevation of 7,100 feet (2,164 m) in the Manti-La Sal National Forest, is a better bet for tents. It has sites with water early May to late October, and no water or fees offseason. A 0.25-mile (0.4 km) nature trail begins at the far end of the campground loop. From Blanding, go north 8 miles (12.9 km) on U.S. 191, then turn west onto a paved road for 1.3 miles (2.1 km); the turnoff from U.S. 191 is between mileposts 60 and 61.

BLUFF

Bluff, a sleepy community of about 300 inhabitants, is nestled in a striking physical location. In the past few years, Bluff has become a rather unlikely mecca for recreationists and escapees from urban congestion. The quality of lodging is better than that of almost any other town of this size in the state, and local outfitters make it easy to get out and enjoy the remarkable scenery hereabouts.

Bluff is the oldest non-Native American community in southeastern Utah; it was settled in 1880 by Mormon pioneers who had traveled the excruciatingly difficult Hole-in-the-Rock Trail from the town of Escalante down into what's now Lake Powell. When the Mormon settlers finally got to the San Juan River valley, they founded **Bluff Fort,** which has been reconstructed (550 E. Black Locust St., 435/672-9995, 9am-5pm Mon.-Sat., free).

Spend an afternoon poking around local washes or examining a large pictograph panel, found along the cliff about 0.3 mile

(0.5 km) downstream from the Sand Island Campground. The visitors center, located in the Bluff Fort complex, is worth a stop; the staff can give you detailed directions for good informal hikes in the nearby washes.

If you want a guided trip into the backcountry of southeastern Utah, **Far Out Expeditions** (425/672-2294, www.faroutexpeditions.com) is a local company with lots of experience leading day trips and overnights in the area. **Wild Expeditions** (435/672-2244, www.riversandruins.com) leads half-day, full-day, and multiday trips to many of the destinations in southeastern Utah, including the Bears Ears area, with your choice of hiking, canyoneering, off-road vehicles, or 4WD touring.

★ Floating the San Juan River

From the high San Juan Mountains in southern Colorado, the San Juan River winds its way into New Mexico, enters Utah near Four Corners, and twists through spectacular canyons before ending at Lake Powell. Most boaters put in at Sand Island Campground near Bluff and take out at the town of Mexican Hat, 26 river miles (42 km) downstream. This trip combines ancient Native American ruins, rock art, and a trip through Monument Upwarp and the Upper Canyon, with some Class III rapids for thrills and weirdly buckled geology to ponder. This portion of the San Juan River can be done as a day trip or a more leisurely multiday trip. Longer trips continue through the famous Goosenecks, the "entrenched meanders" carved thousands of feet below the desert surface, and through more Class III rapids on the way to Clay Hills Crossing or Paiute Farms (not always accessible) on Lake Powell. Allow at least four days for the full trip, though more time will allow for exploration of side canyons and visits to Ancestral Puebloan sites. Rafts, kayaks, and canoes can be used. The season usually lasts March to October despite arid summer conditions because of adequate water flow from Navajo Reservoir upstream.

1: Edge of the Cedars State Park **2:** the Stone Lizard Lodge in Blanding **3:** Bluff Fort **4:** rafting the San Juan River

Several commercial river-running companies offer San Juan trips. If you go on your own, you should have river-running experience or be with someone who does. Private groups need to obtain **permits** ($10-30 pp) from the **Bureau of Land Management's San Juan Resource Area office** (435/587-1544, www.blm.gov); permits are issued through a preseason lottery (via www.recreation.gov), although boaters with flexible schedules can usually get permits close to their time of travel. Permit fees vary depending on how far you're floating.

Some people also like to run the river between Montezuma Creek and Sand Island, a leisurely trip of 20 river miles (32 km). The solitude often makes up for the lack of scenery. It's easy to get a river permit for this section because no use limits or fees apply.

If you're looking for a guided trip on the San Juan River, contact local **Wild Expeditions** (2625 S. U.S. 191, 435/672-2244, www.riversandruins.com), which offers both day and multiday trips out of Bluff; trips run daily in summer, and only a day's notice is usually needed to join a float. On eight-hour, 26-mile (42-km) day excursions to Mexican Hat ($199 adults, $133 under age 15), motors may be used if the water level is low. This highly recommended trip includes lunch plus stops at Ancestral Puebloan ruins and rock-art panels.

Food

A longtime local hangout and a good place for a meal and a friendly vibe is the **Twin Rocks Cafe** (435/672-2341, www.twinrockscafe.com, 8am-8pm Mon.-Sat., $8-20), next to the trading post just below the impossible-to-miss Twin Rocks. Here you can dine on Navajo tacos (fry bread with chili) or Navajo pizza (fry bread with pizza toppings) as well as more standard fare. Be sure to visit the trading post for high-quality Native American crafts, many of them produced locally by Navajo artisans.

Settle in under the big cottonwood tree for a flame-grilled steak dinner at the **Cottonwood Steakhouse** (Main St. and 4th St. E., 435/672-2282, www.cottonwoodsteakhouse.com, 5:30pm-9:30pm daily spring-fall, call for winter hours, $15-26). Dinners come with salad, beans, and potatoes; for $10 you can split an entrée with someone else and get full servings of side dishes. Indoor dining is also an option. Homemade pies are a specialty.

★ **Comb Ridge Eat and Drink** (680 S. U.S. 191, 435/485-5555, 3pm-8:30pm Tues.-Fri.,11:30am-8:30pm Sat.-Sun., $8-15), an artsy café housed in a historic trading post, has lots of character and surprisingly delicious food. Although the menu items are simple (burgers and pub grub), the quality is high. Where else in this part of Utah are you going to find a tabouli bowl? There are several good options for vegetarians here.

On the premises of the Desert Rose Inn find **Duke's** (701 W. Main St., 735/672-2303, www.desertroseinn.com, 5pm-9pm Mon.-Sat., Mar.-Oct., $13-32), with very good burgers and steaks, an attractive dining room, and a lovely patio (but no alcohol).

Accommodations

Attractive ★ **Desert Rose Inn** (701 W. Main St., 735/672-2303 or 888/475-7673, www.desertroseinn.com, $149-230) is one of the nicest lodgings in this corner of the state. The large lodge-like log structure has two-story wraparound porches and guest rooms furnished with pine furniture, quilts, and Southwestern art. An additional wing has an indoor pool and spa, and a handsome restaurant has been added. At the edge of the property are a number of handsome one-bedroom log cabins. This is definitely a class act.

Another classy place to stay is **La Posada Pintada** (239 N. 7th E./Navajo Twins Dr., 435/459-2274, www.laposadapintada.com, $155-175), a stylish, recently built boutique inn with 11 spacious rooms (one a pioneer cabin) and a serious breakfast buffet. This is a refined place: all rooms come with flat screen TVs, Wi-Fi, fridges and microwaves, private patios, large bathrooms, and high-end linens and amenities.

Another great place to stay is **Recapture Lodge** (220 E. Main St., 435/672-2281, www.recapturelodge.com, $98-119). For many years the heart and soul of Bluff, this rustic, comfortable lodge is operated by longtime outfitters and the staff can help you plan an outdoor adventure. Besides guest rooms and kitchenettes, Recapture Lodge has trails out the back door, a swimming pool, a hot tub, and a coin laundry. The Recapture also rents a couple of fully equipped homes in Bluff for families and groups.

Bluff's newest lodging is ★ **Bluff Dwellings Resort and Spa** (2625 S. Hwy. 191, 435/672-2477, www.bluffdwellings.com, $189-289), a large complex centered around a welcoming pool and patio area. The rooms are in a series of structures designed to echo the ancient stone dwellings tucked into local cliffs but with every modern amenity. All rooms have private decks or balconies; some offer kitchenettes. The onsite Hozho Spa offers a number of massage, body, and beauty treatments by appointment.

CAMPGROUNDS

Sand Island Recreation Area (435/587-1500, www.blm.gov, $15) is a Bureau of Land Management (BLM) camping area along the San Juan River, 3 miles (4.8 km) south of town, with piped water. Large cottonwood trees shade this pretty spot, but tenters need to watch for thorns in the grass. River-runners often put in at the campground, so it can be a busy place. Two RV parks are right in town: **Cadillac Ranch RV Park** (U.S. 191, 435/672-2262 or 800/538-6195, www.cadillacranchrv.com, year-round, $22-30) is in the center of town, and **Cottonwood R.V. Park** (U.S. 191, 435/672-2287, http://cottonwoodrvpark.blogspot.com, Mar.-Nov. 15, $35) is at the west end of Bluff.

★ HOVENWEEP NATIONAL MONUMENT

Delve into the region's cultural history and architecture at remote **Hovenweep National Monument** (970/562-4283, www.nps.gov/hove, free), where the Ancestral Puebloans built many impressive masonry buildings during the early-mid-1200s, near the end of their 1,300-year stay in the area. A drought that began in 1274 and lasted 25 years probably hastened their migration from this area. Several centuries of intensive farming, hunting, and woodcutting had already taken a toll on the land. Archaeologists believe the inhabitants retreated south in the late 1200s to sites in northwestern New Mexico and northeastern Arizona. The Ute word *hovenweep* means "deserted valley," an appropriate name for the lonely high desert country they left behind. The Ancestral Puebloans at Hovenweep had much in common with the Mesa Verde culture, although the Dakota sandstone here doesn't form large alcoves suitable for cliff-dweller villages. Ruins at Hovenweep remain essentially unexcavated.

The Ancestral Puebloan farmers had a keen interest in the seasons because of their need to know the best time for planting crops. Astronomical stations (alignments of walls, doorways, and tiny openings) allowed the sun priests to determine the equinoxes and solstices with an accuracy of one or two days. This precision also may have been necessary for a complex ceremonial calendar. Astronomical stations at Hovenweep have been discovered at Hovenweep Castle, House of Square Tower Ruins, and Cajon Ruins.

Planning Your Time

Hovenweep National Monument protects six groups of villages left behind by the Ancestral Puebloans. The sites are near the Colorado border, southeast of Blanding. **Square Tower Ruins Unit,** where the visitors center is located, has the most ruins and the most varied architecture. In fact, you can find all the Hovenweep architectural styles here. There are other ruins that are good to visit if you'd like to spend more time in the area; you'll need a map and directions from a ranger to find them because they aren't signed. One group, the Goodman Point, near Cortez, Colorado, offers relatively little to see except unexcavated mounds.

Visitors Center

The **visitors center** (970/562-4282, 5am-5pm daily Apr.-Oct., 9am-4pm daily Nov.-Mar.) has a few exhibits on the Ancestral Puebloans, photos of local wildlife, and a small bookstore. A ranger can answer your questions, provide brochures and handouts about various aspects of the monument, and give directions for visiting the other groups of ruins.

Square Tower Ruins

This extensive group of Ancestral Puebloan towers and dwellings lines the rim and slopes of Little Ruin Canyon, located a short walk from the visitors center. Obtain a trail-guide booklet from the ranger station. You can take easy walks of less than 0.5 mile (0.8 km) on

the rim. Combine all the trails for a loop of about 2 miles (1.2 km) with only one up-and-down section in the canyon. The booklet has good descriptions of Ancestral Puebloan life and architecture and of the plants growing along the trail. You'll see towers (D-shaped, square, oval, and round), cliff dwellings, surface dwellings, storehouses, kivas, and rock art. Keep an eye out for the prairie rattlesnake, a subspecies of the western rattlesnake, which is active at night in summer and during the day in spring and fall. And stay on the trail: Don't climb the fragile walls of the ruins or walk on rubble mounds.

Holly Ruins

Holly Ruins group is noted for its Great House, Holly Tower, and Tilted Tower. Most of Tilted Tower fell away after the boulder on which it sat shifted. Great piles of rubble mark the sites of structures built on loose ground. Look for remnants of farming terraces in the canyon below the Great House. A hiking trail connects the campground at Square Tower Ruins with Holly Ruins; the route follows canyon bottoms and is about 8 miles (12.9 km) round-trip. Ask a ranger for a map and directions. Hikers can also continue to Horseshoe Ruins (1 mi/1.6 km farther) and Hackberry

The ruins at Hovenweep National Monument date from the 1200s.

Ruins (just beyond Horseshoe). All of these are just across the Colorado border and about 6 miles (9.7 km) one-way by road from the visitors center.

Horseshoe and Hackberry Ruins

Horseshoe Ruins and Hackberry Ruins are best reached by an easy trail (1 mi/1.6 km round-trip) off the road to Holly Ruins. Horseshoe House, built in a horseshoe shape similar to Sun Temple at Mesa Verde, has exceptionally good masonry work. Archaeologists haven't determined the purpose of the structure. An alcove in the canyon below contains a spring and a small shelter. A round tower nearby on the rim has a strategic view. Hackberry House has only one room still intact. Rubble piles and wall remnants abound in the area. The spring under an alcove here still has a good flow and supports lush growths of hackberry and cottonwood trees along with smaller plants.

Cutthroat Castle Ruins

Cutthroat Castle Ruins were remote even in Ancestral Puebloan times. The ruins lie along an intermittent stream rather than at the head of a canyon like most other Hovenweep sites. Cutthroat Castle is a **large multistory** structure with both straight and curved walls. Three round towers stand nearby. Look for wall fragments and the circular depressions of kivas. High-clearance vehicles can get close to the ruins, about 11.5 miles (18.5 km) one-way from the visitors center. Visitors with cars can drive to a trailhead and then walk to the ruins, 1.5 (2.4 km) miles round-trip on foot.

Cajon Ruins

Cajon Ruins are at the head of a little canyon on Cajon Mesa on the Navajo Reservation in Utah, about 9 miles (14.5 km) southwest of the visitors center. The site has a commanding view across the San Juan Valley as far as Monument Valley. Buildings include a large multiroom structure, a round tower, and a tall square tower. An alcove just below has a spring and some rooms. Look for pictographs, petroglyphs, and grooves in the rock used for tool grinding. Farming terraces were located on the canyon's south side.

Camping

A small **campground** (no reservations, $15, no credit cards) near the visitors center has 31 sites geared toward tent campers, although a few sites will accommodate RVs up to 36 feet (11 m) long. Running water is available only during summer, when five gallons are allotted to each camper. Like Hovenweep's ancient inhabitants, campers are often treated to excellent stargazing; the monument is far from light pollution, and the dark night skies are frequently clear.

Getting There

One approach is from U.S. 191 between Blanding and Bluff; head east 9 miles (14.5 km) on Highway 262, continue straight 6 miles (9.7 km) on a small paved road to Hatch Trading Post, and then follow the signs for 16 miles (74 km). A good way in from Bluff is to go east 21 miles (34 km) on paved Highway 162 to Montezuma Creek and Aneth, then follow the signs north for 20 miles (32 km). A scenic 58-mile (93-km) route through Montezuma Canyon begins 5 miles (8 km) south of Monticello and follows unpaved roads to Hatch and on to Hovenweep; you can stop at the BLM's Three Turkey Ruin on the way. From Colorado, take a partly paved road west and north 41 miles (66 km) from U.S. 491 (the turnoff is 4 miles (6.4 km) south of Cortez).

Don't expect your cell phone to work in this remote area.

Cedar Mesa and Vicinity

Head way off the beaten track to explore ancient ruins and stunning geography in the area west of U.S. 191 and east of Glen Canyon and Lake Powell. Experienced hikers can wander deep into this rugged area; those with less experience or fortitude may want to focus on the trails at Natural Bridges National Monument.

CEDAR MESA

Just south of Blanding, Highway 95—here labeled Trail of the Ancients National Scenic Byway—heads west across a high plateau toward the Colorado River, traversing Comb Ridge, Cedar Mesa, and many canyons. This is remote country, so fill up with gas before leaving Blanding; you can't depend on finding gasoline until Hanksville, 122 miles (196 km) away. Hite and the other Lake Powell marinas do have gas and supplies, but their hours are limited.

Cedar Mesa and its canyons have an exceptionally large number of prehistoric Ancestral Puebloan sites. Several ruins are just off the highway, and hikers will discover many more.

Cedar Mesa is also home to **Bears Ears Buttes,** two distinctive outcrops that are visible for miles across southeastern Utah. Native Americans in the area consider just about all of southeastern Utah to be a sacred place, and the Bears Ears have come to represent it. In 2016, 1.35 million acres in this part of the state were designated the Bears Ears National Monument by the Obama administration, to protect the cultural resources of local Native Americans. In 2018, the Trump administration shrank the monument by 85 percent, reopening much of this land to mineral and oil-and-gas extraction. In place of the original Bears Ears monument, the Trump administration designated two smaller monuments: the 71,896-acre Indian Creek National Monument and the 129,980-acre Shash Jaa National Monument.

If you would like to explore the Cedar Mesa and Bears Ears area, be sure to drop in at the BLM's **Kane Gulch Ranger Station** (435/587-1532, www.blm.gov, 8am-noon daily spring and fall), at the west end of Cedar Mesa, 4 miles (6.4 km) south of Highway 95 on Highway 261. BLM staff issue the permits required to explore the Cedar Mesa backcountry for day-use ($5) and for overnight stays ($15 pp) in Grand Gulch, Fish Creek Canyon, and Owl Creek Canyon. The number of people permitted to camp at a given time is limited, so call ahead. BLM staff will also tell you about archaeological sites and their historic value, current hiking conditions, and where to find water. Cedar Mesa is managed for more primitive recreation, so hikers in the area should have good route-finding skills and come prepared with food and water.

If you'd rather leave the logistics to the professionals, the friendly folks at **Wild Expeditions** (435/672-2244, www.riversandruins.com) offer multiday guided trips into the Cedar Mesa and Bears Ears area, and also offer rentals and support for personalized trips into this remote area.

Butler Wash Ruins

Well-preserved pueblo ruins left by the Ancestral Puebloans are tucked under an overhang across the wash. Find the trailhead 11 miles (17.7 km) west of U.S. 191, on the north side of Highway 95, between mileposts 111 and 112. Follow cairns for 0.5 mile (0.8 km) through juniper and piñon pine woodlands and across slickrock to the overlook, where you can see four kivas and several other structures. Parts have been reconstructed, but most of the site is about 900 years old.

Comb Ridge

Geologic forces have squeezed up the earth's crust in a long ridge running 80 miles (129 km) south from the Abajo Peaks into Arizona.

Sheer cliffs plunge 800 feet (244 m) into Comb Wash on the west side. Engineering the highway down these cliffs took considerable effort. A parking area near the top of the grade offers expansive panoramas across Comb Wash. Side roads along the east side of Comb Ridge access a number of Ancestral Puebloan rock-art sites and village ruins. Contact the **Kane Gulch Ranger Station** (435/587-1532, www. blm.gov/visit/kane-gulch-ranger-station) for information about these sites.

Arch Canyon

This tributary canyon of Comb Wash has spectacular scenery and many Native American ruins. Much of the canyon can be seen on a day hike, but 2-3 days are required to explore the upper reaches. (Many visitors shorten the trip by driving a 4WD rig up the canyon for a few miles.) The main streambeds usually have water, but you should purify it before drinking it. To reach the trailhead, turn north onto Comb Wash Road (between mileposts 107 and 108 on Hwy. 95) and go 2.5 miles (4 km) on the dirt road, past a house and a water tank. Park in a grove of cottonwood trees before a stream. The mouth of pretty Arch Canyon is just to the northwest (it's easy to miss). Look for a Native American ruin about 0.25 mile (0.4 km) up Arch Canyon on the right. More ruins are tucked under alcoves farther up-canyon; the canyon's three arches are past the 7-mile (11.3-km) point.

Arch Canyon Overlook

A road and a short trail to the rim of Arch Canyon provide a beautiful view into the depths. Turn north onto Texas Flat Road (County Rd. 263) from Highway 95, between mileposts 102 and 103. Continue 4 miles (6.4 km) and park just before the road begins a steep climb, and then walk east on an old jeep road to the rim. This is a fine place for a picnic, although there are no facilities or guardrails. Texas Flat Road is dirt but passable when dry for cars with good clearance. Trucks can continue up the steep hill to other viewpoints of Arch and Texas Canyons.

Mule Canyon Ruin

Archaeologists have excavated and stabilized this Ancestral Puebloan village on the gentle slope of Mule Canyon's South Fork. A stone kiva, circular tower, and 12-room structure are all visible, and all were originally connected by tunnels. Cave Towers, 2 miles (3.2 km) southeast, would have been visible from the top of the tower here. Signs describe the ruins and periods of Ancestral Puebloan development. Turn north from Highway 95 between mileposts 101 and 102 and continue 0.3 mile (0.5 km) on a paved road. The ruin is right here no hiking required! Hikers can explore other ruins in the North and South Forks of Mule Canyon; check with the Kane Gulch Ranger Station for advice and directions. You might see pieces of pottery and other artifacts in this area. Federal laws prohibit the removal of artifacts. Leave every piece in place so that future visitors can enjoy the discovery. Be sure to have a BLM day-hiking permit when exploring this area.

Shash Jaa National Monument

This national monument, established in 2018, protects 129,980 acres of striking geologic features, juniper forests, canyons, and a cultural and historical legacy that includes an abundance of Ancestral Puebloan ruins and rock art. In addition to the Bears Ears Buttes area, Shash Jaa also protects a long tail of land extending south along Comb Ridge to the San Juan River, another area also rich in ancient remains. The monument includes two tiny satellite units that protect Doll House and Moon House ruins. For recreational information on Shash Jaa, contact **Kane Gulch Ranger Station** (435/587-1532, www.blm. gov/visit/kane-gulch-ranger-station).

GRAND GULCH PRIMITIVE AREA

Within this twisting canyon system are some of the most captivating scenery and largest concentrations of Ancestral Puebloan ruins in southeastern Utah. The main canyon

The Future of Bears Ears

The Bears Ears area is home to two national monuments.

Bears Ears National Monument was established in 2016 in the waning weeks of the Obama administration. It was divided into two much smaller national monuments by President Trump. President Biden has moved to re-instate the original boundaries.

The two new Utah national monuments are the 71,896-acre **Indian Creek National Monument** and the 129,980-acre **Shash Jaa National Monument.** The Indian Creek monument is essentially an eastern annex to the Needles District of Canyonlands National Park and includes noted rock-climbing cliffs and Newspaper Rock, famous for its petroglyphs. Shash Jaa monument protects the area that includes Bears Ears Buttes, parts of Mule and Arch Canyons, and the drainages of Comb Ridge, a sacred landscape for many Indigenous people and an area rich in Ancestral Puebloan ruins and rock art. Notably, this redrawn monument eliminates the earlier designation's protection for Cedar Mesa, another region with a wealth of Ancestral Puebloan remains—and uranium deposits.

The acreage comprising these two new national monuments is a mix of Forest Service, Bureau of Land Management (BLM), state, and private land, and a management plan to administer to these units has been developed but has not been approved. Meanwhile, a number of lawsuits from Native American and environmentalist groups that dispute the legality of the original monument's reduction are making their way through federal court. All publicly accessible sites are expected to remain open in the interim. Specific questions should be directed to the **Kane Gulch Ranger Station** (Hwy. 261, four miles south of Hwy. 95, 435/587-1532, www.blm.gov/visit/kane-gulch-ranger-station), the **BLM field office** in Monticello (365 N. Main St., 435/587-1510, www.blm.gov/programs/recreation/permits-and-passes/lotteries-and-permit-systems), or the **Blanding Visitor Center** (12 N. Grayson Pkwy., 435/678-3662, www.blanding-ut.gov/visitor-s-center.html).

begins only about 6 miles (9.7 km) southeast of Natural Bridges National Monument. From an elevation of 6,400 feet (1,950 m), Grand Gulch cuts deeply into Cedar Mesa on a tortuous path southwest to the San Juan River, dropping 2,700 feet (823 m) in about 53 miles (85 km). Sheer cliffs, alcoves, pinnacles, Ancestral Puebloan cliff dwellings, rock-art sites, arches, and a few natural bridges line Grand Gulch and its many tributaries.

From the Kane Gulch Ranger Station, a trail leads 4 miles (6.4 km) down Kane Gulch to the upper end of Grand Gulch, where a camping area is shaded by cottonwood trees. **Junction Ruin,** a cave dwelling, is visible from here, and less than 1 mile (1.6 km) farther into Grand Gulch are more ruins and an arch.

Kane Gulch and Bullet Canyon provide access to the upper end of Grand Gulch from the east side. A popular loop hike using these canyons is 23 miles (37 km) long (3-4 days); arrange a 7.5-mile (12-km) car shuttle or hitch. Ask at the ranger station if a shuttle service is available. Collins Canyon, reached from the Collins Spring trailhead, leads into lower Grand Gulch from the west side. The hike between the Kane Gulch and Collins Spring trailheads is 38 miles (61 km) one-way (5-7 days). A car shuttle of about 29 miles (47 km), including 8 miles (12.9 km) of dirt road, is required. Be sure to visit the BLM's **Kane Gulch Ranger Station** (435/587 1532, www.blm. gov, 8am-noon daily spring and fall) or the BLM Monticello office for a permit and information. You must have a day-use ($5) or overnight camping permit ($15) to enter the area.

MEXICAN HAT

South of the Kane Gulch Ranger Station, Highway 261 loses its pavement at the Moki Dugway, a series of steeply banked switchbacks incised into the sheer face of Cedar Mesa. Even if you're not given to vertigo, this road will get your attention. Slow down and take this stretch of road (with 1,100 feet/335 meters of elevation change and 5-10 percent grades) at 5-10 mph. About 10 miles (16 km) south of the Dugway is the town of Mexican Hat, a modest trade and tourism center.

Spectacular geology surrounds this tiny community perched on the north bank of the San Juan River. Dramatic folded layers of red and gray rock stand out. Alhambra Rock, a jagged remnant of a volcano, marks the southern approach to Mexican Hat. Another rock, which looks just like an upside-down sombrero, gave Mexican Hat its name; you'll see this formation from U.S. 163, 2 miles (3.2

km) north of town. Monument Valley, Valley of the Gods Scenic Drive, Goosenecks State Park, and Grand Gulch Primitive Area are only short drives away. The riverbanks near town can be a busy place in summer as river-runners on the San Juan put in, take out, or just stop for ice and beer.

Goosenecks State Park

The San Juan River winds through a series of incredibly tight bends 1,000 feet (305 m) below this park. So closely spaced are the bends that the river takes 6 miles (9.7 km) to cover an air distance of only 1.5 miles (2.4 km). The bends and exposed rock layers form exquisitely graceful curves. Geologists know the site as a classic example of entrenched meanders, caused by gradual uplift of a formerly level plain. Signs at the overlook explain the geologic history and identify the rock formations. **Goosenecks State Park** (435/678-2238, http://stateparks.utah.gov, $5 per vehicle) is an undeveloped area with a few picnic tables and vault toilets. A **campground** ($10) is available but has no water. From the junction of U.S. 163 and Highway 261, 4 miles (6.4 km) north of Mexican Hat, go 1 mile (1.6 km) northwest on Highway 261, then turn left and go 3 miles (4.8 km) on Highway 316 to its end.

Muley Point Overlook

One of the great views in the Southwest is just a short drive from Goosenecks State Park and more than 1,000 feet (305 m) higher in elevation. Although the view of the Goosenecks below is less dramatic than at the state park, the 6,200-foot elevation provides a magnificent panorama across the Navajo Reservation to Monument Valley and countless canyons and mountains. To get here, travel northwest 9 miles (14.5 km) on Highway 261 from the Goosenecks turnoff. At the top of the Moki Dugway switchbacks, turn left (southwest) and go 5.3 miles (8.5 km) on gravel County Road 241 (the turnoff may not be signed), and follow it toward the point. This road is not suitable for wet-weather travel.

Food and Accommodations

The **San Juan Inn and Trading Post** (U.S. 163 and San Juan River Rd., 435/683-2220 or 800/447-2022, www.sanjuaninn.net, $98-140), just west of town at a dramatic location above the river, offers clean guest rooms without extras, a few yurts, Native American trade goods, and a restaurant, the **Olde Bridge Grill** (435/683-2322, 7am-10pm daily, $8-15), serving American, Mexican, and Navajo food. **Hat Rock Inn** (120 U.S. 163, 435/683-2221, www.hatrockinn.com, $145-169) offers the nicest guest rooms in town and a swimming pool. **Mexican Hat Lodge** (100 N. Main St., 435/683-2222, www.mexicanhat.net, $84-160) offers guest rooms, a pool, and a fun but somewhat expensive restaurant (lunch and dinner daily) with grilled steaks and burgers.

Valle's Trading Post and RV Park (435/683-2226, year-round, $35) has tent and RV sites with hookups. The camping area is pretty basic, but great scenery surrounds it. The trading post offers crafts, groceries, showers, vehicle storage, and car shuttles. **Goosenecks State Park** has camping ($10) with great views but no amenities.

Valley of the Gods

Great sandstone monoliths, delicate spires, and long rock fins rise from the broad valley. This strange red-rock landscape resembles better-known Monument Valley but on a smaller scale. A 17-mile (27-km) dirt road winds through the spectacular scenery. Cars can usually travel the road at low speeds if the weather is dry (the road crosses washes). Allow 1-1.5 hours for the drive; it's studded with viewpoints, and you'll want to stop at all of them. The east end of the road connects with U.S. 163 at milepost 29 (7.5 mi/12 km northeast of Mexican Hat, 15 mi/24 km southwest of Bluff); the west end connects with Highway 261 just below the Moki Dugway switchbacks (4 mi/6.4 km north of Mexican Hat on U.S. 163, then 6.6 mi/10.6 km northwest on Hwy. 261).

If you're looking to really get away from it all, book a room at the **Valley of the Gods B&B** (970/749-1164, www.valleyofthegodsbandb.com, $175-195), a pretty Southwestern-style solar- and wind-powered ranch house with no TVs.

MONUMENT VALLEY

Towering buttes, jagged pinnacles, and rippled sand dunes make this area along the Utah-Arizona border an otherworldly landscape. Changing colors and shifting shadows during the day add to the enchantment. Most of the natural monuments are remnants of sandstone eroded by wind and water. Agathla Peak and some lesser summits are the roots of ancient volcanoes, whose dark rock contrasts with the pale yellow sandstone of the other formations. The valley is at an elevation of 5,564 feet (1,695 m) in the Upper Sonoran Life Zone; annual rainfall averages about 8.5 inches.

In 1863-1864, when Kit Carson was ravaging Canyon de Chelly in Arizona to round up the Navajo, Chief Hoskinini led his people to the safety and freedom of Monument Valley.

Hollywood movies made the splendor of Monument Valley widely known to the outside world. *Stagecoach*, filmed here in 1938 and directed by John Ford, became the first in a series of Westerns that has continued to the present.

The Navajo have preserved the valley as a park with a scenic drive, visitors center, and campground. From Mexican Hat, drive 22 miles (35 km) southwest on U.S. 163, then turn left and go 3.5 miles (5.6 km) to the visitors center. At the turnoff on U.S. 163 is a village's worth of outdoor market stalls and a modern complex of enclosed shops where you can stop to buy Navajo art and crafts.

Visitors Center

At the entrance to the **Monument Valley Navajo Tribal Park** is a **visitors center** (435/727-5874, www.navajonationparks.org,

---

1: Ancestral Puebloan village along Comb Wash **2:** Mexican Hat's namesake rock formation **3:** the San Juan River winding through Goosenecks State Park **4:** Monument Valley

6am-8pm daily Apr.-Sept., 8am-5pm daily Oct.-Mar., $20 per vehicle with up to 4 people; $6 pp for additional people in the same vehicle) with exhibits and crafts. This is a good place to get a list of Navajo tour guides to lead you on driving or hiking trips into the monument. Lots of folks along the road will also offer these services.

Tours

Take one of several guided tours leaving daily year-round from the visitors center to visit sites such as a hogan, a cliff dwelling, and petroglyphs in areas beyond the self-guided drive. The trips last 1.5-4 hours and cost $55-100 per person. Guided horseback rides from near the visitors center cost around $90 for two hours; longer day and overnight trips can be arranged too. If you'd like to hike in Monument Valley, you must hire a guide. Hiking tours of two hours to a full day or more can be arranged at the visitors center.

Monument Valley Drive

A 17-mile (27-km) **self-guided scenic drive** (6am-8pm daily Apr.-Sept., 8am-4:30pm daily Oct.-Mar.) begins at the visitors center and loops through the heart of the valley. Overlooks provide sweeping views from different vantage points. The dirt road is normally OK for cautiously driven cars. Avoid stopping or you may get stuck in the loose sand that sometimes blows across the road. Allow 90 minutes for the drive. No hiking or driving is allowed off the signed route. Water and restrooms are available only at the visitors center.

Accommodations

Don't be surprised to find that lodgings at Monument Valley are expensive; they're also extremely popular, so be sure to book well ahead.

The Navajo-owned ★ **View Hotel** (435/727-5555, www.monumentvalleyview. com, $119-339) provides the only lodging in Monument Valley Tribal Park. Views are terrific from this stylish newer hotel; reserve a room well in advance. Secluded cabins ($209-279) and camping ($23 tents, $45 RVs) are also available.

★ **Goulding's Lodge and Trading Post** (435/727-3231, www.gouldings.com, $239-317) is another great place to stay in the Monument Valley area. Harry Goulding and his wife, Mike, opened this dramatically located trading post in 1924. It's a large complex tucked under the rimrocks 2 miles (3.2 km) west of the U.S. 163 Monument Valley turnoff, just north of the Arizona-Utah border. Modern motel rooms offer incredible views of Monument Valley. Guests can use a small indoor pool; meals are available in the dining room. A gift shop sells a wide range of souvenirs, books, and Native American crafts. The nearby store has groceries and gas pumps, a restaurant is open daily for all meals, and tours and horseback rides are available. The lodge stays open year-round, and rates drop in winter and early spring. Goulding's Museum, in the old trading post building, displays prehistoric and modern artifacts, movie photos, and memorabilia of the Goulding family. The Gouldings' **campground** ($34-48 without hookups, $55-60 with hookups) is pleasant and well managed.

There are a handful of less costly hotels about 30 minutes south in Kayenta, Arizona. The adobe-style **Hampton Inn** (U.S. 160, 520/697-3170 or 800/426-7866, $199) is the nicest place in town, and it's only a little more expensive than its Kayenta neighbors.

★ NATURAL BRIDGES NATIONAL MONUMENT

Streams in White Canyon and its tributaries cut deep canyons, then formed three impressive bridges, now protected as **Natural Bridges National Monument** (435/692-1234, www.nps.gov/nabr, $20 per vehicle, $15 motorcyclists, $10 cyclists and pedestrians, $55 annual Southeast Utah Parks Pass also includes entrance to Arches and Canyonlands National Parks). When the sun sets, Natural Bridges becomes one of the darkest places in the United States. In fact, the International Dark Sky Association has named this the world's first **dark-sky park.** Come here for some serious **stargazing!**

Silt-laden floodwaters sculpted the bridges by gouging tunnels between closely spaced loops in the meandering canyons. You can distinguish a natural bridge from an arch because the bridge spans a streambed and was initially carved out of the rock by flowing water. In the monument, these bridges illustrate three different stages of development, from the massive, newly formed Kachina Bridge to the middle-aged Sipapu Bridge to the delicate and fragile span of Owachomo. All three natural bridges will continue to widen and eventually collapse under their own weight. A 9-mile (14.5-km) scenic drive has overlooks of the picturesque bridges, Ancestral Puebloan ruins, and twisting canyons. You can follow short trails down from the rim to the base of each bridge or hike through all three bridges on an 8.6-mile (13.8-km) loop.

Ruins, artifacts, and rock art indicate a long occupation by Native Americans, ranging from archaic groups to the Ancestral Puebloans. Many fine cliff dwellings built by the Ancestral Puebloans still stand. In 1883, prospector Cass Hite passed on tales of the huge stone bridges that he had discovered on a trip up White Canyon. Adventurous travelers, including those on a 1904 National Geographic expedition, visited this isolated region to marvel at the bridges. The public's desire for protection of the bridges led President Theodore Roosevelt to proclaim the area a national monument in 1908. Federal administrators then changed the original bridge names from Edwin, Augusta, and Caroline to the Hopi names used today. Although the Hopi never lived here, the Ancestral Puebloans of White Canyon very likely have descendants in the modern Hopi villages in Arizona.

Visitors Center

From the signed junction on Highway 95, it is 4.5 miles (7.2 km) on Highway 275 to the **visitors center** (435/692-1234, 9am-5pm daily April-mid-Oct., 9am-5pm mid-Oct.-Mar. Thurs.-Mon.), at an elevation of 6,505 feet (1,983 m). Exhibits and a short film introduce the people who once lived here, as well as the area's geology, wildlife, and plants. Outside, labels identify native plants of the monument.

The Bridge View Drive is always open, except after heavy snowstorms. A winter visit can be very enjoyable; ice or mud often close the steep Sipapu and Kachina Trails, but the short trail to Owachomo Bridge usually stays open. Pets aren't allowed on the trails or in the backcountry at any time.

Other than the small but popular campground at the national monument, the nearest accommodations are 40 miles (64 km) east near Blanding or a slow 40 miles (64 km) south in Mexican Hat.

Bridge View Drive

This 9-mile (14.5-km) drive begins its one-way loop just past the campground. Allow about 1.5 hours for a quick trip around. To make all the stops and do a bit of leisurely hiking takes about half a day. The cross-bedded sandstone of the bridges and canyons is part of the 265-million-year-old Cedar Mesa Formation.

Sipapu Bridge viewpoint is 2 miles (3.2 km) from the visitors center. The Hopi name refers to the gateway from which their ancestors entered this world from another world below. Sipapu Bridge has reached its mature or middle-age stage of development. The bridge, with a span of 268 feet (82 m) and a height of 220 feet (67 m), is the largest in the monument and, after Rainbow Bridge in Glen Canyon, the second largest in the world. Another view and a trail to the base of Sipapu are 0.8 mile (1.3 km) farther. The viewpoint is about halfway down on an easy trail; allow half an hour. A steeper and rougher trail branches off the viewpoint trail and winds down to the bottom of White Canyon, which is probably the best place to fully appreciate the bridge's size. The total round-trip distance is 1.2 miles (1.9 km), with an elevation change of 600 feet (183 m).

Horse Collar Ruin, built by the Ancestral Puebloans, looks as though it has been abandoned for just a few decades, not 800 years. A short trail leads to an overlook 3.1 miles (5 km) from the visitors center (bring binoculars for a good look). The name comes from the shape of the doorway openings in two storage rooms. Other groups of Ancestral Pueblo dwellings can also be seen in or near the monument; ask a ranger for directions.

The **Kachina Bridge** viewpoint and trailhead are 5.1 miles (8.2 km) from the visitors center. The massive bridge has a span of 204 feet (62 m) and a height of 210 feet (64 m). A trail, 1.5 miles (2.4 km) round-trip, leads to the canyon bottom next to the bridge; the elevation change is 650 feet (198 m). Look for pictographs near the base of the trail. Some of the figures resemble Hopi kachinas (spirits) and inspired the bridge's name. Armstrong Canyon joins White Canyon just downstream from the bridge. Floods in each canyon abraded opposite sides of the rock fin that later became Kachina Bridge.

The **Owachomo Bridge** viewpoint and trailhead are 7.1 miles (11.4 km) from the visitors center. An easy walk leads to Owachomo's base—0.5 mile (0.8 km) round-trip with an elevation change of 180 feet (55 m). Graceful Owachomo spans 180 feet (55 m) and is 106 feet (32 m) high. Erosive forces have worn the venerable bridge to a thickness of only nine feet (2.7 m). Unlike the other two bridges, Owachomo spans a smaller tributary stream instead of a major canyon. Two streams played a role in the bridge's formation. Floods coming down the larger Armstrong Canyon surged against a sandstone fin on one side while floods in a small side canyon wore away the rock on the other side. Eventually a hole formed, and waters flowing down the side canyon took the shorter route through the bridge. The word *owachomo* means "flat-rock

mound" in the Hopi language; a large rock outcrop nearby inspired the name. Toward the end of the one-way loop drive, stop at the **Bears Ears Overlook** to see the twin mesas in the distance.

Natural Bridges Loop Trail

Distance: 8.6 miles (13.8 km) round-trip
Duration: 5-6 hours
Elevation change: 500 feet (152 m)
Effort: moderate-strenuous
Trailhead: Sipapu Bridge

A canyon hike through all three bridges can be the highlight of a visit to the monument. Unmaintained trails make a loop in White and Armstrong Canyons and cross a wooded plateau. The trip is easier if you start from Sipapu and come out on the relatively gentle grades at Owachomo. A path cuts through the center of the driving loop to shorten the return trip to the car; however, you can save 2.5 miles (4 km) by arranging a car shuttle between the Sipapu and Owachomo trailheads. Another option is to go in or out on the Kachina Bridge Trail midway to cut the hiking distance to 5.4 miles (8.7 km). As you near Owachomo Bridge from below, a small sign points out the trail, which bypasses a deep pool. The canyons remain in their wild state; you'll need some hiking experience, water, proper footwear, a compass, and a map (the handout available at the visitors center is adequate).

When hiking in the canyons, keep an eye out for natural arches and Native American writing. Try not to step on midget faded rattlesnakes or other living entities (including the fragile cryptobiotic soil). And beware of flash floods, especially if you see big clouds billowing in the sky in an upstream direction. You don't need a hiking permit, although it's a good idea to talk beforehand with a ranger to find out current conditions. Overnight camping within the monument is permitted only in the campground.

1: Kachina Bridge **2:** Horse Collar Ruin
3: Owachomo Bridge

Campgrounds

The **Natural Bridges Campground** (first come, first served, year-round, $15) is in a forest of piñon pine and juniper. Obtain water from a faucet in front of the visitors center. Rangers give talks several evenings each week during the summer season. The campground is often full, but there is a rather grim designated overflow area near the intersection of Highways 95 and 261. RVs and trailers longer than 26 feet (8 m) must use this parking area. To reach the campground, drive 0.3 mile (0.5 km) past the visitors center and turn right.

Lake Powell and Glen Canyon

Lake Powell is at the center of the **Glen Canyon National Recreation Area** (520/608-6404, www.nps.gov/glca, always open, $30 per vehicle, $25 motorcycles, $15 cyclists and pedestrians, no charge for passing through Page, Arizona, on U.S. 89), a vast preserve covering 1.25 million acres in Arizona and Utah. When the Glen Canyon Dam was completed in 1964, conservationists deplored the loss of the remote and beautiful Glen Canyon of the Colorado River beneath the lake's waters. In terms of beauty and sheer drama, Glen Canyon was considered the equal of the Grand Canyon. Today, we have only words, pictures, and memories to remind us of its wonders. On the other hand, the 186-mile-long lake now provides easy access to an area most had not even known existed. Lake Powell is the second-largest artificial lake in the United States. Only Lake Mead, farther downstream, has a greater water-storage capacity. Lake Powell, however, has three times more shoreline—1,960 miles/3,154 kilometers—and when full, it holds enough water to cover the state of Pennsylvania one foot deep. Just a handful of roads approach the lake, so access is basically limited to boats—bays and coves offer nearly limitless opportunities for exploration by boaters—as well as long-distance hiking trails.

NATURAL BRIDGES TO BULLFROG MARINA BY FERRY

Eight miles (12.9 km) west of the entrance to Natural Bridges National Monument, travelers must make a decision: whether to continue on Highway 95 to cross the Colorado by bridge at Hite or to follow Highway 276 to the Halls Crossing Marina and cross the river, at this point tamed by the Glen Canyon Dam and known as Lake Powell, by car ferry.

Obviously, the ferry is the more exotic choice, and both Halls Crossing and Bullfrog Marinas offer lodging and food, a relative scarcity in this remote area. Crossing the Colorado on the ferry also makes it easy to access Bullfrog-Notom Road, which climbs for 60 miles (97 km) through dramatic landscapes on its way to Capitol Reef National Park's otherwise remote Waterpocket Fold. The road ends at Notom, just 4 miles (6.4 km) from the eastern entrance to Capitol Reef National Park on Highway 24. Drivers can also turn west on the Burr Trail and follow back roads to Boulder, near the Escalante River Canyon.

Halls Crossing and Bullfrog Ferry

At the junction of Highways 95 and 276, a large sign lists the departure times for the ferry; note that these may be different from the times listed in the widely circulated flyer or on the website. Confirm the departure times (435/893-4747, www.udot.utah.gov) before making the 42-mile (68-km) journey to Halls Crossing.

The crossing time for the 3-mile (4.8 km) trip from Halls Crossing to Bullfrog is 27 minutes. Fares are $25 for cars, which includes the driver and all passengers, $10 for bicycles and foot passengers, and $15 for motorcycles. Vehicles longer than 20 feet (6 m) pay $1.50 per foot.

Ferry service runs late April-early October, and there's a trip every other hour daily beginning with the 8am boat from Halls Landing, which then leaves Bullfrog at 9am. In summer high season, the final ferry from Halls Crossing departs at 6pm, and the final ferry from Bullfrog departs at 7pm. The ferry does not run early October-late April.

If drought or downstream demand lowers the level of Lake Powell beyond a certain point, there may not be enough water for the ferry to operate. If this is the case, there will be notices about the ferry's status at just about every park visitors center in Southern Utah.

For reservations and information regarding lodging, camping, tours, boating, and recreation at both Halls Crossing and Bullfrog Marina, contact **Lake Powell Resorts & Marinas** (888/896-3829, www.lakepowell. com).

Arriving at Halls Crossing by road, you'll first reach a small store offering three-bedroom units in trailer houses and an RV park. Continue for 0.5 mile (0.8 km) on the main road to the boat ramp and **Halls Crossing Marina** (435/684-7008). The marina has a larger store (groceries and fishing and boating supplies), a boat-rental office (fishing, waterskiing, and houseboats), a gas dock, slips, and storage. The **ranger station** is nearby, although rangers are usually out on patrol; look for their vehicle in the area if the office is closed.

On the western side of the lake, **Bullfrog Marina** is more like a small town (albeit one run by Aramark), with a **visitors center** (435/684-7423, hours vary May-early Oct.), a clinic, stores, a service station, and a handsome hotel and restaurant. The marina rents boats ranging from kayaks ($50 per day) and paddleboards ($90 per day) to eight-person powerboats ($500 per day) to houseboats ($2,079-10,649 per week), but for guided boat tours of Lake Powell, you'll have to go to the Wahweap Marina near Page, Arizona.

Defiance House Lodge (888/896-3829, www.lakepowell.com, $150-176) offers comfortable lake-view accommodations and the **Anasazi Restaurant** (8am-10am, 11am-1pm, 5pm-9pm daily Apr.-Oct., $12-28). The front desk at the lodge also handles family lodging units (well-equipped trailers, about $270 per night) and an RV park ($46). Showers, a laundry room, a convenience store, and a post office are at **Trailer Village.** Ask the visitors center staff or rangers for directions to primitive camping areas with vehicle access elsewhere along Bullfrog Bay.

Bullfrog Marina can be reached from the north via paved Highway 276. It is 40 miles (64 km) between Bullfrog and the junction with Highway 95. Ticaboo, 20 miles (32 km) north of Bullfrog, has another good lodging option. The **Ticaboo Lodge** (435/788-2110 or 800/842-2267, http://ticaboo.com, $129-151) is a hotel with a swimming pool, a restaurant, and a service-station complex that pretty much constitutes all of Ticaboo.

NATURAL BRIDGES TO LAKE POWELL VIA HIGHWAY 95

If the Lake Powell ferry schedule doesn't match your travel plans, Highway 95 will quickly get you across the Colorado River to the junction with Highway 24 at Hanksville.

Hite

In 1883 Cass Hite came to Glen Canyon in search of gold. He found some at a place later named Hite City, which set off a small gold rush. Cass and a few of his relatives operated a small store and post office, which were the only services for many miles. Travelers who wanted to cross the Colorado River here had the difficult task of swimming their animals across. Arthur Chaffin, a later resident, put through the first road and opened a ferry service in 1946. The Chaffin Ferry served uranium prospectors and adventurous motorists until the lake backed up to the spot in 1964. A steel bridge now spans the Colorado River upstream from Hite Marina. Cass Hite's store and the ferry site are underwater about 5 miles (8 km) down the lake from Hite Marina.

Beyond Hite, on the tiny neck of land between the Colorado River bridge and the Dirty Devil bridge, an unmarked dirt road turns north. Called Hite Road, or Orange Cliffs Road, this long and rugged road eventually links up with backcountry routes—including the Flint Trail—in the Maze District of Canyonlands National Park.

The uppermost marina on Lake Powell, Hite is 141 lake miles (227 km) from Glen Canyon Dam. It is hit hard when water levels drop in Lake Powell, which has been most of the time in recent years. When water is available, boats can continue up the lake to the mouth of Dark Canyon in Cataract Canyon at low water or into Canyonlands National Park at high water. During times of low water, the boat ramp is often high above the lake and the place is pretty desolate. Facilities include a small **store** with gas and a primitive **campground** (free) with no drinking water. Primitive camping is also available nearby, off Highway 95 at Dirty Devil, Farley Canyon, White Canyon, Blue Notch, and other locations. A **ranger station** (435/684-2457) is occasionally open; look for the ranger's vehicle at other times.

PAGE, ARIZONA

Although the town of Page is hot, busy, and not particularly appealing, it is the largest community anywhere near Lake Powell, and it offers travelers a number of places to stay and eat and access to boat tours. The town overlooks Lake Powell and Glen Canyon Dam.

The largest resort in the Glen Canyon National Recreation Area, **Wahweap Resort and Marina** (100 Lakeshore Dr., 928/645-2433, www.lakepowell.com), is just 6 miles (9.7 km) northwest of Page off U.S. 89. Wahweap is a major center for all manner of water sports, including houseboats (from $3,939 for five days in high summer season; they sleep up to 10), kayaks (from $50 per day), and paddleboards ($90 per day). Wahweap also offers an extensive range of boat tours and boat-assisted hiking, among other recreational activities. Wahweap's Lake Powell Resort, a hotel and restaurant complex, offers some of the most comfortable rooms in the area.

Tours

From Wahweap, board a tour boat to really see the special areas of Glen Canyon still visible from Lake Powell. A 1.5-hour tour (10:30am, 2:30pm, and 4:15pm daily Apr.-Oct., $48 adults, $33 children) into the mouth of 10-mile-long **Antelope Canyon** leaves from the Wahweap Marina (928/645-2433). During summer, a 6:15pm tour is added; in the winter, a 10:30am tour runs if there is sufficient demand. Another popular boat tour from Wahweap motors to **Rainbow Bridge National Monument** (Wahweap Marina, 928/645-2433, 7:30am daily April-Oct., with an additional tour at 12:30pm June-Sept. 15, $126 adults, $79 children). This tour, which takes around six hours and includes a 1.25-mile (2 km) round trip hike, cruises 50 miles (81 km) of shoreline to reach Rainbow Bridge, one of the largest known natural bridges in the world, at 290 feet (88 m) high and spanning 275 feet (84 m). If the price seems too stiff, or the boat ride too tame, a couple of rugged 17-mile-long trails leave from Page and travel across Navajo lands to the bridge. See the monument's website (www.nps.gov/rabr) for details on these trails.

Quite a different Antelope Canyon is the focus of a land-based tour to a famed slot canyon east of Page, beloved by multitudes of photographers seeking to capture the canyon's supple curves and pink-gold hues. Travel to Upper Antelope Canyon by truck with **Antelope Canyon Tours** (22 S. Lake Powell Blvd., 928/645-9102, www.antelopecanyon.com, $54-67). Tours last about 1.5 hours and run several times a day year-round.

Food

If you've been traveling through remote rural Utah for a while, dipping into Page, Arizona, can seem like a gastronomic mecca. The

Ranch House Grill (819 N. Navajo Dr., 928/645-1420, 6am-3pm daily, $7-15) serves breakfast all day plus sandwiches, burgers, steaks, and chops during the day. After a few days of abstemious travel in Southern Utah, **Blue Wine Bar** (644 N. Navajo Dr., 928/608-0707, 6pm-11pm Tues.-Sat., $5-12) is a real treat. The tapas and small plates are excellent, as is the wine selection. In the same Dam Plaza complex, the stylish **Blue Buddha** (644 N. Navajo Dr., 928/608-0707, 5pm-9pm Tues.-Sat., $10-20) serves cocktails and Japanese food, including sushi. For steaks and Italian food, **Bonkers Restaurant** (810 N. Navajo Dr., 928/645-2706, 4pm-9pm Tues.-Sat., $19-44) is a small but classy operation with good salads, pasta and old-time favorites like chicken Marsala. **Fiesta Mexicana** (125 S. Lake Powell Blvd., 928/645-4082, 11am-9pm Sun.-Thurs., 11am-10:30pm Fri.-Sat., $9-15) is a busy but friendly little Mexican place (and here in Arizona, it's easy to get a margarita).

Accommodations

Nearly all Page motels are on or near Lake Powell Boulevard (U.S. 89L), a 3.25-mile (5.2-km) loop that branches off the main highway. Page is a busy place in summer, however, and a call ahead is a good idea if you don't want to chase around town looking for vacancies. Expect to pay top dollar for views of the lake. The summer rates listed here drop in winter (Nov.-Mar.).

In a way, the most appealing lodgings are in the small apartments-turned-motels on and around 8th Avenue, a quiet residential area two blocks off Lake Powell Boulevard. These apartments date back to 1958-1959, when they housed supervisors for the dam construction project. One such place is the **Lake Powell Motel** (750 S. Navajo Dr., 480/452-9895, https://lakepowellmotel.net, $99-159), a nicely remodeled property with standard motel rooms and stylish one- and two-bedroom apartments with kitchenettes. Another vintage motel that's been freshly updated, the **Red Rock Motel** (114 8th Ave., 928/645-0062, https://redrockmotel.com, $69-139) offers everything from small basic rooms to two-bedroom apartments with kitchens and living rooms. All rooms have private patios, some with BBQs.

If you prefer the standard comforts of chain motels, a quick search of hotel booking websites will reveal that Page has all the usual suspects, plus some upscale resorts if you're looking for luxury. **Courtyard Page** (600 Clubhouse Dr., 928/645-5000, www.marriott.com, $209-239) is a good option in a great setting, with views, a restaurant, pool, spa, an exercise room, and an adjacent 18-hole golf course.

If you want to play in the water, there's no better spot to spend the night than the **Lake Powell Resort** at Wahweap Marina (6 mi/9.7 km north of Page off U.S. 89 at 100 Lakeshore Dr., 928/645-2433, www.lakepowell.com, $229-309), with access to lake recreation, tours and a lively drinking and dining scene right out your front door.

West of Canyonlands

It's a lonely road that leads north from the Glen Canyon National Recreation Area and Lake Powell to I-70, just west of the town of Green River. The crossroads town of Hanksville is a good place to gas up (don't expect any bargains on fuel) and grab a burger, and Goblin Valley State Park and Little Wild Horse Canyon are worthwhile detours. Highway 24 north of Hanksville also provides access to Canyonlands National Park's Maze District and the incredible rock art in the park's Horseshoe Canyon Unit.

HANKSVILLE

Even by Utah standards, tiny Hanksville (pop. just over 200) is pretty remote. Ebenezer Hanks and other Mormon settlers founded this out-of-the-way community in 1882 along the Fremont River, then known as the Dirty Devil River. The isolation attracted polygamists like Hanks and other fugitives from the law. Butch Cassidy and his gang found refuge in the rugged canyon country of "Robbers' Roost," east of town. Several houses and the old stone church on Center Street, one block south of the highway, survive from the 19th century.

Travelers exploring this scenic region find Hanksville a handy if lackluster stopover; Capitol Reef National Park is to the west, Lake Powell and the Henry Mountains are to the south, the remote Maze District of Canyonlands National Park is to the east, and Goblin Valley State Park is to the north. Because Hanksville is a true crossroads, the few lodgings here are often booked up well in advance, so plan ahead.

Wolverton Mill

E. T. Wolverton built this ingenious mill during the 1920s at his gold-mining claims in the Henry Mountains. A 20-foot waterwheel, still perfectly balanced, powered ore-crushing machinery and a sawmill. Owners of claims at the mill's original site didn't like a steady stream of tourists coming through to see the mill, so it was moved to the BLM office at Hanksville. Drive south 0.5 mile (0.8 km) on 100 West to see the mill and some of its original interior mechanism.

Food

Hanksville's restaurants cluster at the south end of town; don't expect anything fancy. **Stan's Burger Shack** (150 S. Hwy. 95, 435/542-3330, 10am-10pm Mon.-Sat., noon-10pm Sun., $5-9), at the Chevron station, is full of locals and a step up from the chains. The classiest spot for dinner is **Duke's Slickrock Grill** (275 Hwy. 24, 435/542-3235, 7am-10pm daily, $9-28), with steaks, barbecue, and burgers.

Accommodations

Hanksville is a busy crossroads with just two lodging options, so rooms go fast. Book in advance if your plans call for spending a night here, even though accommodations are pretty basic. At **Whispering Sands Motel** (90 S. Hwy. 95, 435/542-3238, $99-129) you'll have a choice of rooms in the motel or in "cabins" that look a lot like garden sheds. Never mind—by the time you arrive, you'll be glad to see them. Though most people would call this a motel, **OYO Hotel** (280 E. 100 N., 435/542-3471, www.oyorooms.com/us, $89-122) is the other option, also basic but serviceable.

In the center of town, behind Duke's Slickrock Grill, is **Duke's Slickrock Campground & RV Park** (275 Hwy. 24, 435/542-3235 or 800/894-3242, mid-Mar.-Oct., $15-20 tents, $35 RVs) has showers and a laundry, and also a number of new cabins that are easily the nicest places to stay in Hanksville. Each of the cabins has two queen beds, private bath, and a porch with a table and chairs.

It's also good to know about the **Rodeway Inn Capitol Reef** (25 E. Hwy. 24, 435/456-9900, www.choicehotels.com, $94-99), 15 miles (24 km) west of Hanksville in Caineville, another pleasant but standard lodging, but note that the nearest actual restaurant is in Hanksville. Fortunately, there's a small breakfast served; even better, the Mesa Farm Market is nearby on the road to Capitol Reef National Park with excellent homemade bread and cheese.

Information and Services

The **Bureau of Land Management** (435/542-3461, www.blm.gov) has a field station 0.5 mile (0.8 km) south of Highway 24 on 100 West, with information on road conditions, hiking, camping, and the buffalo herd in the Henry Mountains.

★ GOBLIN VALLEY STATE PARK

Thousands of rock formations, many with goblin-like "faces," inhabit **Goblin Valley State Park** (435/275-4584, reservations 800/322-3770, www.reserveamerica.com, year-round, $20 per vehicle day use, $30 camping, $100 yurts). All of these so-called goblins have weathered out of the Entrada Formation, here a soft red sandstone and even softer siltstone. The **Carmel Canyon Trail** (1.5-mi/2.4-km loop) begins at the northeast side of the parking lot at road's end, then drops down to the desert floor and a strange landscape of goblins, spires, and balanced rocks. Just wander around at your whim; this is a great place for the imagination. A 1.3-mile (2.1-km) trail connects the campground and the goblin-studded Carmel Canyon Trail.

Curtis Bench Trail begins on the road between the parking lot and the campground and goes south to a viewpoint of the Henry Mountains; cairns mark the 1.5-mile/2.4-kilometer (one-way) route.

The turnoff from Highway 24 is at milepost 137, which is 21 miles (34 km) north of Hanksville and 24 miles (39 km) south of I-70; follow signs west 5 miles (8 km) on a paved road, then south 7 miles (11.3 km) on a gravel road.

Although there are off-road vehicle and motorcycle riding areas just west of the park, bicycling is limited to the park's roads. However, 12 miles (19.3 km) north, the **Temple Mountain Bike Trail** traverses old mining roads, ridges, and wash bottoms. Popular hikes near the state park include the Little Wild Horse and Bell Canyons Loop, Chute and Crack Canyons Loop, and Wild Horse Canyon. The park is also a good base for exploring the **San Rafael Swell** area to the northwest.

Camping at Goblin Valley is a real treat; the late-evening and early-morning sun makes the sandstone spires glow. If you're not much of a camper, consider booking one of the park's two yurts ($100). They're tucked back among the rock formations, and each is equipped with bunk beds and a futon, a swamp cooler, and propane stove. There are only 26 camping sites, so it's best to reserve well in advance.

LITTLE WILD HORSE CANYON

About 6 miles (9.7 km) west of Goblin Valley, Little Wild Horse is a good slot canyon hike for people without technical experience, though obstacles do require a little scrambling. Hike in as far as you like and turn around to exit or make a loop with Bell Canyon. Hiking is best in spring and fall; avoid the area when there's a chance of rain, which is often the case in August. Reach the trailhead by traveling west on Goblin Valley Road; turn right on Wild Horse Road before you reach the Goblin Valley State Park entrance.

GREEN RIVER

Green River (population about 950) is, except for a handful of motels and a lively tavern, pretty run-down, but it's the only real settlement on the stretch of I-70 between Salina and the Colorado border. Travelers can stop for a night or a meal, set off on a trip down the Green River, or use the town as a base for exploring the scenic San Rafael Swell country nearby.

Green River is known for its melons. In summer, stop at roadside stands and partake of wondrous cantaloupes and watermelons. The blazing summer heat and ample irrigation water make such delicacies possible. **Melon Days** (3rd weekend in Sept.) celebrate the harvest with a parade, a city fair, music, a canoe race, games, and lots of melons.

John Wesley Powell River History Museum

Stop by the fine **John Wesley Powell River History Museum** (1765 E. Main St., 435/564-3427, http://johnwesleypowell.com, 9am-5pm Mon.-Sat., $6 adults, $2 ages 3-12) to learn about Powell's daring expeditions down the Green and Colorado Rivers in 1869 and 1871-1872. An excellent multimedia presentation about both rivers uses narratives from Powell's trips. Historic riverboats on display include a replica of Powell's *Emma Dean*.

Labyrinth and Stillwater Canyons

The Green River's Labyrinth and Stillwater Canyons are downstream, between the town of Green River and the river's confluence with the Colorado River in Canyonlands National Park. Primarily a canoeing or kayaking river, the Green River at this point is calm and wide as it passes into increasingly deep, rust-colored canyons. This isn't a wilderness river; regular powerboats can also follow the river below town to the confluence with the Colorado River and head up the Colorado to Moab, two or three days and 186 river miles (300 km) away.

The most common trip on this portion of the Green River begins just south of town and runs south through the Labyrinth Canyon, ending at Mineral Bottom (68 river mi/109 km). **Moab Rafting and Canoe Company** (420 Kane Creek Blvd., Moab, 435/259-7722, http://moab-rafting.com, four-day guided trip from $999 pp, depending on group size) offers this trip in canoes and offers unguided raft rentals too. **Tex's Riverways** (691 N. 500 West, Moab, 435/259-5101, www.texsriverways.com) offers canoe and touring kayak rentals and all the other equipment you need to outfit a self-guided multiday trip, plus shuttle services to and from the river. Permits are required to paddle in Labyrinth Canyon; they're free and available to download from the BLM website (www.blm.gov) or can be picked up in town at the John Wesley Powell Museum (1765 E. Main St.) or Green River State Park (150 S. Green River Blvd.).

Crystal Geyser

With some luck, you'll catch the spectacle of this cold-water geyser on the bank of the Green River. The carbon-dioxide-powered gusher occasionally shoots as high as 60 feet (18 m), but it's pretty unpredictable, so you may just see burbles. This isn't a natural geothermal geyser; it was created by an oil drill in the 1930s, and water shoots out from a rusty pipe.

Even if the geyser is only putting out a few little spurts, its setting is beautiful. Colorful travertine terraces around the opening and down to the river make this a pretty spot, even if the geyser is quiet.

Crystal Geyser is 10 miles (16 km) south of Green River by road; boaters should look for the geyser deposits on the left, about 4.5 river miles (7.2 km) downstream from Green River. From downtown, drive east 1 mile (1.6 km) on Main Street, turn left, and go 3 miles (4.8 km) on signed Frontage Road (near milepost 4), then turn right and go 6 miles (9.7 km) on a narrow paved road just after going under a railroad overpass. The road goes under I-70; keep right at a fork near some power lines. Some washes must be crossed, so the drive isn't recommended after rains. When the weather is fair, cars shouldn't have a problem.

1: Little Wild Horse Canyon **2:** Goblin Valley State Park **3:** eroded mudstone spires near Hanksville

Food

Other than motel restaurants and fast food, the one really notable place to eat in Green River is ★ **Ray's Tavern** (25 S. Broadway, 435/564-3511, 11am-9pm daily, $8-27). Ray's doesn't look like much from the outside, but inside you'll find a friendly welcome, tables made from tree trunks, and some of the best steaks, chops, and burgers in this part of the state. Don't expect haute cuisine, but the food is good, and the atmosphere is truly Western; beer drinkers will be glad for the selection of regional microbrews after a long day navigating the river or driving desert roads.

Grab a taco from **La Pasadita** (215 E. Main St., 435/564-8159, 8am-10pm Sun.-Thurs., 9am-10pm Fri.-Sat., $6-10), a taco truck in the parking lot of an old gas station. The food is tasty, and the scene is convivial at the picnic tables set up for diners.

Directly adjacent to the River Terrace hotel is a decent American-style restaurant, **The Tamarisk** (1710 E. Main St., 435/564-8109, 7am-10pm daily, $12-19), with riverfront views.

Accommodations

Green River has a few rather shabby older motels as well as newer chain motels to choose from. Unless noted, each of the following has a swimming pool—a major consideration in this often-sweltering desert valley.

If you're on a budget, try the basic **Robber's Roost Motel** (325 W. Main St., 435/564-3452, www.rrmotel.com, $44-58), which is right in the center of town; it does not

have a pool. Green River's newer motels are on the east end of town. The **Super 8** (1248 E. Main St., 435/564-8888 or 800/888-8888, $63-75), out by I-70 exit 162, is a good value, with spacious, comfortable guest rooms.

The nicest place to stay in town is the ★ **River Terrace** (1740 E. Main St., 435/564-3401 or 877/564-3401, www.river-terrace.com, $140-150), with somewhat older but large guest rooms, some of which overlook the Green River and some with balconies. Breakfast is included, with a restaurant adjacent to the hotel. The very pleasant outdoor pool area is flanked by patios, gardens, and shaded tables.

CAMPGROUNDS

Several campgrounds, all with showers, offer sites for tents and RVs year-round. **Green River State Park** (150 S. Green River Blvd., 435/564-3633 or 800/322-3770, www.reserveamerica.com, year-round, $7 day use, $35 with hookups, $75 cabins) has a great setting near the river; it's shaded by large cottonwoods and has a boat ramp and a nine-hole golf course. **Shady Acres RV Park** (350 E. Main St., 435/564-8290 or 800/537-8674, www.shadyacresrv.com, year-round, $25-30 tents, $43-47 with hookups, $55 cabins) is not all that shady and may be a bit too close to the noisy road for tent campers; it has a store, showers, and a laundry. **Green River KOA** (235 S. 1780 E., 435/564-3651, $29 tents, $50-68 with hookups, $71-81 cabins) has campsites and cabins (bring sleeping bags) across from the John Wesley Powell Museum and next to the Tamarisk restaurant.

Background

The Landscape

Southeastern Utah's national parks and its preserves of public land are all part of the **Colorado Plateau,** a high, broad physiographic province that includes Southern Utah, northern Arizona, southwestern Colorado, and northwestern New Mexico. This roughly circular plateau, nearly the size of Montana, also contains the Grand Canyon, the Navajo Nation, and the Hopi Reservation.

Created by a slow but tremendous uplift and carved by magnificent rivers, the plateau is mostly between 3,000 and 6,000 feet elevation (915-1,830 m), with some peaks reaching nearly 13,000 feet (3,962 m).

Although much of the terrain is gently rolling, the Green and Colorado Rivers have sculpted remarkable canyons, buttes, mesas, arches, and badlands.

Canyonlands is noted for its synclines, anticlines, and folds. Nongeologists can picture the rock layers as blankets on a bed, and then imagine how they look before the bed is made in the morning. This warping, which goes on deep beneath the earth's surface, has affected the overlying rocks, permitting the development of deeply incised canyons.

Isolated uplifts and foldings have formed such features as the rock arches in Arches National Park, while the rounded Abajo and La Sal Mountains are examples of intrusive rock—an igneous layer that was formed below the earth's surface and later exposed by erosion.

GEOLOGY

When you visit any one of Utah's national parks, the first things you're likely to notice are rocks. Vegetation is sparse and the soil is thin, so there's not much to hide the geology here. Particularly stunning views are found where rivers have carved deep canyons through the rock layers.

The clean, orderly stairsteps from the young rocks in canyons show off the clearly defined layers of rock. Weird crenellations, hoodoos, and arches occur as a result of the way erosion acted on the various rocks that make up this big Colorado Plateau layer cake.

Sedimentation

Water made this desert what it is today. Back before the continents broke apart and began drifting to their present-day locations, Utah was near the equator, just east of a warm ocean. Ancient seas washed over the land, depositing sand, silt, and mud. Layer upon layer, the soils piled up and were—over time—compressed into sandstones, limestones, and shales.

The ancestral Rocky Mountains rose to the east of the ocean, and, just to their west, a trough-like basin formed and was intermittently flushed with sea water. Evaporation caused salts and other minerals to collect on the basin floor; when the climate became wetter, more water rushed in.

As the ancestral Rockies eroded, their bulk washed down into the basin. The sea level rose, washing in more mud and sand. When the seas receded, dry winds blew sand across the region, creating enormous dunes.

Over time, the North American continent drifted north, away from the equator, but this region remained near the sea and was regularly washed by tides, leaving more sand and silt. Just inland, freshwater lakes filled, then dried, and the lakebeds consolidated into shales. During wet periods, streams coursed across the area, carrying and then dropping their loads of mud, silt, and sand.

As the ancestral Rockies wore down to mere hills, other mountains rose, then eroded, contributing their sediments. A turn toward dry weather meant more dry winds, kicking up the sand and building it into massive dunes. Then, about 15 million years ago, the sea-level plateau began to lift, slowly, steadily, and, by geologic standards, incredibly gently. Some areas were hoisted as high as 10,000 feet above sea level.

Erosion

As the Colorado Plateau rose, its big rivers carved deep gorges through the uplifting rocks. Today, the Green, Colorado, and San Juan Rivers are responsible for much of the dramatic scenery here.

More subtle forms of erosion have also contributed to the plateau's present-day form. Water percolating down through the rock layers is one of the main erosive forces, washing away loose material and dissolving ancient salts, often leaving odd formations, such as thin fins of resistant rock.

The Colorado Plateau

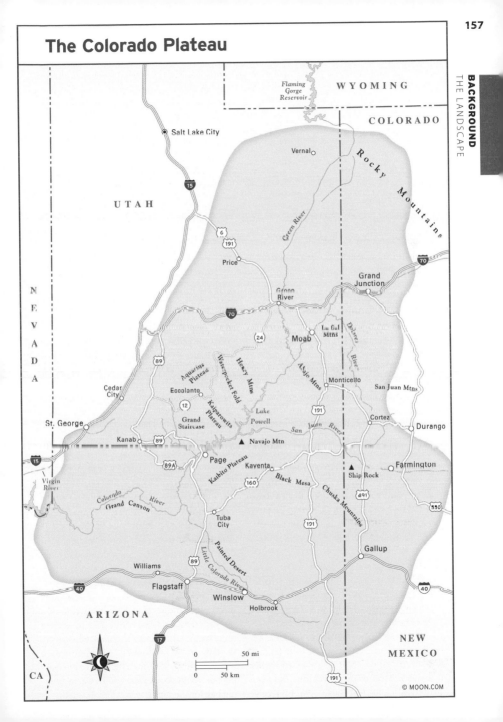

WYOMING

COLORADO

Flaming Gorge Reservoir

Salt Lake City

Vernal

Rocky Mountains

UTAH

15

Green River

6
191

Price

70

Grand Junction

Green River

NEVADA

24

Moab

La Sal Mtns

Dolores River

89

Aquarius Plateau

Waterpocket Fold

Henry Mtns

Abajo Mtns

Monticello

San Juan Mtns

Cedar City

Escalanto

12

Kaiparowits Plateau

Lake Powell

191

Cortez

Durango

St. George

Grand Staircase

San Juan River

Kanab

89

Navajo Mtn

89A

Page

Kaibito Plateau

Kayenta

Black Mesa

Ship Rock

Farmington

15

Virgin River

Colorado River

Grand Canyon

160

Chuska Mountains

491

550

Tuba City

Painted Desert

Gallup

Williams

89

Little Colorado River

191

Flagstaff

40

Winslow

Holbrook

40

ARIZONA

17

NEW MEXICO

CA

0   50 mi

0   50 km

191

© MOON.COM

Nature's Palette

In Utah, you'll get used to seeing a lot of colorful rock formations. The color gives you clues to the composition and geologic history of the rock. In general:

- **Red rocks** are stained by rusty iron-rich sediments washed down from mountains, and they are a clue that erosion has occurred.

- **Gray or brown rocks** were deposited by ancient seas.

- **White rocks** are colored by their "glue," the limey remains of dissolved seashells that leach down and harden sandstones.

- **Black rocks** are volcanic in origin, though not all volcanic, or igneous, rocks are black. Igneous rocks are present in the La Sal, Abajo, and Henry Mountains near Canyonlands. These mountains are "laccoliths," formed by molten magma that pushed through the sedimentary layers, leaking deeper into some layers than others and eventually forming broad dome-shaped protuberances, which were eroded into soft peaks, then carved by glaciers into the sharp peaks we see today.

The many layers of sedimentary rocks forming the Colorado Plateau are all composed of different minerals and have varying densities, so it's not surprising that erosion affects each layer a bit differently. For instance, sandstones and limestones erode more readily than the harder mudstones or shales.

Erosion isn't limited to the force of water against rock. Rocks may be worn down or eaten away by a variety of forces, including wind, freezing and thawing, exfoliation (when sheets of rock peel off), oxidation, hydration and carbonation (chemical weathering), plant roots or animal burrows, and dissolving of soft rocks. The ever-deepening channel of the Colorado River through Canyonlands, and the slow thinning of pedestals supporting Arches' balanced rocks are all clues that erosion continues unabated.

CLIMATE

The main thing for Utah travelers to remember is that they're in the desert.

The high-desert country of the Colorado Plateau lies mostly between 3,000 and 6,000 feet (915-1,830 m) in elevation. Annual precipitation ranges from an extremely dry 3 inches in some areas to about 10 inches in others. Mountainous regions between 10,000 and 13,000 feet (3,048-3,962 m) receive abundant rainfall in summer and heavy snows in winter.

Sunny skies prevail through all four seasons. Spring comes early to the canyon country, with weather that's often windy and rapidly changing. Summer can make its presence known in April, although the real desert heat doesn't set in until late May-early June. Temperatures then soar into the 90s and 100s at midday, although the dry air makes the heat more bearable. Early morning is the choice time for travel in summer. A canyon seep surrounded by hanging gardens or a mountain meadow filled with wildflowers provides a refreshing contrast to the parched desert; other ways to beat the heat include hiking in the mountains and river rafting.

Summer thunderstorm season begins anywhere mid-June-August; huge billowing thunderstorm clouds bring refreshing rains and coolness. During this season, canyon hikers should be alert for flash flooding.

Fall begins after the rains cease, usually in October, and lasts into November or even December; days are bright and sunny with ideal temperatures, but nights become cold. In all of the parks, evenings will be cool even in midsummer. Although the day may be baking hot, you'll need a jacket and a warm sleeping bag for the night.

Mormon Tea

Although it's not the showiest wildflower in the desert, Mormon tea (*Ephedra viridis*) is widespread across Southern Utah, and it's particularly common in Arches National park. This broom-like plant is remarkably well adapted to the desert, and many desert-dwelling humans have adapted themselves to enjoy drinking it as a tea.

The plant's branches contain chlorophyll and are able to conduct photosynthesis. The leaves are like tiny scales or bracts; their small size reduces the amount of moisture the plant loses to transpiration. Male and female flowers grow on separate plants.

Native Americans used this plant medicinally as a tea for stomach and bowel disorders as well as for colds, fever, and headaches. Some used it to control bleeding and as a poultice for burns.

Mormon tea is related to ma huang, a Chinese herb that is traditionally used to treat hay fever. All parts of the plant contain a small amount of ephedrine, a stimulant that in large concentrations can be quite harmful. Pioneers in Southern Utah were mostly Mormons, who are forbidden to drink coffee or similar stimulants. When they learned that drinking the boiled stems of *Ephedra viridis* gave them a mild lift, they approached Brigham Young, the head of the Latter-Day Saints. Young gave the tea his stamp of approval, and the plant's common name grew out of its widespread use by Mormons. In Utah it's also sometimes called Brigham tea.

The tea itself is yellowish and, as one local puts it, tastes something like what she imagines boiled socks would taste like. To increase the tea's palatability, it's often mixed with mint, lemon, and sugar or honey. Pioneers liked to add strawberry jam to their Mormon tea.

If you are tempted to try this tea for yourself, make certain not to harvest plants in a national park. Women who are pregnant or nursing and people with high blood pressure, heart disease, diabetes, glaucoma, or other health problems should definitely avoid even the small amounts of ephedrine present in Mormon tea.

Winter lasts only about two months at the lower elevations. Light snows on the canyon walls add new beauty to the rock layers. Nighttime temperatures commonly dip into the teens, which is too cold for most campers. Otherwise, winter can be a fine time for travel. Heavy snows rarely occur below 8,000 feet (2,438 m).

Flash Floods

Rainwater runs quickly off the rocky desert surfaces and into gullies and canyons. A summer thunderstorm or a rapid late-winter snowmelt can send torrents of mud and boulders rumbling down dry washes and canyons. Backcountry drivers, horseback riders, and hikers need to avoid hazardous locations when storms threaten or unseasonably warm winds blow on the winter snowpack.

Flash floods can sweep away anything in their path, including boulders, cars, and campsites. Do not camp or park in potential flash flood areas. If you come to a section of flooded roadway—a common occurrence on desert roads after storms—wait until the water goes down before crossing (it shouldn't take long). Summer lightning causes forest and brush fires, posing a danger to hikers who are foolish enough to climb mountains when storms threaten.

The bare rock and loose soils so common in the canyon country do little to hold back the flow of rain or meltwater. In fact, slickrock is effective at shedding water as fast as it comes in contact. Logs and other debris wedged high on canyon walls give proof enough of past floods.

PLANTS

Within the physiographic province of the Colorado Plateau, several different life zones are represented.

In the low desert, shrubs eke out a meager existence. Climbing higher, you'll pass through grassy steppe, sage, and piñon-juniper woodlands to ponderosa pine. Of all these zones, the piñon-juniper is most common.

But it's not a lockstep progression of plant A at elevation X and plant B at elevation Z. Soils are an important consideration, with sandstones being more hospitable than shales. Plants will grow wherever the conditions will support them. Utah's parks have many micro-environments that can lead to surprising plant discoveries. Look for different plants in these different habitats: slickrock (where cracks can gather enough soil to host a few plants), riparian (moist areas with the greatest diversity of life), and terraces and open space (the area between riverbank and slickrock, where shrubs dominate).

How Plants Survive in the Desert

Most of the plants you'll see are well adapted to desert life. Many are succulents, which have their own water storage systems in their fleshy stems or leaves. Cacti are the most obvious succulents; they swell with stored moisture during the spring, then slowly shrink and wrinkle as the stored moisture is used.

Other plants have different strategies for making the most of scarce water. Some, such as yucca, have deep roots, taking advantage of what moisture exists in the soil. The leaves of desert plants are often spiny, exposing less surface area to the sun. Leaves may also have very small pores, slowing transpiration, or stems coated with a resinous substance, which also slows water loss. Hairy or light-colored leaves help reflect sunlight.

Most desert wildflowers are annuals. They bloom in the spring when water is available, form seeds that can survive the dry, hot summer, and then die. A particularly wet spring means a bumper crop of wildflowers.

Even though mosses aren't usually thought of as desert plants, they are found growing in seeps along canyon walls and in cryptobiotic soils. When water is unavailable, mosses dry up; when the water returns, the moss quickly plumps up again.

Junipers have a fairly drastic way of dealing with water shortage: self-pruning. During a prolonged dry spell, a juniper tree can shut off the flow of water to one or more of its branches, sacrificing these branches to keep the tree alive.

Hanging Gardens

Look for clumps of ferns and mosses lit with maidenhair ferns, shooting stars, monkey flowers, columbine, orchids, and bluebells. These unexpectedly lush pockets are called "hanging gardens," gemlike islands of plant life nestled into desert cliffs.

Hanging gardens take advantage of a unique microclimate created by the meeting of two rock layers: Navajo sandstone and Kayenta shale. Water percolates down through porous sandstone and, when it hits the denser shale layer, travels laterally along the top of the harder rock and emerges at cliff's edge. These little springs support lush plant life.

Tamarisk

One of the Colorado Plateau's most common trees, the nonnative tamarisk is also one of the peskiest. Imported from the Mediterranean and widely planted along the Colorado River to control erosion, the tamarisk has spread wildly, and its dense stands have crowded out native trees such as cottonwoods. Tamarisks are notoriously thirsty trees, sucking up vast amounts of water, but they give back little in the way of food or habitat for local wildlife. Their thick growth also increases the risk of fire. State and federal agencies are taking steps to control tamarisk.

Cryptobiotic Soil

Over much of the Colorado Plateau, the soil is alive. What looks like a grayish-brown crust is actually a dense network of filament-forming blue-green algae intertwined with soil particles, lichens, moss, green algae, and microfungi. This slightly sticky, crusty mass holds the soil together, slowing erosion. Its spongelike consistency allows it to soak up water and hold it. Plants growing in cryptobiotic soil have a great advantage over plants rooted in dry sandy soil.

Cryptobiotic soils take a long time to develop and are extremely fragile. Make every effort to avoid stepping on them—stick to trails, slickrock, or rocks instead.

ANIMALS

Although they're not thought of as great "wildlife parks" like Yellowstone or Denali, Utah's national parks are home to plenty of animals. However, desert animals are often nocturnal and go unseen by park visitors.

Rodents

Rodents include squirrels, packrats, kangaroo rats, chipmunks, and porcupines, most of which spend their days in burrows.

One of the few desert rodents out foraging during the day is the white-tailed antelope squirrel, which looks much like a chipmunk. Its white tail reflects the sunlight, and when it needs to cool down a bit, an antelope squirrel smears its face with saliva (yes, that probably would work for you too, but that's why you have sweat glands). The antelope squirrel lives at lower elevations; higher up you'll see golden-mantled ground squirrels.

Look for rabbits—desert cottontails and jackrabbits—at dawn and dusk. If you're rafting the Green or Colorado Rivers, keep an eye out for beavers.

Kangaroo rats are particularly well adapted to desert life. They spend their days in cool burrows, eat only plants, and never drink water. Instead, a kangaroo rat metabolizes dry food in a way that produces water.

Prairie dogs live together in social groups called colonies or towns, which are laced with burrows, featuring a network of entrances for quickly popping in and out of the ground. Prairie dogs are preyed on by badgers, coyotes, hawks, and snakes, so a colony will post lookouts that are constantly searching for danger. When threatened, the lookouts "bark" to warn the colony. Utah prairie dogs hibernate during the winter and emerge from their burrows to mate furiously in early April.

Bats

As night falls in canyon country, bats emerge from the nooks and crannies that protect them from the day's heat and begin to feed on mosquitoes and other insects. The tiny gray western pipistrelle is common. It flies early in the evening, feeding near streams, and can be spotted by its somewhat erratic flight. The pallid bat spends a lot of its time creeping across the ground in search of food, feeding late at night.

Large Mammals

Mule deer are common. Other large mammals include predators such as mountain lions and coyotes. If you're lucky, you'll get a glimpse of a bobcat or a fox.

If you're hiking the trails early in the morning and see something that looks like a small dog in a tree, it's probably a gray fox. These small (5-10 pounds) foxes live in forested areas and have the catlike ability to climb trees. Kit foxes, which are even tinier than gray foxes, with prominent ears and a big bushy tail, are common. Red foxes also live throughout the plateau.

Look for desert bighorn sheep trotting across steep, rocky ledges. In Arches, they're frequently sighted along U.S. 191 south of the visitors center. They also roam the talus slopes and side canyons near the Colorado River.

Reptiles

Reptiles are well suited to desert life. As cold-blooded, or ectothermic, animals, their body temperature depends on the environment, rather than on internal metabolism, and it's easy for them to keep warm in the desert heat. When it's cold, reptiles hibernate or drastically slow their metabolism.

The western whiptail lizard is common in Arches. You'll recognize it because its tail is twice as long as its body. Also notable is the western collared lizard, with a bright green body set off by a black collar.

Less flashy but particularly fascinating are the several species of parthenogenetic lizards. All of these lizards are female, and they reproduce by laying eggs that are clones of themselves. Best known is the plateau striped whiptail, but 6 of the 12 species of whiptail present in the area are all-female.

The northern plateau lizard is common at altitudes of about 3,000-6,000 feet (915-1,830 m). It's not choosy about its habitat—juniper-piñon woodlands, prairies, riparian woodlands, and rocky hillsides are all perfectly acceptable. This is the lizard you'll most often see scurrying across your campsite.

Rattlesnakes are present across the area, but given a chance, they'll get out of your way rather than strike. (Still, they're another good reason to wear sturdy boots.) The midget faded rattlesnake, a small subspecies of the western rattlesnake, lives in burrows and rock crevices and is mostly active at night. Although this snake has especially toxic venom, full venom injections occur in only one-third of all bites.

Amphibians

Although they're not usually thought of as desert animals, a variety of frogs and toads live on the Colorado Plateau. Tadpoles live in wet springtime potholes as well as in streams and seeps. If you're camping in a canyon, you may be lucky enough to be serenaded by a toad chorus.

Bullfrogs are not native to the western United States, but since they were introduced in the early 1900s, they have flourished at the expense of native frogs and toads, whose eggs and tadpoles they eat.

The big round toes of the small spotted canyon tree frog make it easy to identify—that is, if you can see this well-camouflaged frog in the first place. These frogs are most active at night, spending their days on streamside rocks or trees.

Toads present include the Great Basin spadefoot, red spotted toad, and western woodhouse toad.

Birds

Have you ever seen a bird pant? Believe it or not, that's how desert birds expel heat from their bodies. They allow heat to escape by drooping their wings away from their bodies, exposing thinly feathered areas (sort of like pulling up your shirt and using it to fan your torso).

The various habitats across the Colorado Plateau, such as piñon-juniper, perennial streams, dry washes, and rock cliffs, allow many species of bird to find homes. Birders will find the greatest variety of birds near rivers and streams. Other birds, such as golden eagles, kestrels (small falcons), and peregrine falcons nest high on cliffs and patrol open areas for prey. Commonly seen hawks include the red-tailed hawk and northern harrier; late-evening strollers may see great horned owls.

People usually detect the canyon wren by its lovely song; this small, long-beaked bird nests in cavities along cliff faces. The related rock wren is—as its name implies—a rock collector: It paves a trail to its nest with pebbles, and the nest itself is lined with rocks. Another canyon bird, the white-throated swift, swoops and calls as it chases insects and mates, rather dramatically, in flight. Swifts are often seen near violet-green swallows, which are equally gymnastic fliers.

Several species of hummingbird (mostly black-chinned, but also broad-tailed and rufous) are often seen in the summer. Woodpeckers are also common, including the northern flicker and red-naped sapsucker, and flycatchers like Say's phoebe, western kingbird, and western wood pewee can be spotted too. Two warblers—the yellow and the yellow-rumped—are common in the summer, and Wilson's warbler stops in during spring and fall migrations. Horned larks are present year-round.

Mountain bluebirds are colorful, easy for a novice to identify.

Both the well-known scrub jay and its local cousin, the piñon jay, are noisy visitors to almost every picnic. Other icons of Western avian life—the turkey vulture, the raven, and the magpie—are widespread and easily spotted.

Edward Abbey: "Resist Much, Obey Little"

Edward Abbey spent two summers in the late 1950s living in a trailer in Arches National Park. From this experience, he wrote *Desert Solitaire,* which, when it was published in 1968, introduced many readers to the beauties of Utah's slickrock country and to the need to preserve it. In the introduction to this book, he gives a word of caution to slickrock pilgrims:

> Do not jump into your automobile next June and rush out to the Canyon country hoping to see some of that which I have attempted to evoke in these pages. In the first place you can't see anything from a car; you've got to get out of the goddamned contraption and walk, better yet crawl, on hands and knees, over the sandstone and through the . . . cactus. When traces of blood begin to mark your trail you'll see something, maybe.

This sense of letting the outdoors affect you—right down to the bone—pervades Abbey's writing. He advocated responding to assaults on the environment in an equally raw, gutsy way. Convinced that the only way to confront rampant development in the American West was by preserving its wilderness, he was a pioneer of radical environmentalism, a "desert anarchist." Long before Earth First!, Abbey's fictional characters blew up dams and created a holy environmentalist ruckus in *The Monkey Wrench Gang.* Some of his ideas were radical, others reactionary, and he seemed deeply committed to raising a stir. Abbey's writing did a lot to change the way people think about the American West, its development, and staying true to values derived from the natural world.

Two biographies, *Edward Abbey: A Life,* by James M. Cahalan (Tucson: University of Arizona Press, 2001), and the less academic *Adventures with Ed,* by Abbey's good friend Jack Loeffler (Albuquerque: University of New Mexico Press, 2002), help readers see the person behind the icon.

Fish

Obviously, deserts aren't particularly known for their aquatic life, and the big rivers of the Colorado Plateau are now dominated by nonnative species such as channel catfish and carp. Many of these fish were introduced as game fish. Native fish, like the six-foot, 100-pound Colorado pikeminnow, are now uncommon.

Spiders and Scorpions

Tarantulas, black widow spiders, and scorpions all live across the Colorado Plateau, and all are objects of many a visitor's phobias. Although the black widow spider's venom is toxic, tarantulas deliver only a mildly toxic bite (and they rarely bite humans), and a scorpion's sting is about like that of a bee.

ENVIRONMENTAL ISSUES

Utah's national parks have generally been shielded from the environmental issues that play out in the rest of the state, which has always been business-oriented, with a heavy emphasis on extractive industries such as mining and logging.

The main environmental threats to the parks are the consequences of becoming too popular. During the summer, auto and RV traffic can clog park roads, with particularly bad snarls at viewpoint parking areas.

Hikers also have an impact, especially when they tread on fragile cryptobiotic soil. Killing this living soil crust drastically increases erosion in an already easily eroded environment.

ATV Overkill

Off-road vehicles, or ATVs (all-terrain vehicles), have gone from being the hobby of a small group of enthusiasts to being one of the fastest-growing recreational markets in the country. Although use of ATVs is prohibited in the national parks, these dune buggies on steroids are having a huge impact on public lands adjacent to the parks and on Bureau of Land Management (BLM) lands that are currently under study for designation as wilderness. The scope of the issue is easy to measure: In 1979 there were 9,000 ATVs registered in Utah; in 2018 there were over 202,000. In addition, the power and dexterity of the machines has greatly increased. Now essentially military-style machines that can climb near-vertical cliffs and clamber over any kind of terrain, ATVs are the new "extreme sports" toy of choice, and towns like Moab are now seeing more visitors coming to tear up the backcountry on ATVs than to mountain bike. The problem is that ATVs are extremely destructive to the delicate natural environment of the Colorado Plateau deserts and canyon lands, and the more powerful, roaring, exhaust-belching machines put even the most remote and isolated areas within reach of large numbers of potentially destructive revelers.

Between the two camps—one that would preserve the public land and protect the ancient human artifacts found in remote canyons, the other that sees public land as a playground to be zipped over at high speed—is the BLM. The Moab BLM office has seemed to favor the ATV set, abdicating its role to protect the land and environment for all. Groups like Southern Utah Wilderness Alliance (SUWA, www.suwa.org) are constantly strategizing to force the BLM to comply with its responsibility for environmental stewardship of public land.

Nonnative Species

Nonnative species don't respect park boundaries, and several nonnative animals and plants have established strongholds in Utah's national parks, altering the local ecology by outcompeting native plants and animals.

Particularly invasive plants include tamarisk (salt cedar), cheatgrass, Russian knapweed, and Russian olive. Tamarisk is often seen as the most troublesome invader. This thirsty Mediterranean plant was imported in the 1800s as an ornamental shrub and was later planted by the Department of Agriculture to slow erosion along the banks of the Colorado River in Arizona. It rapidly took hold, spreading upriver at roughly 12 miles (19.3 km) per year, and is now firmly established on all of the Colorado's tributaries, where it grows in dense stands. Tamarisk consumes a great deal of water and rarely provides the food and shelter necessary for the survival of wildlife. It also outcompetes cottonwoods because tamarisk shade inhibits the growth of cottonwood seedlings.

Courthouse Wash in Arches is one of several sites where the National Park Service has made an effort to control tamarisk. Similar control experiments have been established in nearby areas, mostly in small tributary canyons of the Colorado River.

History

The landscape isn't the only vivid aspect of Utah—the area's human history is also noteworthy. This part of the West has been inhabited for over 10,000 years, and there are remnants of ancient villages and panels of mysterious rock art in now-remote canyons. More recently, colonization by Mormon settlers and the establishment of the national parks have brought attention to the human history in this dramatic corner of the Colorado Plateau.

PREHISTORY

Beginning about 15,000 years ago, nomadic groups of Paleo-Indians traveled across the Colorado Plateau in search of game animals and wild plants, but they left few traces.

Nomadic bands of hunter-gatherers

roamed the Colorado Plateau for at least 5,000 years. The climate was probably cooler and wetter when these first people arrived, with both food plants and game animals more abundant than today.

Agriculture was introduced from the south about 2,000 years ago and brought about a slow transition to a settled village life. The Fremont culture emerged in the northern part of the region and the Ancestral Puebloans resided in the southern part. In some areas, the groups lived contemporaneously. Although both groups made pots, baskets, bowls, and jewelry, only the Ancestral Puebloans constructed masonry villages. Thousands of stone dwellings, ceremonial kivas, and towers built by the Ancestral Puebloans still stand. Both groups left behind intriguing rock art, either pecked in (petroglyphs) or painted (pictographs).

The Ancestral Puebloans and Fremont people departed from this region about 800 years ago, perhaps because of drought, warfare, or disease. Some of the Ancestral Puebloans moved south and joined the Pueblo people of present-day Arizona and New Mexico. The fate of the Fremont people remains a mystery.

After the mid-1200s and until white settlers arrived in the late 1800s, small bands of nomadic Ute and Paiute moved through Southern Utah. The Navajo began to enter Utah in the early 1800s. None of the three groups established firm control of the region north of the San Juan River, where the present-day national parks are located.

SPANISH ARRIVAL

In 1776, Spanish explorers of the Dominguez-Escalante Expedition were the first Europeans to visit and describe the region. They had given up partway through a proposed journey from Santa Fe to California and returned to Santa Fe along a route passing through the sites of present-day Cedar City and Hurricane, crossing the Colorado River in a place that is now covered by Lake Powell.

The Old Spanish Trail, used from 1829 to 1848, ran through Utah to connect New Mexico with California, crossing the Colorado River near present-day Moab. Fur trappers and mountain men, including Jedediah Smith, also traveled Southern Utah's canyons in search of beaver and other animals during the early 1800s; inscriptions carved into the sandstone record their passage. In 1859 the U.S. Army's Macomb Expedition made the first documented description of what is now Canyonlands National Park. Major John Wesley Powell's pioneering river expeditions down the Green and Colorado Rivers in 1869 and 1871-1872 filled in many blank areas on the maps.

MORMON SETTLEMENT

In 1849-1850, Mormon leaders in Salt Lake City took the first steps toward colonizing Southern Utah. Parowan, now a sleepy community along I-15, became the first Mormon settlement in Southern Utah, and Cedar City the second—both were established in 1851. In 1855 a successful experiment in growing cotton along Santa Clara Creek near present-day St. George aroused considerable interest among the Mormons. New settlements soon arose in the Virgin River Valley. Poor roads hindered development, and floods, droughts, and disease, and resistance from the local Indigenous people discouraged some Mormon settlers, but many of those who stayed prospered by raising food crops and livestock.

Also in 1855, the Elk Ridge Mission was founded near present-day Moab, but it lasted only a few months. Conflict with the local Ute people resulted in three deaths and led the Mormon settlers to abandon the mission. Church members later had greater success in the Escalante area in 1876 before returning to Moab in 1877.

For sheer exertion and endurance, the efforts of the Hole-in-the-Rock Expedition of 1879-1880 are remarkable. Sixty families with 83 wagons and more than 1,000 head of livestock crossed some of the West's most rugged canyon country in an attempt to settle at Montezuma Creek on the San Juan

Anasazi or Ancestral Puebloan?

As you travel through the Southwest, you may hear reference to the Anasazi, otherwise known as Ancestral Puebloans. The word *anasazi* is actually a Navajo term that archaeologists chose, thinking it meant "old people." A more literal translation is "enemy ancestors." For this reason, some consider the name inaccurate or even offensive. The terminology is in flux, and which name you hear depends on whom you're talking to or where you are. The National Park Service now uses the more descriptive term Ancestral Puebloan, and that's the term we've chosen to use in this book. These ancient people built masonry villages and eventually moved south to Arizona and New Mexico, where their descendants, such as the Acoma, Cochiti, Santa Clara, Taos, and Hopi Mesas, live in modern-day pueblos.

River. They almost didn't make it: A journey expected to take six weeks turned into a six-month ordeal. The exhausted company arrived on the banks of the San Juan on April 5, 1880. Too tired to continue just 20 easy miles (32 km) to Montezuma Creek, they stayed and founded the town of Bluff. The Mormons also established other towns in southeastern Utah, relying on ranching, farming, and mining for their livelihoods. None of the communities in the region ever reached a large size; Moab is the biggest, with a current population of 5,500.

NATIONAL PARK MOVEMENT IN UTAH

In the early 1900s, people other than Native Americans, Mormon settlers, and explorers began to notice that Southern Utah was a remarkably scenic place and that it might be developed for tourism.

In 1909, President William Howard Taft issued an executive order designating Mukuntuweap (now Zion) a national monument in Zion Canyon. Roads were built to improve access, and by 1917 a tent camping resort was operating in the canyon. Two years later, Congress passed a bill forming Zion National Park. In the 1920s, the Union Pacific Railroad completed a rail line to Cedar City and Zion; Zion Lodge was built; and the technically challenging construction of the Zion-Mt. Carmel Highway, including its impressive 1.1-mile (1.8-km) tunnel, began.

Early homesteaders around Bryce took

visiting friends and relatives to see the incredible rock formations, and pretty soon they found themselves in the tourism business. In 1923, when Warren G. Harding created Bryce Canyon National Monument, the Union Pacific Railroad took over the fledgling tourist camp and began building Bryce Lodge. Tours of the hoodoos proved to be spectacularly popular, and Bryce became a national park in 1928.

Like Bryce and Zion, Arches was also helped along by railroad executives looking to develop their own businesses. In 1929 President Herbert Hoover signed the legislation creating Arches National Monument.

Capitol Reef became a national monument in 1937, under President Franklin Roosevelt, and for years it was loved passionately by a handful of Utah archaeology buffs but largely ignored by the federal government, which put it under the administrative control of Zion National Park.

During the 1960s the National Park Service responded to a huge increase in park visitation nationwide by expanding facilities, spurring Congress to change the status of several national monuments to national parks. Canyonlands became a national park in the 1960s, and after a spate of uranium prospecting in the nuclear-giddy 1950s, Capitol Reef and Arches gained national park status in 1971.

As visitors continued to flood the parks during the 1980s and 1990s, park managers realized they needed to develop strategies to deal with the crowds, especially the traffic.

New trails, campgrounds, and visitors centers were built, and Zion and Bryce have both made attempts to control traffic on their scenic roads.

In 1996, President Bill Clinton used provisions of the Antiquities Act to establish the Grand Staircase-Escalante National Monument, a sudden announcement that angered many locals, as it limited possible development in these areas. This vast tract, which totaled nearly 1.9 million acres, was the largest national monument land grouping in the Lower 48, bringing together Department of the Interior management land previously administered by the Bureau of Land Management, the U.S. Forest Service, and the State of Utah.

President Barack Obama used similar provisions in 2016 to create the Bears Ears National Monument to protect 1.35 million acres of land rich in ancient Ancestral Puebloan sites. Both these national monuments were greatly reduced in size and divided into much smaller units under executive orders issued by President Donald Trump in 2018.

The People

One of the oddest statistics about Utah is that it's the most urban state in the country. According to 2015 statistics from the U.S. Census Bureau, 88.4 percent of Utah's nearly 3 million residents live in cities and towns rather than unincorporated areas. That means that there aren't many people in remote Southern Utah. With the exception of St. George, Cedar City, Kanab, and Moab, there are no sizable communities in this part of the state. Even the undaunted Mormon settlers found this a forbidding place to settle during their 19th-century agrarian colonization of Utah.

Moab is known as a youthful and dynamic town, and its mountain bikers set the civic tone more than the Mormon Church. However, outside Moab, most small ranching communities in southeastern Utah are still deeply Mormon. It's a good idea to develop an understanding of Utah's predominant religion if you plan on spending any time here outside the parks.

LATTER-DAY SAINTS

One of the first things to know is that the term *Mormon* is rarely used by church members themselves. The church's proper title is the Church of Jesus Christ of Latter-Day Saints, and members prefer to be called Latter-Day Saints, Saints (usually this term is just used among church members), or LDS. While calling someone a Mormon isn't wrong, it's not quite as respectful.

The religion is based in part on the Book of Mormon, the name given to a text derived from a set of golden plates found by Joseph Smith in 1827 in western New York State. Smith claimed to have been led by an angel to the plates, which were covered with a text written in "reformed Egyptian." A farmer by upbringing, Smith translated the plates and published an English-language version of the Book of Mormon in 1830.

The Book of Mormon tells the story of the lost tribes of Israel, which, according to Mormon teachings, migrated to North America and became the ancestors of today's Native Americans. According to the Book of Mormon, Jesus also journeyed to North America, and the book includes teachings and prophecies that Christ supposedly gave to the ancient Native Americans.

The most stirring and unifying aspect of Mormon history is the incredible westward migration made by the small, fiercely dedicated band of Mormon pioneers in the 1840s. Smith and his followers were persecuted in New York and then in their newly founded utopian communities in Ohio, Missouri, and Illinois. After Smith was murdered near Carthage, Illinois, in 1844, the group decided to press even farther westward toward the frontier, led by church president Brigham Young. The journey across the then very Wild West to the Great Salt Lake basin was made by horse, wagon, or handcart—hundreds of Mormon pioneers pulled their belongings across the Great Plains in small carts. The first group of Mormon pioneers reached what is now the Salt Lake City area in 1847. The bravery and tenacity of the group's two-year migration forms the basis of many Utah residents' fierce pride in their state and their religion.

Most people know that LDS members are clean-living, family-focused people who eschew alcohol, tobacco, and stimulants, including caffeine. This can make it a little tough for visitors to feed their own vices, and indeed, it may make what formerly seemed like a normal habit feel a little more sinister. But Utah has loosened up a lot in the last couple decades, and it's really not too hard to find a place to have a beer with dinner, although you may have to make a special request. Towns near the national parks are particularly used to hosting non-Mormons, and residents attach virtually no stigma to others waking up with a cup of coffee or winding down with a glass of wine.

SOUTHERN UTAH'S NATIVE AMERICANS

It's an oddity of history that most visitors to Utah's national parks will see much more evidence of the state's ancient Indigenous residents—in the form of eerie rock art, stone pueblos, and storehouses—than they will of today's remaining Native Americans. The prehistoric residents of the canyons of southeastern Utah left their mark on the land but largely moved on. The fate of the ancient Fremont people has been lost to history, and

the abandonment of Ancestral Puebloan villages is a mystery still being unearthed by archaeologists. When the Mormons arrived in the 1840s, isolated bands of Native Americans lived in the river canyons. Federal reservations were granted to several of these groups.

Ute

Several bands of Utes, or Núuci, ranged over large areas of central and eastern Utah and adjacent Colorado. Originally hunter-gatherers, they acquired horses around 1800 and became skilled raiders. Customs adopted from Plains people included the use of rawhide, tepees, and the travois, a sled used to carry goods. The discovery of gold in southern Colorado and the pressures of farmers there and in Utah forced the Utes to move and renegotiate treaties many times. They now have the large Uintah and Ouray Indian Reservation in northeast Utah, the small White Mesa Indian Reservation in southeast Utah, and the Ute Mountain Indian Reservation in southwest Colorado and northwest New Mexico.

Navajo

Calling themselves Diné, the Navajo moved into the San Juan River area around 1600. The Navajo have proved exceptionally adaptable in learning new skills from other cultures: Many Navajo crafts, clothing, and religious practices have come from Native American, Spanish, and Anglo neighbors. The Navajo were the first in the area to move away from hunting and gathering lifestyles, relying instead on the farming and shepherding techniques they had learned from the Spanish. The Navajo are one of the largest Native American groups in the country, with 16 million acres of exceptionally scenic land in southeast Utah and adjacent Arizona and New Mexico. The Navajo Nation's headquarters is at Window Rock, Arizona.

Essentials

Getting There

If you're driving from other points in North America, Utah is easy to reach. The parks are east of I-15, which runs parallel to the Rocky Mountains from Montana to Southern California. And they're south of I-70, which links Denver to I-15.

International travelers flying into the region have numerous options. Salt Lake City is convenient as a terminus for travelers who want to make a road-trip loop tour through all of Utah's parks. For other travelers, These parks may be best seen as part of a longer U.S. road trip.

Public transportation, except for regularly scheduled flights, is

almost nonexistent in Southern Utah and the parks; you'll need your own vehicle to explore the area.

FROM SALT LAKE CITY

Many tours of These parks begin in Salt Lake City. Its busy airport and plethora of hotels make it an easy place to begin and end a trip.

Airport

Salt Lake City is a hub for Delta Airlines, and all other major airlines have regular flights into **Salt Lake City International Airport** (SLC, 776 N. Terminal Dr., 801/575-2400, https://slcairport.com). The airport is an easy 7 miles (11.3 km) west of downtown; reach it via I-80 or North Temple Boulevard or take the Green Line TRAX light rail train operated by the Utah Transit Authority (UTA, www.rideuta.com).

SkyWest Airlines (800/453-9417, www.skywest.com) offers flights between Denver and **Canyonlands Field** (CNY, U.S. 191, 16 mi/25.7 km north of Moab, 435/259-4849).

The Salt Lake City airport has three terminals; in each you'll find a ground transportation information desk, restaurants, motel and hotel courtesy phones, and car rentals (all the major companies are either on-site or a short shuttle ride away). Terminal 2 houses Zion's First National Bank for currency exchange. Terminal 3 is dedicated to international arrivals and departures.

Train

The only passenger train through Salt Lake City is Amtrak's California Zephyr, which heads west to Reno and Oakland and east to Denver and Chicago three times a week. **Amtrak** (station 340 S. 600 W., 800/872-7245, www.amtrak.com) prices tickets as airlines do, with special seasonal fares and advance-booking and other discounts. Amtrak office hours are irregular and timed to meet the trains, so call first.

Long-Distance Bus

Salt Lake City is at a crossroads of several major highways and has good bus service from **Greyhound** (160 W. South Temple St., 801/355-9579 or 800/231-2222, www.greyhound.com). Generally speaking, buses run north and south along I-15 and east and west along I-80; you won't be able to take the bus to any of Utah's national parks.

Car

From Salt Lake City, it's a long 238-mile drive to Moab, the center for exploring Arches and Canyonlands National Parks. The fastest route takes you south from Salt Lake City on I-15, cutting east at Spanish Fork on U.S. 6/89 to Price, south to Green River and I-70, and then to Moab on U.S. 191. Dramatic scenery highlights the entire length of this four-hour drive.

You'll find all of the major car rental companies at the Salt Lake City airport (www.slcairport.com).

RV and Motorcycle Rentals

Expect to pay $1,200-1,800 per week to rent an RV, depending on the season and the size of the vehicle; small travel trailers are less expensive but are frequently unavailable.

Access RV Rental (2240 S. State St., Salt Lake City, 801/936-1200 or 800/327-6910, http://accessrvrental.com) is a local company with relatively good rates on RV rentals. **Cruise America** (4125 S. State St., Salt Lake City, 801/288-0930, www.cruiseamerica.com) is a larger company with RV rentals available. **El Monte RV** (3490 W. 1820 S., Salt Lake City, 888/337-2214, www.elmonterv.com) also provides rentals.

For automobile campers not quite ready to join the RV set, a popular option is the camper van experience. Camper vans are smaller than RVs and can be parked in regular tent parking spots in most campgrounds, with artfully designed sleeping spaces within the

Utah Driving Distances

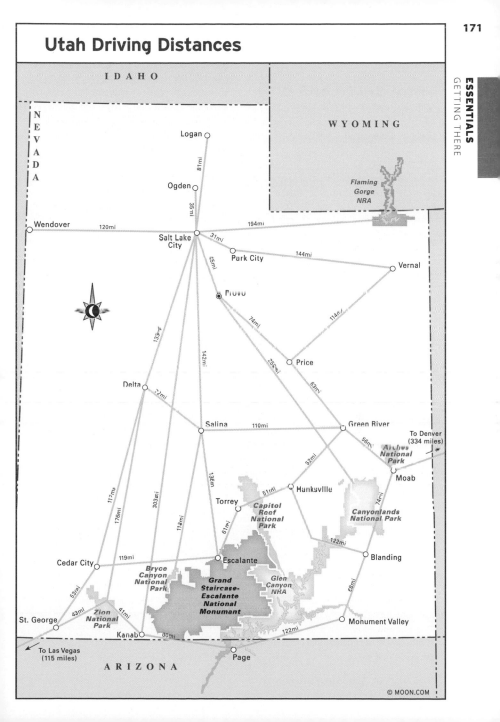

IDAHO

NEVADA

WYOMING

Logan

Flaming Gorge NRA

81mi

Ogden

35 mi

Wendover — 120mi — Salt Lake City

194mi

31mi

Park City — 144mi — Vernal

45mi

Provo

74mi

114mi

133mi

142mi

Price

255mi

63mi

Delta

72mi

Salina — 110mi — Green River

To Denver (334 miles)

86mi

52mi

Archos National Park

117mi

303mi

136mi

51mi

Hanksville

74mi

Moab

176mi

114mi

Torrey

Capitol Reef National Park

Canyonlands National Park

61mi

122mi

Cedar City — 119mi — Escalante

Blanding

Bryce Canyon National Park

Grand Staircase-Escalante National Monument

Glen Canyon NHA

68mi

53mi

43mi

41mi

Zion National Park

Kanab

90mi

122mi

Monument Valley

St. George

To Las Vegas (115 miles)

Page

ARIZONA

© MOON.COM

body of the van. These vans typically come with bedding, a propane stove, cooking gear, and camp chairs. **Basecamper Vans** (423 E. 600 S., Salt Lake City, 801/938-4433, www.basecampervans.com) offers several lines of camper vans, with prices starting at $99 per day.

Rent a motorcycle from **EagleRider/Harley-Davidson of Salt Lake City** (2900 S. State St., Sandy, 385/831-7253, www.eaglerider.com, from $99 per day).

Food

If you're going to be camping on your trip through these parks, you may want to pick up some provisions in Salt Lake City before hitting the road south. Just east of I-15, off I-80 in the Sugar House district, **Whole Foods Market** (1131 E. Wilmington Ave., 801/359-7913) has a good deli, lots of organic produce, bulk foods, and good bread (likely the last you'll see for a while). It's in a complex that also contains some good restaurants, a camping supply store, and the brightest, shiniest tattoo parlor you'll ever lay eyes on.

Downtown, stop at **Tony Caputo Market & Deli** (308 W. Broadway, 801/531-8669, www.caputosdeli.com, 9am-7pm Mon.-Sat., 10am-5pm Sun.), an old-style Italian deli brimming with delicious sausages, cheeses, and olives. Don't forget to get a sandwich to go.

Red Iguana (736 W. North Temple St., 801/322-1489, www.rediguana.com, 11am-10pm Mon.-Thurs., 11am-11pm Fri., 10am-11pm Sat., 10am-9pm Sun., $8-22), on the way in from the airport, is one of the city's favorite Mexican restaurants and offers excellent south-of-the-border cooking with a specialty in Mayan and regional foods. Best of all, the flavors are crisp, fresh, and earthy. The Red Iguana is very popular, so arrive early—especially at lunch—to avoid the lines.

The Copper Onion (111 E. Broadway, 801/355-3282, http://thecopperonion.com, 4pm-9pm Wed.-Sun., $12-29) always gets a mention when people talk about the best restaurant in Salt Lake City. Emphasizing full-flavored New American cooking, the Copper Onion offers a choice of small and large plates, with such delights as a pork chop with farro, wild mushrooms and pumpkin seed vinaigrette. For the quality, the prices are very reasonable.

In the Hotel Monaco, **Bambara** (202 S. Main St., 801/363-5454, www.bambara-slc.com, 5pm-9pm Tues.-Sat., $20-25) has a menu that emphasizes the freshest and most flavorful local meats and produce, with preparations in a wide-awake New American style that is equal parts tradition and innovation.

Utah's oldest brewpub is **Squatters Pub Brewery** (147 W. Broadway, 801/363-2739, www.squatters.com, noon-8pm Sun.-Wed., noon-9pm Thurs., noon-10pm Fri.-Sat., $8-18). In addition to fine beers and ales, the pub serves sandwiches, burgers, and other light entrées in a handsome old warehouse. In summer there's seating on the back deck. Another popular brewpub is the **Red Rock Brewing Company** (254 S. 200 W., 801/521-7446, www.redrockbrewing.com, 11:30am-8pm Sun.-Thurs., 11:30am-10pm Fri.-Sat., $10-20), offering pasta, salads, and sandwiches, including an excellent variation on the hamburger, baked in a wood-fired oven inside a bread pocket.

Accommodations

Salt Lake City has many hotel rooms across all price categories. We've included a few of our favorites here. Although most aren't airport hotels, the airport is pretty easy to get to from all of them.

If you're driving into town and just want to find a hotel room fast, head south and west of downtown, where chain hotels proliferate. The area around 600 South and 200 West is especially fertile ground for mid-priced hotels.

UNDER $50

The Avenues Hostel (107 F St., 801/363-3855, www.saltlakehostel.com, $27-47, only half have private baths), 1 mile (1.6 km) east of Temple Square, offers lodging with the use of a kitchen, a TV room, and laundry. Information-packed bulletin boards list city sights and goings-on, and you'll meet travelers from all over the world. Reservations (with first night's deposit) are advised in the busy summer travel and winter ski seasons. From downtown, head east on South Temple Street to F Street, then turn north and go two blocks.

$50-100

One of the most affordable lodging options in central Salt Lake City is the **Metropolitan Inn** (524 S. West Temple St., 801/531-7100, www.metropolitaninn.com, $72-110), with clean simple rooms, an outdoor pool, guest laundry, and buffet breakfast.

$100-150

If you're looking for comfortable rooms without breaking the bank, the ★ **Little America Hotel and Towers** (500 S. Main St., 801/363-6781 or 800/304-8970, http://saltlake.littleamerica.com, $110-269) is a great place to stay. This large lodging complex, with nearly 850 guest rooms, offers three types of rooms: Courtside rooms and garden suites are scattered around the hotel's nicely manicured grounds, with most guest rooms overlooking a pool or a fountain. Tower suites are executive-level suites in a 17-story block offering some of SLC's best views. All guests share the hotel's elegant public areas, two pools, health club, and workout facility. The restaurant is better than average, and there is free airport transfer.

Another of the nicer for the money hotels in this part of Salt Lake City is the **Crystal Inn** (230 W. 500 S., 801/328-4466 or 800/366-4466, www.crystalinnsaltlake.com, $146-191). Guest rooms are very large and nicely furnished; all come with fridges and microwaves. There's a free hot breakfast buffet for all guests. For recreation, there's an indoor pool, an exercise room, a sauna, and a hot tub.

On the campus of the University of Utah, the **University Guest House and Conference Center** (110 S. Ft. Douglas Blvd., 801/587-1000 or 888/416-4075, www.universityguesthouse.com, $155-186) is a good choice if you want a comfortable room, free parking, and nice walks in the neighborhood

(check out the Red Butte Garden). Good restaurants are nearby, and downtown is a short drive or light-rail trip away.

At the **DoubleTree by Hilton SLC Airport** (5151 Wiley Post Way, 801/539-1515 or 800/999-3736, www.hilton.com, $95-179), guest rooms are spacious and nicely furnished, and facilities include two pools, a putting green, a sports court, and an exercise room and whirlpool. The hotel even has its own lake. Practically next door to the airport terminal is the **Ramada Salt Lake City Airport** (5575 W. Amelia Earhart Dr., 801/537-7020 or 800/272-6232, www.ramada.com, $79-109), with a pool and a spa.

OVER $150

If you really want to do Salt Lake City in style, two downtown hotels are good places to splurge. **Hotel Monaco** (15 W. 200 S., 801/595-0000 or 877/294-9710, www.monaco-saltlakecity.com, $236-305) occupies a grandly renovated historic office building in a convenient spot in the middle of downtown; on the main floor is Bambara, one of the most sophisticated restaurants in Utah. Guest rooms are sumptuously furnished with real élan. Facilities include an on-site fitness center, meeting rooms, and concierge and valet services. Pets are welcome, and if you forgot your own pet, the hotel will deliver a companion goldfish to your room.

The gigantic **Grand America Hotel and Suites** (75 E. 600 S., 800/533-3525, www.grandamerica.com, $339-414) is Salt Lake City's take on the Vegas fantasy hotel. A block square (that's 10 acres in this land of long blocks), its 24 stories contain 775 guest rooms, more than half of them suites. Guest rooms have luxury-level amenities; expect all the perks and niceties that modern hotels can offer. On the campus of the University of Utah, the **Salt Lake City Marriott University Park Hotel** (480 Wakara Way, 801/581-1000 or 800/637-4390, www.marriott.com, $200-256) is one of the city's best-kept secrets for luxurious lodgings in a lovely setting. You can't miss with the views: All guest rooms either overlook the city or look onto the soaring peaks of the Wasatch Range, directly behind the hotel. Guest rooms are very nicely appointed—the suites are some of the best in the city. All guest rooms have minibars, fridges, and coffeemakers; there's an exercise room, and bicycles are available for rent.

Camping

Of the several commercial campgrounds around the periphery of Salt Lake City, **Salt Lake City KOA** (1400 W. North Temple St., 801/328-0224, www.koa.com, year-round, from $37 tents, from $64-84 RVs) is the most convenient, located between downtown and the airport. It offers showers, a swimming pool, a game room, a playground, a store, and laundry. From I-15 northbound, take exit 311 for I-80; go west 1.3 miles (2.1 km) on I-80, exit north for 0.5 mile (0.8 km) on Redwood Road (Hwy. 68), then turn right and continue another 0.5 mile (0.8 km) on North Temple Street. From I-15 southbound, take exit 313 and go south 1.5 miles (2.4 km) on 900 West, then turn right and drive less than 1 mile (1.6 km) on North Temple Street. From I-80, either take the North Temple exit or the one for Redwood Road (Hwy. 68).

There are two good U.S. Forest Service campgrounds in Big Cottonwood Canyon, about 15 miles (24. km) southeast of downtown Salt Lake City, and another two in Little Cottonwood Canyon, about 19 miles (31 km) southeast of town. All have drinking water, and all prohibit pets because of local watershed regulations; rates range $19-23, and some can be reserved (877/444-6777, www.recreation.gov, reservation fee $9 online, $10 phone). In Big Cottonwood Canyon, **Spruces Campground** (9.1 mi/14.7 km up the canyon, elevation 7,400 ft/2,253 m) is open early June-mid-October. The season at **Redman Campground** (elev. 8,300 ft/2,530 m, first come, first served) is mid-June-early October. It's between Solitude and Brighton, 14 mi/22.5 km up Big Cottonwood Canyon. Little Cottonwood Canyon's **Tanners Flat Campground** (4.3 mi/6.9 km up the canyon,

elev. 7,200 ft/2,195 m, first come, first served) is open mid-May-mid-October. **Albion Basin Campground** (elev. 9,500 ft/2,895 m), first come, first served) is high in the mountains a few miles past Alta Ski Area and is open early July-late September; go 11 miles (17.7 km) up the canyon (the last 2.5 mi/4 km are gravel).

FROM DENVER

Although it may not seem intuitive to start your tour of These parks in Denver, that's exactly what works best for many folks, especially those who fly from European capital cities to Denver International Airport. From there, it's easy to rent a car or RV and begin a tour that typically includes Rocky Mountain National Park, Utah's five national parks, and the Grand Canyon before terminating at Las Vegas.

Airport

Locals joke that **Denver International Airport** (DEN, 8500 Peña Blvd., 303/342-2000, www.flydenver.com), often referred to as DIA, is in Kansas; it's actually 23 miles (37 km) northeast of downtown Denver on Highway 470, north of I-70. Major airlines using DIA include American, British Airways, Delta, and United.

DIA's Jeppesen Terminal has a giant atrium and three concourses connected by a light-rail train. Car-rental counters are in the central terminal atrium between security screening areas.

Car

To drive from Denver to the parks, follow I-70 west, up over the Continental Divide along the Rocky Mountains, and down to the Colorado River. Cross into Utah and take I-70 exit 212 at Cisco. From Denver to Cisco is 297 miles (478 km), all on the freeway. From Cisco, follow Highway 128 for 37 highly scenic miles (60 km) through red-rock canyons to Moab. Allow 5.5 hours of driving time between Moab and Denver.

All major car rental agencies have facilities near DIA.

RV Rentals

Regional corporations with offices in Denver include **Cruise America** (8950 N. Federal Blvd., Denver, 303/650-2865, www.cruiseamerica.com) and **El Monte RV** (5989 Main St., Louviers, 303/426-7998 or 888/337-2214, www.elmonterv.com).

Food

Denver has a large Hispanic population, so it's no surprise that there are lots of Latin American restaurants, and these are often good and reliable places for inexpensive meals. Indeed, some of Denver's most exciting restaurants are Nuevo Latin American restaurants—where familiar tacos, tortillas, and enchiladas are updated into zippy fine dining. One of the best is **Lola** (1575 Boulder St., 720/570-8686, www.loladenver.com, 4pm-10pm Mon. Thurs., 4pm-11pm Fri., 10am-11pm Sat., 10am-9pm Sun., entrées under $25), a hip and happening restaurant with over 150 tequilas to choose from and main courses like grilled pork with habanero sauce. Guacamole is prepared table-side. More upscale is **Tamayo** (1400 Larimer St., 720/946-1433, www.richardsandoval.com, noon-8pm Tues.-Thurs., noon-10pm Fri., 11am-10pm Sat., 11am-8pm Sun., entrées $20-28), a hybrid of French refinement and zesty Mexican flavors. Views from this rooftop dining room overlook Larimer Square and the Rockies, making it a top spot for margaritas and appetizers, particularly the excellent shrimp tacos.

The **Barolo Grill** (3030 E. 6th Ave., 303/393-1040, http://barologrilldenver.com, 5:30pm-9:30pm Tues.-Thurs., 5pm-10pm Fri.-Sat., $15-30) is a comfortable northern Italian restaurant with good salads and pasta as well as grilled fish, game, and chicken main courses.

The wine list is outstanding. Denver is known for its steak houses, and one of the best is the **Capital Grille** (1450 Larimer St., 303/539-2500, www.thecapitalgrille.com, 11am-10pm Mon.-Thurs., 11am-11pm Fri., 4:30pm-11pm Sat., 4pm-9pm Sun., $19-40), with swank surroundings, an attentive staff, and excellent steaks, prime rib, and chops. For a lighter meal, go to **Falling Rock Tap House** (1919 Blake St., 303/293-8338, http://fallingrocktaphouse.com, 5pm-10pm Thurs., 5pm-11pm Fri., noon-11pm Sat., noon-8pm Sun., $8-20), one of Denver's top regional beer pubs, with over 75 brews on tap and tasty pub grub.

Accommodations

Chain hotels have set up shop in the area surrounding DIA. Almost all offer shuttles to and from the airport.

For budget travelers, the **11th Avenue Hotel and Hostel** (1112 N. Broadway, 303/861-7777, http://innkeeperrockies.com, $33 dorm, $66-99 pp private rooms) is a 1903 hotel on the edge of downtown that's now a blend of hotel and hostel. Facilities include laundry, Internet access, and cable TV. There's no kitchen, but guests have access to a barbecue grill, microwave, and toaster oven.

The closest lodgings to DIA are about 6 miles (10 km) from the airport. The **DIA Microtel Inn** (18600 E. 63rd Ave., 303/371-8300 or 800/771-7171, www.microtelinn.com, $109-179) includes breakfast. The **Quality Inn** (6890 Tower Rd., 303/371-5300 or 877/424-6423, www.qualityinn.com, $85-189) is easy to find north of I-70 exit 286. About 12 miles (19 km) south of the airport, near the intersection of I-70 and Peña Boulevard, is a cluster of chain motels, including **Red Lion Inn and Suites** (16921 E. 32nd Ave., 303/367-5000, www.redlion.com, $109-139).

Getting Around

For most travelers, getting around Utah requires using some form of automobile. Public transportation is nonexistent between the parks, and distances are great—although the parks cover a relatively compact area, the geography of the land is so contorted that there are few roads that connect the dots. For instance, from Moab to the Arizona border, nearly 130 miles (209 km), only one bridge crosses the Colorado River once it drops into its canyon. Cars are easily rented in gateway cities, and in towns like Moab there is a plethora of jeep and Humvee rentals as well.

Bicycle touring is certainly an excellent option, but cyclists need to be in good shape and be prepared for intense heat during summer trips. For detailed information on cycling Utah, read the classic *Bicycle Touring in Utah* by Dennis Coello, now out of print but available from libraries and used from online sources.

STREET NUMBERING AND GRID ADDRESSES

Many towns founded by Mormon settlers share a street-numbering scheme that can be confusing to first-time visitors but quickly becomes intuitive. A city's address grid will generally have its temple at the center, with blocks numbered by hundreds out in every direction. For instance, 100 West is one block west of the center of town, then comes 200 West, and so on. In conversation, you may hear the shorthand "4th South," "3rd West," and so on to indicate 400 South or 300 West.

While this street-numbering system is a picture of precision, it's also confusing at first. All addresses have four parts: When you see the address 436 North 100 West, for instance, the system tells you that the address will be found four blocks north of the center of town, on 100 West. One rule of thumb is to remember that the last two segments of

an address (300 South, 500 East, 2300 West) are the street's actual name—the equivalent of a single street signifier such as Oak Street or Front Avenue.

TRAVELING BY RV

Traveling the Southwest's national parks in an RV is a time-honored tradition, and travelers will have no problem finding RV rentals in major cities like Denver and Salt Lake City. The parks have good campgrounds, and towns like Moab have some very spiffy campground options with extras like swimming pools and fine-dining cookouts.

DRIVING THE PARKS

During the summer, patience is the key to driving in These parks. Roads are often crowded with slow-moving RVs, and traffic jams are not uncommon.

If you're traveling on back roads, make sure you have plenty of gas, even if it means paying top dollar at a small-town gas pump.

Summer heat in the desert puts an extra strain on both cars and drivers. It's worth double-checking your vehicle's cooling system, engine oil, transmission fluid, fan belts, and tires to make sure they are in top condition. Carry several gallons of water in case of a breakdown or radiator trouble. Never leave children or pets in a parked car during warm weather; temperatures inside can cause fatal heatstroke in minutes.

At times the desert has too much water, when late-summer storms frequently flood low spots in the road. Wait for the water level to subside before crossing. Dust storms can completely block visibility but tend to be short-lived. During such storms, pull completely off the road, stop, and turn off your lights so as not to confuse other drivers. Radio stations carry frequent weather updates when weather hazards exist.

If stranded, stay with your vehicle unless

Visitor Information

General tourism literature and maps are available from the **Utah Travel Council** (Council Hall/Capitol Hill, Salt Lake City, UT 84114-7420, tel. 801/538-1030, fax 801/538-1399, www.utah.com). Call or write in advance of your visit to obtain maps and brochures from the parks.

Arches National Park
P.O. Box 907
Moab, UT 84532-0907
435/719-2299
www.nps.gov/arch

Canyonlands National Park
2282 SW Resource Blvd.
Moab, UT 84532-3298
435/719-2100
www.nps.gov/cany

you're positive of where to go for help, then leave a note explaining your route and departure time. Airplanes can easily spot a stranded car (tie a piece of cloth to your antenna), but a person walking is more difficult to see. It's best to carry emergency supplies: blankets or sleeping bags, a first-aid kit, tools, jumper cables, a shovel, traction mats or chains, a flashlight, rain gear, water, food, and a can opener.

Maps
The Utah Department of Transportation prints and distributes a free, regularly updated map of Utah. Ask for it when you call for information or when you stop at a visitor information office. Benchmark Maps' *Utah Road and Recreation Atlas* is loaded with beautiful maps, recreation information, and global positioning system (GPS) grids. If you're planning on extensive backcountry exploration, be sure to ask locally about conditions.

If you're looking for USGS topo maps, you can download them for free at www.topozone.com.

Off-Road Driving

Here are some tips for safely traversing the backcountry in a vehicle (preferably one with four-wheel drive):

- Drive slowly enough to choose a safe path and avoid obstacles such as rocks or giant potholes, but keep up enough speed to propel yourself through sand or mud.

- Keep an eye on the route ahead of you. If there are obstacles, stop, get out of your vehicle, and survey the situation.

- Reduce the tire pressure if you're driving across sand.

- Drive directly up or down the fall line of a slope. Cutting across diagonally may seem less frightening, but it puts you in a position to slide or roll over.

If you really want to learn to drive your 4WD rig, consider signing up for a class.

TOURS

Bus tours, often in conjunction with Grand Canyon National Park, are available from several regional tour companies. **Southern Utah Scenic Tours** (435/656-1504 or 888/404-8687, http://utahscenictours.com) offers multiday scenic and thematic tours of the Southwest, including the Utah national parks.

Road Scholar (800/454-5768, www.roadscholar.org) operates programs out of St. George, including a bus tour of Southern Utah and northern Arizona's national parks and monuments. These trips are geared toward older adults (this is the organization formerly known as Elderhostel) and involve a bit of easy hiking.

For a truly unusual bus tour, consider the **Adventure Bus** (375 S. Main St., Moab, 909/633-7225 or 888/737-5263, www.adventurebus.com), a bus that's had most of its seats removed to make lounge and sleeping areas. Guests live on the bus (some meals are provided) as it makes tours of Utah and other Southwest hot spots.

Recreation

These epic landscapes—red-rock canyons, towering arches, and needles of sandstone—are best explored by foot, by bike, or on the water. Hikers will find a variety of trails, ranging from paved all-abilities paths to remote backcountry tracks. Rafts and jet boats out of Moab provide another means to explore rugged canyons otherwise inaccessible to all but the hardiest trekkers. The sheer rock cliff faces and promontories in the parks provide abundant challenges to experienced rock climbers; be certain to check park regulations before climbing, however, as restrictions may apply.

HIKING

The parks offer lots of opportunities for hikers and backcountry enthusiasts interested in exploring the scenery on foot. Each of the parks has a variety of well-maintained hiking trails, ranging from easy strolls to multiday backcountry treks. In fact, much of the Needles and Maze Districts in Canyonlands are accessible only by foot; visits to remote Ancestral Puebloan ruins and petroglyphs are among the rewards for the long-distance hiker.

One popular activity is canyoneering—exploring mazelike slot canyons. Hundreds of feet deep but sometimes only wide enough for a hiker to squeeze through, these canyons are located across Southern Utah. You'll need to be fit to explore these regions—and watch the weather carefully for flash floods.

CAMPING

All of Utah's national parks have campgrounds, with each park keeping at least one campground open year-round. Some campgrounds are first come, first served; **reservations** (877/444-6777, www.recreation.gov, reservation fee $9 online, $10 phone) are accepted seasonally at Arches' Devils Garden Campground. During the summer and on holiday weekends during the spring and fall, it's best to arrive at the park early in the day and select a campsite immediately. Don't expect to find hookups or showers at National Park Service campgrounds. For these comforts, look just outside the park entrance, where you'll generally find at least one full-service commercial campground.

Backcountry Camping

Backcountry campers in national parks must stop by the park visitors center for a backcountry permit. Backcountry camping may be limited to specific sites in order to spread people out a bit; if so, a park ranger will consult with you and assign you a campground.

Before heading into the backcountry, check with a ranger about weather, water sources, fire danger, trail conditions, and regulations. Backpacking stores are also good sources of information. Here are some tips for traveling safely and respectfully in the backcountry:

- Tell rangers or other reliable people where you are going and when you expect to return; they'll alert rescuers if you go missing.

- Travel in small groups for the best experience (group size may also be regulated).

- Avoid stepping on—or camping on—fragile cryptobiotic soils.

- Use a portable stove to avoid leaving fire scars.

- Resist the temptation to shortcut switchbacks; this causes erosion and can be dangerous.

- Avoid digging tent trenches or cutting vegetation.

- Help preserve old Native American and other historic ruins.

- Camp at least 300 feet (91 m) away from springs, creeks, and trails. Camp at least 0.25 mile (0.4 km) from a lone water source to avoid scaring away wildlife and livestock.

The America the Beautiful Pass

The U.S. government has revamped its park pass system, inaugurating a new set of annual passes that are the result of a cooperative effort between the National Park Service, the U.S. Forest Service, the U.S. Fish and Wildlife Service, the Bureau of Land Management, and the Bureau of Reclamation.

The basic pass is called the **America the Beautiful—National Parks and Federal Recreational Lands Pass** (valid for 1 year from date of purchase, $80 plus a $5 processing and handling fee), which is available to the general public and provides access to, and use of, federal recreation sites that charge an entrance or standard amenity fee. Passes can be obtained in person at a park; by calling 888/ASK-USGS (888/275-8747, ext. 1); or at http://store.usgs.gov/pass.

U.S. citizens or permanent residents age 62 or older can purchase a lifetime version of the America the Beautiful pass for $80. This pass can only be obtained in person at a park. The Senior Pass provides free access to federal parks and recreational areas, plus a 50 percent discount on some fees, such as camping, swimming, boat launch, and specialized interpretive services.

Both passes are good for the cardholder plus three adults (children 15 and under are free). The pass is nontransferable and generally does not cover or reduce special recreation permit fees or fees charged by park concessionaires.

U.S. citizens or permanent residents with permanent disabilities are eligible for a free lifetime America the Beautiful Access Pass. Documentation such as a statement from a licensed physician, the Veterans Administration, or Social Security is required to obtain this pass, which can only be obtained in person at a park. Like the Senior Pass, the Access Pass provides free access to federal parks and recreational areas, plus a 50 percent discount on some fees, such as camping, swimming, boat launch, and specialized interpretive services. Free annual passes are also available to members of the U.S. military and their families.

Volunteers who have amassed 250 service hours with one of the participating federal agencies are eligible for a free one-year pass, which is available through their supervisor.

- Avoid camping in washes at any time; be alert to thunderstorms.

- Take care not to throw or kick rocks off trails—someone might be below you.

- Don't drink water directly from streams or lakes, no matter how clean the water appears; it may contain the parasitic protozoan *Giardia lamblia*, which causes giardiasis. Boiling water for several minutes will kill giardia as well as most other bacterial or viral pathogens. Chemical treatments and water filters usually work too, although they're not as reliable as boiling (giardia spends part of its life in a hard shell that protects it from most chemicals).

- Bathe and wash dishes away from lakes, streams, and springs. Use biodegradable soap, and scatter your wash water.

- Bring a trowel for personal sanitation. Dig 6-8 inches deep and cover your waste; in some areas, you'll be required to carry portable human waste disposal systems.

- Pack out all your trash, including toilet paper and feminine hygiene items.

- Bring plenty of feed for your horses and mules.

- Leave dogs at home; they're not permitted on national park trails.

- If you realize you're lost, find shelter. If you're sure of a way to civilization and plan to walk out, leave a note with your departure time and planned route.

- Visit the Leave No Trace website (www.lnt.org) for more details on responsible backcountry travel.

CLIMBING

Most visitors enjoy spotting rock climbers scaling canyon walls and sandstone pillars, but for a few, the whole reason to visit Southern Utah is to climb. These folks need a climbing guide, either the classic *Desert Rock* by Eric Bjørnstad or *Rock Climbing Utah* by Stewart M. Green.

Prospective climbers should take note: Just because you're the star of the local rock gym, don't think that climbing Canyonlands' remote sandstone towers is going to be simple. Sandstone poses its own set of challenges; it weakens when wet, so it's wise to avoid climbing in damp areas or after rain. The Entrada sandstone in Arches is particularly tough to climb.

Climbers in the national parks should take care to use clean climbing techniques. Approach climbs via established trails to prevent further erosion of slopes. Camp in park campgrounds or, on multiday climbs, get a backcountry permit. Because white chalk leaves unsightly marks on canyon walls, add red pigment to your chalk. Do not disturb vegetation growing in cracks along your route. Tube or bag human waste and carry it out. Remove all old worn rope and equipment, but do not remove fixed pins. Make sure your climb is adequately protected by visually inspecting any preexisting bolts or fixed pins. It is illegal to use a power drill to place bolts. Never climb directly above trails, where hikers may be hit by dislodged rocks.

In Canyonlands, strict regulations are in place. No new climbing hardware may be left in a fixed location; protection may not be placed with the use of a hammer except to replace existing belay and rappel anchors and bolts on established routes (or for emergency self-rescue); and unsafe slings must be replaced with earth-colored slings.

Plan to climb in the spring or fall. During the summer, the walls become extremely hot. Some climbing areas may be closed during the spring to protect nesting raptors. Check at the visitors centers for current closures.

Travel Tips

This may seem a remote, uninhabited, and even hostile destination, but it sees hundreds of thousands of travelers each year and has sufficient facilities to ensure that visitors have a pleasant vacation. Before you visit, here are a few tips to ensure that your Utah vacation goes well.

INTERNATIONAL VISITORS
Entering the United States
Citizens of Canada must provide a passport to enter the United States, but a visa is not required for Canadian citizens.

Citizens of 28 other countries can enter the United States under a reciprocal visa-waiver program. These citizens can enter for up to 90 days for tourism or business with a valid passport, and no visa is required. These countries include most of Western Europe plus Japan, Australia, New Zealand, and Singapore. For a full list of reciprocal visa-waiver countries (along with other late-breaking news for travelers to the United States), check out http://travel.state.gov. Visitors on this program who arrive by sea or air must show round-trip tickets out of the United States dated within 90 days, and they must present proof of financial solvency (credit cards are usually sufficient). If citizens of these countries are staying longer than 90 days, they must apply for and present a visa.

Citizens of countries not covered by the reciprocal visa-waiver program are required to present both a valid passport and a visa to enter the United States. These are obtained from U.S. embassies and consulates. These travelers are also required to offer proof of financial solvency and show a round-trip ticket out of the United States dated within the timeline of the visa.

Coronavirus in Utah and the National Parks

At the time of writing, Utah was managing the effects of the coronavirus, with the situation constantly evolving. Most, if not all, destinations required that **face masks** be worn in enclosed spaces and **social distancing** was encouraged. As Utah's Department of Health monitors COVID-19 cases and transmission through the state, phased guidelines may change locally, so check the websites below regularly. The National Park Service also emphasizes the importance of park visitors wearing masks.

Now more than ever, Moon encourages its readers to be courteous and ethical in their travel. We ask travelers to be respectful to residents, and mindful of the evolving situation in their chosen destination when planning their trip.

BEFORE YOU GO

- Check relevant websites (listed below) for **updated local restrictions** and the overall health status of the destination.

- If you plan to fly, check with your **airline** and the **local health authorities** for updated recommendation requirements.

- Check the websites of any venues you wish to patronize to confirm that they're open, if their hours have been adjusted, and to learn about any specific visitation requirements, such as mandatory **reservations.**

- Pack **hand sanitizer, a thermometer,** and plenty of **face masks.** Road trippers may want to bring a **cooler** to limit the number of stops along their route.

- Assess the risk of entering **crowded spaces,** joining **tours,** and taking **public transit.**

- Expect **general disruptions.** Events may be postponed or cancelled. Some tours and venues may require reservations, enforce limits on the number of guests, or operate during different hours than the ones listed. Some may be closed entirely.

RESOURCES

Monitor the following websites to keep track of the evolving COVID-19 situation in Utah:

- **Utah Health Department** (https://coronavirus.utah.gov)

- **Utah State Travel Bureau** (https://www.visitutah.com/plan-your-trip/covid-19)

- **National Park Service** (https://www.nps.gov/planyourvisit/alerts.htm)

Once in the United States, foreign visitors can travel freely among states without restrictions.

Customs

U.S. Customs allows each person over the age of 21 to bring one liter of liquor and 200 cigarettes into the country duty-free. Non-U.S. citizens can bring in $100 worth of gifts without paying duty. If you are carrying more than $10,000 in cash or traveler's checks, you are required to declare it.

Money and Currency Exchange

Except in Salt Lake City, there are few opportunities to exchange foreign currency or traveler's checks in non U.S. funds at Utah banks or exchanges. Traveler's checks in U.S. dollars are accepted at face value in most businesses without additional transaction fees.

By far the best way to keep yourself in cash is by using bank, debit, or cash cards at ATMs (automated teller machines). Not only does withdrawing funds from your own home account save on fees, but you also often get a better rate of exchange. Nearly every town in Utah has an ATM. Most ATMs at banks require a small fee to dispense cash. Most grocery stores allow you to use a debit or cash card to purchase food, with the option of adding a cash withdrawal. These transactions are free to the withdrawer.

Credit cards are accepted nearly everywhere in Utah. The most common are Visa and MasterCard. American Express, Diners Club, and Discover are also used, although these aren't as ubiquitous

Electricity

As in all of the United States, electricity is 110 volts, 60 hertz. Plugs have either two flat prongs or two flat prongs plus one round prong. Older homes and hotels may only have two-prong outlets. If you're traveling with computers or appliances that have three-prong plugs, ask your hotel or motel manager for an adapter. You may need to buy a three-prong adapter, but the cost is small.

ACCESS FOR TRAVELERS WITH DISABILITIES

Travelers with disabilities will find Utah progressive when it comes to accessibility. The parks have all-abilities trails and services. All five national parks have reasonably good facilities for visitors with limited mobility. Visitors centers are all accessible, and at least a couple of trails in each park are paved or smooth enough for wheelchair users to navigate with some assistance. Each park has a few accessible campsites.

Most hotels also offer some form of barrier-free lodging. It's best to call ahead and inquire what these accommodations are, however, because these services can vary quite a bit from one establishment to another.

Accessibility information for each park can also be found on the National Parks Service website (www.nps.gov).

TRAVELING WITH CHILDREN

The parks are filled with dramatic vistas and exciting recreation. The parks provide lots of opportunities for adventures, whether it's rafting the Colorado River or hiking to ancient Ancestral Puebloan ruins, and most children will have the time of their young lives in Utah.

Utah is a family-vacation type of place, and no special planning is required to make a national park holiday exciting for children. Children do receive discounts on a number of things, ranging from motel rooms (where they often stay for free, but inquire about age restrictions, which vary) to museum admissions. One exception to this family-friendly rule is B&Bs, which frequently don't allow children at all.

Utah law requires all children age four or younger to be restrained in a child safety seat. Child seats can be rented from car-rental agencies—ask when making a car reservation.

SENIOR TRAVELERS

The parks and Utah in general are hospitable for senior travelers. The National Parks and Federal Recreational Lands Senior Pass is a lifetime pass for U.S. citizens or permanent residents age 62 or over. The pass provides access to, and use of, federal parks and recreation sites that charge an entrance fee or standard amenity. The pass admits the pass holder and passengers in a noncommercial vehicle at per-vehicle fee areas, not to exceed four adults. The pass costs $80 and can only be obtained in person at a park. There is a similar discount program at Utah state parks.

LGBTQ TRAVELERS

Utah is not the most enlightened place in the world when it comes to equality issues, but that shouldn't be an issue for travelers to the national parks. Needless to say, a little discretion is a good idea in most public situations, and don't expect to find much of a gay scene anywhere in southeastern Utah. Moab is notably more progressive than anywhere else in this part of the state, but there are no gay bars or gathering places.

PETS

Unless you really have no other option, it's best not to bring your dog (or cat, or bird, or ferret) along on a national park vacation. Although pets are allowed in national parks, they aren't permitted on the trails. This limits you and your dog to leashed walks along the roads, around campground loops, and in parking areas. During much of the year, it's far too hot to leave an animal in a parked car.

Several pet boarding services are available in Moab:

- **Karen's Canine Campground** (2781 S. Roberts Rd., 435/259-7922, https://karenolt9campground.wordpress.com)

- **Moab Veterinary Clinic** (4575 Spanish Valley Dr., 435/259-8710, http://moabvetclinic.com)

- When in Moab, visit the **Moab Bark Park** (300 S. 100 E.), a fenced off-leash dog park.

CONDUCT AND CUSTOMS
Alcohol and Nightlife

Observant Mormons don't drink alcoholic beverages and **Utah's liquor laws** can seem confusing to outsiders. Changes to Utah's once prohibitive rules have made it easier to buy and consume alcohol. Note that it's no longer necessary to be a member of a private club in order to consume alcohol in a bar—no more buying a temporary membership or signing in on someone else's membership just to enjoy a drink. Several different kinds of establishments are licensed to sell alcoholic beverages:

Taverns, which include brewpubs, can sell only 3.2 percent beer (beer that is 3.2 percent alcohol by volume). Taverns can't sell wine, which is classed as hard liquor in Utah. Stronger beer is available in Utah, but only in bottles, and this beer is also regulated as hard liquor. You don't need to purchase food

to have a beer in a tavern. With the exception of brewpubs, taverns are usually fairly derelict and not especially cheery places to hang out.

Licensed restaurants are able to sell beer, wine, and hard liquor, but only with food orders. In many parts of Utah, you'll need to specifically ask for a drink or the drink menu to begin the process. In Salt Lake City, Moab, and Park City, most restaurants have liquor licenses. In small towns, few eating establishments offer alcohol.

Cocktail bars, lounges, live music venues, and nightclubs, which once operated on the private-club system, can now serve alcohol without asking for membership. However, some continue the income flow by demanding a cover charge for entry. Depending on which county you are in, you may still be required to order some food to have a drink.

Nearly all towns will have a state-owned liquor store. They can be difficult to find. 3.2 percent beer is available in most grocery stores and gas station minimarts. Many travelers find that carrying a bottle of your favorite beverage to your room is the easiest way to enjoy an evening drink. The state drinking age is 21.

If going out for drinks and nightclubbing is part of your idea of entertainment, you'll find that only Moab offers much in the way of nightspots. Outside Moab, many restaurants in Southern Utah don't serve alcohol.

Smoking

Smoking is taboo for observant Mormons, and smoking is prohibited in almost all public places. You're also not allowed to smoke on church grounds. Obviously, take care when smoking in national parks and pick up your own butts. Besides the risk of fire, there's nothing that ruins a natural experience more than windblown piles of cigarette filters.

Small-Town Utah

If you've never traveled in Utah before, you may find that Utahans don't initially seem as welcoming and outgoing as people in other Western states. In many smaller towns, visitors from outside the community are a relatively new phenomenon, and not everyone in the state is anxious to have their towns turned into tourism or recreational meccas. Mormons are very family- and community-oriented, and if certain individuals initially seem insular and uninterested in travelers, don't take it as unfriendliness.

Mormons are also orderly and socially conservative people. Brash displays of rudeness or use of foul language in public will not make you popular.

Health and Safety

There's nothing inherently dangerous about These parks, though a few precautions can help minimize what risks do exist. For the most part, using common sense about the dangers of extreme temperatures, remote backcountry exploration, and encounters with wildlife will ensure a safe and healthy trip.

HEAT AND WATER

Southern Utah in summer is a very hot place. Be sure to use sunscreen, or else you risk having an uncomfortable vacation. Wearing a wide-brimmed hat and good sunglasses, with full UV protection, can shield you from the sun's harmful effects. Heat exhaustion can also be a problem if you're hiking in the hot sun. In midsummer, try to get an early start if you're hiking in full sun. If you're out during the heat of the afternoon, look for a shady spot and rest until the sun begins to drop.

Drink steadily throughout the day, whether you are thirsty or not, rather than gulping huge amounts of water once you feel thirsty. For hikers, one of the best ways to drink enough is to carry water in a hydration pack (the two top brands are CamelBak and Platypus). These collapsible plastic bladders come with a hose and a mouthpiece, so you can carry your water in your pack, threading the hose out the top of the pack and over your shoulder, which keeps the mouthpiece handy for frequent sips of water. One easy way to tell if you're getting enough to drink is to monitor your urine output. If you're only urinating a couple of times a day, and the color and odor of your urine are both strong, it's time to start drinking more water.

HYPOTHERMIA

Don't think that just because you're in the Utah desert that you're immune to hypothermia. This lowering of the body's temperature below 95°F causes disorientation, uncontrollable shivering, slurred speech, and drowsiness. The victim may not even realize what's wrong. Unless corrective action is taken immediately, hypothermia can lead to death. Hikers should therefore travel with companions and always carry wind and rain protection. Space blankets are lightweight and cheap and offer protection against the cold in emergencies. Remember that temperatures can plummet rapidly in Utah's dry climate—a drop of 40 degrees between day and night is common. Be especially careful at high elevations, where sunshine can quickly change into freezing rain or a blizzard. Simply falling into a mountain stream can also lead to hypothermia and death unless proper action is taken. If you're cold and tired, don't waste time: Seek shelter and build a fire, change into dry clothes, and drink warm liquids. If a victim isn't fully conscious, warm him or her by skin-to-skin contact in a sleeping bag. Try to keep the victim awake and offer plenty of warm liquids.

GIARDIA

Giardia lamblia is a protozoan that has become common in even the remotest mountain streams. It is carried in animal or human waste that is deposited or washed into the water. When ingested, it begins reproducing, causing intense cramping and diarrhea in the host; this can become serious and may require medical attention.

No matter how clear a stream looks, it's best to assume that it is contaminated and to take precautions against giardia by filtering, boiling, or treating water with chemicals before drinking it. A high-quality filter will remove giardia and a host of other things you don't want to be drinking. (Spend a bit extra for one that removes particles down to one micrometer in size.) It's also effective to simply boil your water; two to five minutes at a rolling boil will kill giardia even in the cyst stage. Because water boils at a lower temperature as elevation increases, increase the boiling time to 15 minutes if you're at 9,000 feet (2,743 m). Two drops of bleach left in a quart of water for 30 minutes will remove most giardia, although some microorganisms are resistant to chemicals.

HANTAVIRUS

Hantavirus is an infectious disease agent that was first isolated during the Korean War and then discovered in the Americas in 1993 by a task force of scientists in New Mexico. This disease agent occurs naturally throughout most of North and South America, especially in dry desert conditions. The infectious agent is airborne, and in the absence of prompt medical attention, its infections are usually fatal. This disease is called hantavirus pulmonary syndrome (HPS). It can affect anyone, but given some fundamental knowledge, it can also easily be prevented.

The natural host of the hantavirus appears to be rodents, especially mice and rats. The virus is not usually transmitted directly from rodents to humans; rather, the rodents shed hantavirus particles in their saliva, urine, and droppings. Humans usually contract HPS by inhaling particles that are infected with the hantavirus. The virus becomes airborne when the particles dry out and get stirred into the air (especially from sweeping a floor or shaking a rug). Humans then inhale these particles, which leads to the infection.

HPS is not considered a highly infectious disease, so people usually contract HPS from long-term exposure. Because transmission usually occurs through inhalation, it is easiest for a human being to contract hantavirus within a contained environment, where the virus-infected particles are not thoroughly dispersed. Being in a cabin or barn where rodents can be found poses elevated risks for contracting the infection.

Simply traveling to a place where the hantavirus is known to occur is not considered a risk factor. Camping, hiking, and other outdoor activities also pose low risk, especially if steps are taken to reduce rodent contact. If you happen to stay in a rodent-infested cabin, thoroughly wet any droppings and dead rodents with a chlorine bleach solution (one cup of bleach per gallon of water) and let them stand for a few minutes before cleaning them up. Be sure to wear rubber gloves for this task, and double-bag your garbage.

The first symptoms of HPS can occur anywhere between five days and three weeks after infection. They almost always include fever, fatigue, aching muscles (usually in the back, shoulders, or thighs), and other flu-like symptoms. Other early symptoms may include headaches, dizziness, chills, and abdominal discomfort such as vomiting, nausea, or diarrhea. These symptoms are shortly followed by intense coughing and shortness of breath. If you have these symptoms, seek medical help immediately. Untreated infections of hantavirus are almost always fatal.

THINGS THAT BITE OR STING

Although travelers in these parks are not going to get attacked by a grizzly bear, and encounters with mountain lions are rare, there are a few animals to watch out for. Snakes, scorpions, and spiders are all present in considerable numbers, and there are a few key things to know about dealing with this phobia-inducing trio.

Snakes

Rattlesnakes, including the particularly venomous midget faded rattlesnake, are present throughout Southern Utah. The midget faded snakes live in Arches and Canyonlands, where they frequent burrows and rock crevices and are mostly active at night. Even though their venom is toxic, full venom injections are relatively uncommon, and, like all rattlesnakes, they pose little threat unless they're provoked.

If you see a rattlesnake, observe it at a safe distance. Be careful where you put your hands when canyoneering or scrambling—it's not a good idea to reach above your head and blindly plant your hands on a sunny rock ledge. Hikers should wear sturdy boots to minimize the chance that a snake's fangs will reach the skin if a bite occurs. Do not walk barefoot outside after dark, as this is when snakes hunt for prey.

First aid for rattlesnake bites is full of conflicting ideas: to suck or not to suck; to apply a constricting bandage or not; to take time treating in the field versus rushing to the hospital. Most people who receive medical treatment after being bitten by a rattlesnake live to tell the story. Prompt administration of antivenin is the most important treatment, and the most important aspect of first aid is to arrange transportation of the victim to a hospital as quickly as possible.

Scorpions

A scorpion's sting isn't as painful as you'd expect (it's about like a bee sting), and the venom is insufficient to cause any real harm. Still, it's not what you'd call pleasant, and experienced desert campers know to shake out their boots every morning, as scorpions and spiders are attracted to warm, moist, dark places.

Spiders

Tarantulas and black widow spiders are present across much of the Colorado Plateau. Believe it or not, a tarantula's bite does not poison humans; the enzymes secreted when they bite turn the insides of frogs, lizards, and insects to a soft mush, allowing the tarantula to suck the guts from its prey. Another interesting tarantula fact: While males live about as long as you'd expect a spider to live, female tarantulas can live for up to 25 years. Females do sometimes eat the males, which may account for some of this disparity in longevity.

Black widow spiders, on the other hand, have a toxic bite. Although the bite is usually painless, it delivers a potent neurotoxin, which quickly causes pain, nausea, and vomiting. It is important to seek immediate treatment for a black widow bite; although few people actually die from these bites, recovery is helped along considerably by antivenin.

Resources

Suggested Reading

ARCHAEOLOGY

Childs, Craig. *House of Rain: Tracking a Vanished Civilization across the American Southwest*. New York: Back Bay Books, 2008. Only part of this book deals with Utah, but it's a great read about the Ancestral Puebloans.

Jones, Kevin T., and Miller, Layne. *Standing on the Walls of Time: Ancient Art of Utah's Cliffs and Canyons*. Salt Lake City, University of Utah Press, 2019. With sumptuous photos, this book looks at the artistry of Utah's rock art; written by the former Utah state archeologist.

Lister, Robert, and Florence Lister. *Those Who Came Before*. Tucson: Southwest Parks and Monuments, 1993. A well-illustrated guide to the history, artifacts, and ruins of prehistoric Southwestern people. The author also describes parks and monuments containing archeological sites.

Simms, Steven R. *Traces of Fremont: Society and Rock Art in Ancient Utah*. Salt Lake City: University of Utah Press and Price, UT: College of Eastern Utah Prehistoric Museum, 2010. Great photos accompany the text in this look into Fremont culture.

MAPS AND GUIDEBOOKS

Benchmark Maps. *Utah Road & Recreation Atlas*. Medford, OR: Benchmark Maps, 2017. Shaded relief maps emphasize landforms, and recreational information is abundant. Use the atlas to locate campgrounds, back roads, and major trailheads, although there's not enough detail to rely on it for hiking.

Huegel, Tony. *Utah Byways: 65 of Utah's Best Backcountry Drives*. Berkeley, CA: Wilderness Press, 2006. If you're looking for off-highway adventure, this is your guide. The spiral-bound book includes detailed directions, human and natural history, outstanding photography, full-page maps for each of the 65 routes, and an extensive how-to chapter for beginners

HISTORY AND CURRENT EVENTS

Dellenbaugh, Frederick S. *A Canyon Voyage: The Narrative of the Second Powell Expedition*. Tucson: University of Arizona Press, 2017. A well-written account of John Wesley Powell's second expedition down the Green and Colorado Rivers, 1871-1872. The members took the first Grand Canyon photographs and obtained much valuable scientific knowledge.

Stegner, Wallace. *Beyond the Hundredth Meridian: John Wesley Powell and the Second Opening of the West*. New York: Penguin Books, reprinted 1992 (first published in 1954). Stegner's book tells the story of Powell's wild rides down the Colorado River, then goes on to point out why the United States should have listened to what Powell had to say about the U.S. Southwest.

MEMOIRS

Abbey, Edward. *Desert Solitaire*. New York: Ballantine Books, 1991. A meditation on the red-rock canyon country of Utah. Abbey brings his fiery prose to the service of the American outback, while excoriating the commercialization of the West.

Childs, Craig. *The Secret Knowledge of Water.* Boston: Back Bay Books, 2001. Childs looks for water in the desert, and finds plenty of it.

Zwinger, Ann. *Run, River, Run: A Naturalist's Journey down One of the Great Rivers of the American West.* Tucson: University of Arizona Press, 1984. An excellent description of the author's experiences along the Green River, from its source in the Wind River Range of Wyoming to the Colorado River in southeastern Utah. The author weaves geology, Native American ruins, plants, wildlife, and her personal feelings into the text and drawings.

NATURAL SCIENCES

Chronic, Lucy, and Felicie Williams. *Roadside Geology of Utah.* Missoula, MT: Mountain Press Publishing, 2014. This layperson's guide tells the story of the state's fascinating geology as seen by following major roadways.

Fagan, Damian. *Canyon Country Wildflowers.* Helena, MT: Falcon Publishing, 2012. A comprehensive field guide to the diverse flora of the Four Corners area.

Fagan, Damian, and David Williams. *A Naturalist's Guide to the White Rim Trail.* Seattle: Wingate Ink, 2007. Take your time to explore nature on the White Rim Trail.

Williams, David, and Gloria Brown. *A Naturalist's Guide to Canyon Country.* Helena, MT: Falcon Publishing, 2020. If you want to buy just one field guide, this is the one to get. It's well written, beautifully illustrated, and a delight to use.

OUTDOOR ACTIVITIES

Crowell, David. *Mountain Biking Moab.* Helena, MT: Falcon Guides, 2019. A guide to the many trails around Moab, from the most popular to the little explored, in a handy size—small enough to take on the bike with you.

Day, David. *Utah's Favorite Hiking Trails.* Provo, UT: Rincon Publishing, 2002. Good simple maps and detailed descriptions of trails all over the state, including many in Southern Utah's national parks and monuments.

Green, Stewart M. *Rock Climbing Utah.* Helena, MT: Falcon Publishing, 2012. Good detail on climbs in all of Utah's national parks, including many line drawings and photos with climbing routes highlighted.

Kelsey, Michael R. *Canyon Hiking Guide to the Colorado Plateau.* Provo, UT: Brigham Distributing, 2018. One of the best guides to hiking in southeastern Utah's canyon country. Geologic cross sections show the formations you'll be walking through.

Molvar, Erik. *Best Easy Day Hikes Zion and Bryce Canyon National Parks.* Helena, MT: Falcon Publishing, 2014. Features concise descriptions and easy-to-follow maps for 22 easily manageable hikes in two of Utah's most popular national parks.

Schneider, Bill. *Best Easy Day Hikes Canyonlands and Arches.* Helena, MT: Falcon Publishing, 2017. Twenty hikes in this popular vacation area, geared to travelers who are short on time or aren't able to explore the canyons on more difficult trails.

Wells, Charles A., and Shelly Mayer. *Guide to Moab, UT Backroads & 4-Wheel Drive Trails.* Monument, CO: Funtreks, 2016. Good descriptions and GPS waypoints for Moab-area four-wheelers.

Witt, Greg. *50 Best Hikes in Utah's National Parks.* Birmingham, AL: Wilderness Press, 2014. A veteran hiking guide shares his favorite routes in Utah's five national parks.

Internet Resources

The American Southwest
www.americansouthwest.net/utah
This online Utah guide provides an overview of national parks, national recreation areas, and some state parks.

Desert USA
www.desertusa.com
Desert USA's Utah section discusses places to visit and what plants and animals you might meet there. Here's the best part of this site: You can find out what's in bloom at www.desertusa.com/wildflo/nv.html.

Moab Area Travel Council
http://discovermoab.com
Upcoming events, mountain bike trails, local restaurants and lodging, and outfitters are all easy to find at this comprehensive site.

National Park Service
www.nps.gov
The National Park Service offers pages for all its parks at this site. Trail conditions, maps, accessible features, and other helpful information are included. You can also enter this address followed by a slash and the first two letters of the first two words of the place (first four letters if there's just a one-word name); for example, www.nps.gov/arch takes you to Arches Canyon National Park and www.nps.gov/cany leads to Canyonlands National Park.

Recreation.gov
www.recreation.gov
If a campground is operated by the federal government, this is the place to make a reservation. You can expect to pay close to $10 for this convenience.

Reserve America
www.reserveamerica.com
Use this website to reserve campsites in state campgrounds. It costs a few extra bucks to reserve a campsite, but compare that with the cost of being skunked out of a site and having to resort to a motel room.

State of Utah
www.utah.gov
The official State of Utah website has information on travel, agencies, programs, and what the legislature is up to.

U.S. Forest Service
www.fs.fed.us/r4
Utah falls within U.S. Forest Service Region 4. The Manti La Sal National Forest (www.fs.fed.us/r4/mantilasal) is in southeast Utah around Moab and Monticello.

Utah Mountain Biking
www.utahmountainbiking.com
Details mountain biking routes listed in this book as well as other local trails.

Utah State Parks
http://stateparks.utah.gov
The Utah State Parks site offers details on the large park system, including links to reserve campsites.

Utah Travel Council
https://utah.com
The Utah Travel Council is a one-stop shop for all sorts of information on Utah. It takes you around the state to sights, activities, events, and maps, and offers links to local tourism offices. The accommodations listings are the most up-to-date source for current room rates and options.

Index

List of Maps

Photo Credits

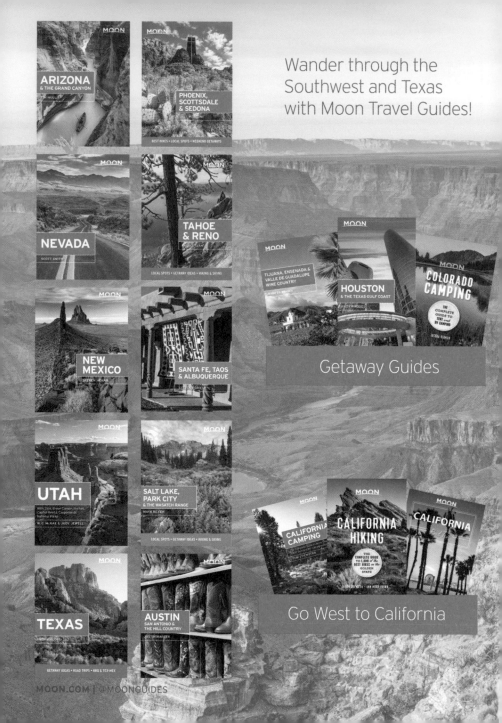

Wander through the
Southwest and Texas
with Moon Travel Guides!

MOON
ARIZONA
& THE GRAND CANYON
TIM HULL

MOON
PHOENIX,
SCOTTSDALE
& SEDONA

BEST HIKES • LOCAL SPOTS • WEEKEND GETAWAYS

MOON
NEVADA
SCOTT SMITH

MOON
TAHOE
& RENO

LOCAL SPOTS • GETAWAY IDEAS • HIKING & SKIING

MOON
NEW
MEXICO
STEVEN HORAK

MOON
SANTA FE, TAOS
& ALBUQUERQUE

MOON
TIJUANA, ENSENADA &
VALLE DE GUADALUPE
WINE COUNTRY

MOON
HOUSTON
& THE TEXAS GULF COAST
ANDY RHODES

MOON
COLORADO
CAMPING
THE
COMPLETE
GUIDE TO
TENT and
RV CAMPING

Getaway Guides

MOON
UTAH
With Zion, Bryce Canyon, Arches,
Capitol Reef & Canyonlands
National Parks
W. C. McRAE & JUDY JEWELL

MOON
SALT LAKE,
PARK CITY
& THE WASATCH RANGE
MARK BLEVINS

LOCAL SPOTS • GETAWAY IDEAS • HIKING & SKIING

MOON
CALIFORNIA
CAMPING
TOM STIENSTRA

MOON
CALIFORNIA
HIKING
THE
COMPLETE GUIDE
TO 1,000 of the
BEST HIKES in the
GOLDEN
STATE

MOON
CALIFORNIA

MOON
TEXAS
ANDY RHODES

MOON
AUSTIN
SAN ANTONIO &
THE HILL COUNTRY
JUSTIN MARLER

GETAWAY IDEAS • ROAD TRIPS • BBQ & TEX-MEX

Go West to California

MAP SYMBOLS

≡≡≡	Expressway	○	City/Town	✈	Airport	⚱	Golf Course
≡≡≡	Primary Road	◉	State Capital	✈	Airfield	▣	Parking Area
≡≡≡	Secondary Road	⊛	National Capital	▲	Mountain	⚊	Archaeological Site
▪▪▪▪	Unpaved Road	✪	Highlight	✦	Unique Natural Feature	♠	Church
------	Trail	★	Point of Interest			▇	Gas Station
··········	Ferry	•	Accommodation	⛆	Waterfall	◌	Glacier
►◄►◄	Railroad	▼	Restaurant/Bar	⛫	Park	▨	Mangrove
▨▨▨	Pedestrian Walkway	■	Other Location	🛈	Trailhead	◿	Reef
▥▥▥	Stairs	Λ	Campground	⛷	Skiing Area	▭	Swamp

CONVERSION TABLES

°C = (°F - 32) / 1.8
°F = (°C x 1.8) + 32
1 inch = 2.54 centimeters (cm)
1 foot = 0.304 meters (m)
1 yard = 0.914 meters
1 mile = 1.6093 kilometers (km)
1 km = 0.6214 miles
1 fathom = 1.8288 m
1 chain = 20.1168 m
1 furlong = 201.168 m
1 acre = 0.4047 hectares
1 sq km = 100 hectares
1 sq mile = 2.59 square km
1 ounce = 28.35 grams
1 pound = 0.4536 kilograms
1 short ton = 0.90718 metric ton
1 short ton = 2,000 pounds
1 long ton = 1.016 metric tons
1 long ton = 2,240 pounds
1 metric ton = 1,000 kilograms
1 quart = 0.94635 liters
1 US gallon = 3.7854 liters
1 Imperial gallon = 4.5459 liters
1 nautical mile = 1.852 km

MOON ARCHES & CANYONLANDS NATIONAL PARKS

Avalon Travel
Hachette Book Group
1700 Fourth Street
Berkeley, CA 94710, USA
www.moon.com

Editor: Diana Smith
Acquiring Editor: Nikki Ioakimedes
Copy Editor: Rachael Sablik
Graphics and Production Coordinator: Rue Flaherty
Cover Design: Kimberly Glyder Design
Interior Design: Domini Dragoone
Moon Logo: Tim McGrath
Map Editor: Mike Morgenfeld
Cartographer: Brian Shotwell
Indexer: Rachel Kuhn

ISBN-13: 978-1-64049-469-5

Printing History
1st Edition — 2013
3rd Edition — September 2021
5 4 3 2 1

Front cover photo: Delicate Arch in Arches National Park © S.& S. Grunig-Karp / Huber / eStock Photo

Back cover photo: Shafer Trail road in Canyonlands National Park © Maksershov | Dreamstime.com

Printed in Malaysia for Imago

Avalon Travel is a division of Hachette Book Group, Inc. Moon and the Moon logo are trademarks of Hachette Book Group, Inc. All other marks and logos depicted are the property of the original owners.